LATE VICTORIAN BRITAIN
1875 – 1901

J.F.C. HARRISON, who is Emeritus Professor of History at the University of Sussex, was born in Leicester in 1921 and educated at City Boys' School, Leicester, and at Selwyn College, Cambridge. He served as an infantry captain in the Second World War before becoming a lecturer, and then Deputy Director, in the Deparment of Adult Education at Leeds University. From 1961 until 1970 he was Professor of History at the University of Wisconsin. He has travelled widely and has held visiting appointments at Harvard University, the Australian National University and the Institute for Research in the Humanities at the University of Wisconsin.

Among his books are *Learning and Living, 1790–1960* (1961); *Society and Politics in England, 1780–1960* (1965); *Robert Owen and the Owenites in Britain and America* (1969); *The Early Victorians, 1832–51* (1971; published by Fontana as *Early Victorian Britain* in 1979); *The Second Coming: Popular Millenarianism, 1780–1850* (1979); and *The Common People: A History from the Norman Conquest to the Present* (1984).

J.F.C. HARRISON

Late Victorian Britain

1875 – 1901

LONDON AND NEW YORK

First published 1991
by Routledge
11 New Fetter Lane, London EC4P 4EE
29 West 35th Street, New York, NY 10001

Printed and bound in Great Britain by
William Collins Sons & Co. Ltd, Glasgow

A CIP catalogue record for this book is
available from the British Library

A Library of Congress catalogue record for this
book is available from the Library of Congress

Contents

Introduction

There are many possible excuses or self-justifications for writing a book. Mine is simply that I have enjoyed making it. After spending a considerable part of my professional life with the early Victorians and speculating about the mid-Victorians who succeeded them, I have long been curious to know what happened to them all in the later part of the nineteenth century. How did the story end, how did the logic of the earlier years work itself out, what became of all those confident hopes and haunting anxieties that beset the men and women of the 1830s and 1840s? Like all modern social historians I am concerned with the process of social change. But a word of caution is perhaps in order when dealing with the relatively short period of twenty-five or thirty years. There is plenty of evidence that many views and attitudes which we think of as late Victorian were present throughout the whole of the period 1837–1901 and beyond. This is certainly true of some religious views for instance. To a considerable extent we are victims of our own periodization in dividing up the nineteenth century into three neat categories of early, mid and late Victorian. We have always to remember that for individuals the unit of time is not the historian's decade or generation, but a lifetime of experiences. Men and women whose formative ideas came out of the 'Hungry Forties' were still alive and active fifty years later in the 'Age of Imperialism'. While the general directions of Victorian social change are not in doubt it is clear that there was also continuity in many fields between the late Victorians and their predecessors.

There is another, more personal reason for my interest in late Victorian Britain. This was the period when my grandparents were in their prime and my parents were growing up. My father was born in 1882 and my mother in 1890. For me late Victorian Britain was therefore part of that dimly-perceived world to which

9

our parents and grandparents from time to time make reference but which we have never experienced first-hand. It is a world which is somehow familiar and yet unknown.

In my quest for enlightenment I have shamelessly plundered the work of others. In some places I have also drawn upon material which I have used elsewhere. Essentially this is a work of synthesis and interpretation. The book is a collection of themes and events which seem to me to illuminate late Victorian society. It is not a text book but rather a series of vignettes intended as an introductory temptation to the late Victorian age. It is basically social history but of a rather eclectic and untheoretical kind. Throughout the book my concern has been to reconstruct a past age, to convey its tone and flavour as it appeared to those who lived at the time. Wherever possible I have tried to let the people speak for themselves, even when this has entailed numerous and sometimes lengthy quotations. At the same time I have tried 'to make sense' of it all.

The Victorians frequently used the word England interchangeably with Britain; and I have not managed to escape the usual historian's Anglocentric approach. The confusion is compounded by having to rely on statistics which are sometimes for England and Wales, at others for Great Britain, the United Kingdom or the British Isles. The book is intended to complement the two previous social histories in the Fontana series, my own *Early Victorian Britain, 1832–51* and Geoffrey Best's *Mid-Victorian Britain, 1851–75*, and therefore follows much the same format.

Sussex, February 1990   J.F.C.H.

I

The Victorian Achievement

1

Progress and Poverty

In December 1881 there appeared in London a book with the challenging title *Progress and Poverty*. It was written by an American, Henry George, and proceeded from the observation that in the midst of the most bounteous material conditions the world had ever seen there remained widespread want. Steam, electricity, and labour-saving machinery promised to usher in the golden age of which mankind had always dreamed. Yet poverty, unemployment and a fierce struggle for existence were the reality for the majority of Britons. The association of poverty with progress was the great enigma of the times. George was preoccupied with propounding a remedy for the poverty of the working classes; but his title neatly encapsulates both the late Victorian achievement and its limitations. A deep belief in the reality of progress in all aspects of life continued in most quarters until the end of the century, despite doubts and questionings. The constituents of this progress will therefore be our point of departure; from which the working-out of the logic of mid-Victorianism will follow.

We shall begin with demographic progress. During the previous hundred years the population of Great Britain had been increasing rapidly, and this growth continued during the last quarter of the century. A high birth rate of over 30 per thousand throughout the nineteenth century and a steadily falling death rate (from 22 per thousand in 1871 to 16.1 in 1901) ensured that Britain became ever more crowded, despite considerable emigration to America and Australasia. Between 1871 and 1901 another 10 million was added to the population, making a total of 37 million for Great Britain. Before the end of the century, however, there were signs that the rate of growth was slackening. The birth rate, which had reached a maximum of over 35 per thousand in the

1870s, began to fall, and after 1900 declined rapidly. Nevertheless the effects of this fall were not perceptible for some time, and each year the population of the British Isles (with the exception of Ireland) was larger than ever before. In this primary sense late Victorian Britain continued to be an expanding society.

Beyond the broad contours of population change the census figures can be made to yield other clues of social significance. The fall in fertility rates, for example, resulted in smaller families. Marriages in the late 1860s produced an average of 6.16 children; by 1881 this had fallen to 5.27, and in 1914 to 2.73. Put another way, 43 per cent of the women married in 1870–9 had between five and nine children and nearly 18 per cent had ten or more. Thirty years later this pattern had changed dramatically, and the trend towards the one- or two-child family soon became established. Within these overall fertility figures there were important social differentials. The decline in fertility and therefore in size of families began amongst the middle and upper classes and reached manual workers later. In 1900–9 the average miner or labourer had almost twice the number of children as the average professional man. Twenty-five years is too short a period for the assessment of long-term demographic change, and the true significance of the years 1875–1901 can be seen only in comparison with what came before and after. Table 4 shows changes in the life cycle over a period of one hundred years. By comparing the profile of an average person born in 1850 with someone born in 1950 the late Victorian years fall into perspective. Nevertheless, although the full implications of the decline in fertility were not apparent until after World War I, in the last quarter of the nineteenth century some of the effects were already beginning to be observable in changes in the family and in social structure, occupational patterns, and ways of living.

The census of 1851 had shown that for the first time just over half the population of England and Wales was living in urban areas (that is, in towns of 20,000 people or larger). Early Victorian Britain had become the world's first urbanized society. In the last thirty years of the century this progress (if progress it was) towards general settlement in what the early Victorians called 'large towns and populous districts' continued; by 1901 the proportion of population classified by the census as urban had risen to three-quarters. Traditionally 'Town' meant London, since it was the only very large town in Britain. At the end of the century, with a population of over 4.5 million, it was still unique. But between 1871 and 1901 a group of great towns increased considerably in size. Liverpool, Manchester and Birmingham grew to between 500,000 and 800,000 apiece; Leeds, Sheffield and Bristol had populations of 300,000 to 500,000; and the total number of towns with more than 50,000 inhabitants increased from 37 to 75 (see Table 7). The fastest rate of growth in this period was exhibited by towns like Leicester, Nottingham, Hull and Bradford, which in 1871 had populations of between 50,000 and 200,000. By 1901, 45 per cent of the total population of England and Wales was living in London and the 74 large towns of more than 50,000 inhabitants.

This urban transformation in late Victorian Britain had important social ramifications. First and most obviously, the increase in population resulted in an increase in population density, especially in the largest towns. This can perhaps be measured more usefully in terms of overcrowding than as persons per square mile. Taking the definition of overcrowding as more than two persons per room, the 1901 census reported that 8.2 per cent of the population of England and Wales lived in an overcrowded environment. Within this overall figure, however, were considerable variations, ranging from Gateshead with 35.5 per cent and Newcastle with 30.5 per cent to Leicester (1.0 per cent) and Bournemouth (0.6 per cent). London as a whole had 16 per cent overcrowding, but the figure for Finsbury was 35.2 per cent. Secondly, the development and reluctant acceptance of the megalopolis marked a new stage in Victorian consciousness of progress and poverty. The early Victorians had thought of the city as a problem. Although they were aware of the relationship between mortality and environment, attempts to improve the living conditions of the urban poor were defeated by poor housing, impure water and a lack of open space. However, the final great cholera epidemic happened in 1866, and the high rate of urban infant mortality finally began to fall at the end of the century. But the improvement in public health was not matched by success in tackling the more intractable problems of housing and poverty. To many late Victorians the industrial city seemed essential for the progress of society and yet dangerous for civilization, about which they talked much.

Just as the population continued to increase but at a decreasing rate during the last third of the century, so the economy continued to grow but unevenly and at a slower pace than formerly. Indeed, so marked was the change in economic tempo that economic historians have called the years 1873–96 the Great Depression. In fact it was not a depression of the magnitude of those of the 1830s and 1840s or the 1930s, but was rather a recognition that a new phase in the development of the economy had been reached. Something akin to stagnation, compared with the previous tremendous advance, seemed to have set in. Prices, interest rates and profits fell or remained at a low level. To the articulate middle classes and the farming community this amounted to a depression; though for working people the fall in prices meant a rise in wages in real terms. The Victorian belief in virtually unlimited progress was for the first time checked by serious doubts and questionings. With hindsight we can see that what had happened was that the world monopoly position of British industrial capitalism had come to an end, and the long lead of the world's first industrial revolution was no more; bullish, competitive, young industrial nations had caught up.

The British industrial revolution had been built on textiles, coal, iron and steel, shipbuilding and machinery; and the economy was geared to selling these products cheaply to a worldwide market. Production continued to expand throughout the later nineteenth century. Coal output rose from 110 million tons in 1870 to 225 million tons in 1900 and 287 million tons by 1913, and exports of coal also increased. Iron and steel production grew from 6 million tons in 1870 to 10 million tons in 1913. In 1880 John Ruskin lamented 'the ferruginous temper' of the age which had 'changed our Merry England into the Man in the Iron Mask'. Between 1880 and 1900 the value of exports of iron, steel, machinery and coal doubled to £95 million. Textiles were not so buoyant and their traditionally dominant share of the export trade declined from 55 per cent in value in 1870 to 34 per cent in 1909–13. Nevertheless the total output and value of textiles was maintained, and in some sectors, including cotton, it increased. The years 1875–1900 were, overall, a period of economic progress, with rising productivity and national income (see Table 8).

But whereas hitherto Britain had had virtually no rivals, after 1870 other nations, especially America and Germany, began to overtake the level of British production and pioneered new areas. For instance, in 1880 Britain produced one third of the world's steel. By 1902, despite an almost fivefold increase, this proportion had shrunk to one seventh of the world total, and both Germany and the USA produced more than Britain. Similarly, although Britain remained the world's greatest trading nation, the value of her exports increased by only 6.4 per cent between 1880–84 and 1894–1900, whereas in the same period German exports rose by 23 per cent and the United States' gains were 42.8 per cent. Critics argued that the British economy had lost its earlier dynamism and speculated as to why this should be so.

To some extent of course Britain was paying the price for being first in the field. When larger nations followed the British example and industrialized it was inevitable that they would surpass her in certain respects. Moreover the phenomenal rate of growth of British industry, especially textiles, in the middle years of the century could not be sustained indefinitely. Even if the late Victorians had adopted new techniques more energetically than was in fact the case, they could not have hoped to match the growth rate achieved by their fathers. There was also the burden of established and tried techniques, entrenched attitudes and heavy investment to be borne. Why re-equip with new technology if the old could be made to last a little longer? It was a temptation to which older manufacturers might succumb, for in the short run it was cheaper and easier than root-and-branch innovation. This was not by any means an unreasonable response. It made good economic sense in that it minimized costs and maintained profits, at least for the foreseeable future. Nineteenth-century machines were often superbly built and, with occasional replacement of worn parts, could last a long time – witness, for example, the pumping engines at waterworks, now preserved as museums

17

but still in full working order a hundred years later. Furthermore, Britain had the advantage of a large and skilled industrial labour force and an established dominance in world shipping. As the winds of competition blew keenly after 1870, and the more recently industrialized countries erected tariff barriers to keep out foreign goods, the vulnerability of an economy so dependent on exports began to appear. There was no inherent reason why Britain did not respond more vigorously and successfully to this challenge of competition, she simply did not.

The failure to innovate and the consequent falling behind America and Germany in industry after industry exposed weaknesses in the British economy. Iron and steel provide a classic example. All the great innovations in steel making were developed in Britain: Bessemer's converter (1856) made mass production possible, the Siemens-Martin open-hearth furnace (1866) greatly increased productivity, and Gilchrist-Thomas in 1879 solved the problem of how to use low-grade phosphoric ore. Yet after adapting to the converter British steelmakers made relatively little use of the other inventions, which were enthusiastically taken up in Germany and France. Again, the first aniline dye was discovered in 1859 by a British chemist, W. H. Perkin. Yet although Britain had the world's largest textile industry and therefore the largest market for dyes, the development of the dye industry was left to Germany – which also took the lead in the general production of chemicals. Similarly in the case of the electrical industries, British pioneers like Faraday and Clerk-Maxwell had laid the foundations, but American and German firms developed the technology and provided the investment. When the London underground railway was electrified in 1900–14, the process relied heavily on American expertise and finance. The British economy neither kept abreast of the development of new industries nor adopted new techniques in the older industries to the same extent as her competitors.

The reasons for this failure are complex, and no single-cause explanation seems adequate. Failure is, in any case, a relative term. It can be employed usefully only when measured against some attainable goal, which in this instance could not be a repetition of the early Victorian industrial achievement. In the later stages of development in an industrial economy, the tertiary or services sector tends to grow more rapidly than manufacturing, and such a structural shift may result in lower growth rates, since productivity is not usually so high in the tertiary sector, which tends to be more labour-intensive. Trade, banking, insurance and finance expanded during this period; capital was exported in great quantities; and a favourable balance of trade (exports over imports) was maintained by 'invisible' exports such as shipping and profits from investments abroad. Nevertheless the deceleration of the rate of industrial growth after 1873 caused concern to contemporaries, and its explanation has been much debated by historians. The subject has a particularly modern relevance if the events of the late nineteenth century are seen as the beginning of a process extending over the next hundred years, for then the roots of today's economic problems can be traced to choices and decisions made in late Victorian times. It would be easy, for instance, to blame management and attribute the shortcomings of the economy to a lack of enterprise among businessmen. This certainly seems to have been a factor in some of the new industries requiring much research and development, such as chemicals and electrical engineering. But in the basic heavy industry of shipbuilding British efficiency was unchallenged; and in light industries and processing, like pharmaceuticals and brewing, British entrepreneurship was second to none. It was in this period that firms such as Beecham, Lever, Rowntree, Cadbury, Guinness, Bass, Coats, Lipton, and Lyons became household names.

The doubts about late Victorian entrepreneurship, however, can be extended beyond purely economic evidence to wider, cultural factors. It has been argued that the dominance of aristocratic values and styles of life, which the English middle classes increasingly aspired to emulate, was inimical to dynamic economic progress. [1] Gentlemanly ideals, which denigrated trade and industry, became accepted among the children of successful businessmen, and there was a similar 'gentrification' among the upper echelons of the professions. A new, homogeneous elite of landed aristocrats, industrialists, financiers, civil servants and professional men was forged by a common education in the public schools and ancient universities. This education, heavily

biased towards classical and literary studies and against science
and technology, inculcated attitudes which were unfavourable to
industry and commerce. British economic endeavour was thus
hampered by a prevailing system of social values which was at
odds with those qualities most requisite for business success.

The paradox of a non-, or even anti-, industrial cultural establishment being present at the core of the world's most intensely
industrialized country has not gone unnoticed. Fifty years ago
the social historian G. M. Young remarked how 'in a money-
making age, opinion was, on the whole, more deferential to birth
than to money, and . . . in a mobile and progressive society, most
regard was had to the element which represented immobility,
tradition, and the past.'[2] By the last quarter of the nineteenth
century this attitude was reflected in families where the second
or third generation of mill owners deserted their industry, the
source of their wealth, for the life of country gentry, as with the
Marshalls of Leeds, whose wealth from flax-spinning enabled
them to become Yorkshire squires and intermarry with the aristocracy. Within industry the liberal education which the sons of
industrialists received in public schools fitted them for leisure,
public service and gentlemanly pursuits, rather than for the
hurly-burly of mill and marketplace. A hierarchy of status among
businessmen is perceptible by the end of the century, with those
engaged in finance and commerce, centred on London, regarded
as superior to the manufacturers of the Midlands and the North.
The Victorians' neglect of technical and scientific education,
particularly when compared with Germany, was frequently commented on by contemporary critics. But as long as engineers and
industrialists were regarded as inferior in prestige and status to
the gentry and the gentrified professions, little change was to be
expected. This was in sharp contrast to the situation in America,
and Germany. Whether this elitist cultural conservatism is the
crucial factor in the explanation of Britian's economic decline is
difficult to determine. At the least such attitudes did nothing to
assist – and may well have hindered – Britain's adaptation to the
economic realities of the late nineteenth and early twentieth
centuries.

Yet whatever status landowning conferred it did not bring

much economic prosperity in late Victorian Britain. As industrialization proceeded apace, the relative importance of agriculture declined. From being the framework of the whole economy it shrank to just one sector of production, albeit still a very large one. In 1851 one fifth of the gross national income came from agriculture; by 1891 this figure had fallen to one thirteenth. Until 1873 farming enjoyed its full share of mid-Victorian prosperity, with high prices and an expanding demand for food. The Great Depression marked an end to this golden age: wheat prices tumbled, rents fell, and small farmers and agricultural labourers left the land. A flood of cheap food imports, aggravated by a series of poor harvests in the late 1870s, was unchecked by tariff protection. As the vast new arable lands of the American and Canadian prairies came into production, British cereal farming was badly hit. The effect of this was to force a shift in agricultural production from arable to livestock, from wheat and barley to cattle-raising and dairying. In late Victorian Britain the economic basis of agriculture was gravely weakened and therewith the age-old dominance of the landed interest.

Material progress as a whole continued to be made in the later years of the nineteenth century. Britain was still one of the wealthiest countries in the world and the national income increased year by year (see Table 8). Nevertheless this progress was criticized as deficient in two respects: first, the rate of increase was slower than previously; and secondly, the wealth was not spread sufficiently widely among all classes. The failure of late Victorian society to remedy the effects of the poverty and gross inequalities whose existence had been acknowledged fifty years earlier raised doubts about the economic and social changes claimed as progress. Was progress always to be accompanied by (perhaps even conditional on) poverty, as unavoidable as the reverse side of a coin? Such disturbing thoughts were later to fuel movements for more radical change.

When Victorians talked about progress they usually had in mind more than economic growth and an increase in material comfort, though these were always the most obvious and most readily measurable benefits. Moral progress, the progress of the race, and the progress of civilization were also compelling issues for thousands of the Queen's subjects. In the sphere of politics progress was generally perceived to be dependent on a widening of the boundaries of democracy. Chartism had failed in its immediate political objectives; but it was followed by a gradual and piecemeal extension of the franchise and by reform of the worst abuses of the old pre–1832 political system. The 1867 Reform Act had given the vote to respectable urban working-class men, specifically borough householders with a one-year residential qualification, and lodgers who paid an annual rent of £10 for at least a year. In the counties the franchise was limited to occupiers of land worth £12 a year, which effectively excluded the agricultural labourers. By 1884 the time was judged to be ripe for a further extension, and in that year the Reform Act enfranchised householders and lodgers in the counties on the same basis as in the towns. This meant that about 5 million males in Great Britain were qualified to vote, which amounted to two out of three men in England and Wales and three in five in Scotland, or about 28 per cent of the United Kingdom's population above twenty years of age. A majority of the electors were now working men, but women remained excluded until 1918. Measures to ensure a secret ballot (1872), check corruption and illegal electoral practices (1883), and redistribute seats (1885) helped to create a new electoral system and necessitated new forms of political organization. Local government was similarly overhauled, with the establishment of elected county councils in 1888 to replace the county magistrates meeting at Quarter Sessions. Elected district and parish councils were added in 1894. By the end of the century the opportunities for popular participation in politics had been considerably increased. Progress in this area of national life was understood to mean a continuing and inevitable process, and it bore the stamp of an irreversible trend, which was simultaneously heartening to reformers and alarming to conservatives.

Although the mid-Victorian champions of extension of the franchise, like John Stuart Mill, argued their case on the grounds of right and human dignity, they were at pains to emphasize that the increase in popular political involvement would also ensure the stability of the existing system. By incorporating working men within the political structure, it was argued, more radical change would be avoided. This in fact was what happened in the later nineteenth century. The 1884–5 Reform Acts did not change the type of wealthy member elected to Parliament in the counties, nor did the redistribution of seats in the towns upset the traditional divide between Conservatives and Liberals. But the increase in the size of the electorate intensified the need for party organization which developed after 1867. The Liberals set the pace in the 1870s with Joseph Chamberlain's Birmingham caucus, and under Gladstone's leadership the National Liberal Federation was established. The Conservatives countered with the creation of Conservative Working Men's Associations, the National Union of Conservative and Constitutional Associations, and, most effective of all, the Primrose League (the latter in 1883). The country was covered at regional and local level with political associations which provided opportunities for activists to engage in a variety of types of voluntary party work: holding meetings, canvassing, petitioning, missionizing on bicycles. Somewhat wider in their appeal were the thousands of Liberal, Conservative and Radical clubs which were established as social centres to attract the new electors. Well might it be wondered

> How nature always does contrive
> That every boy and every gal,
> That's born into the world alive,
> Is either a little Liberal,
> Or else a little Conservative![3]

It is by no means certain however just how far the political nation, in the sense of those active or at least interested in politics, extended. The number of voters was still only a minority of the total adult population. First, all women were excluded. Secondly, male householders who had not occupied premises for twelve months did not qualify. Thirdly, certain groups such as domestic servants resident with employers and sons living with their parents could not vote because they did not fit into any of the franchise categories. Fourthly, the complications and inconveniences of getting enrolled as a voter deterred poorer people. By 1911 there were only about 8 million voters in the U.K., or

29.7 per cent of the total adult population and 63.3 per cent of the total adult male population. However, since there were at least half a million plural voters (that is, persons who qualified for more than one vote) only about 59 per cent of adult males were actually enfranchised.[4] To the deficiencies in the franchise laws were added the intricacies of voter registration, with the result that a quarter of a century after the 1884–5 reforms some 40 per cent of all adult males, and all women were still not on the electoral register. The gap between the ideals and the practice of liberal democracy was large. Political progress there had undoubtedly been; but political poverty was there too.

The last thirty years of the nineteenth century are usually regarded as the golden age of the two-party system, when the pendulum swung between Conservatives and Liberals, under the leadership of their two champion gladiators, Benjamin Disraeli ('Dizzy') and William Gladstone ('the people's William'); cartoonists portrayed the two great adversaries as prize fighters in the boxing ring. As time went on new men such as Joseph Chamberlain, Lord Randolph Churchill and Charles Stewart Parnell joined the ranks of the leadership; but the succession of men like the Marquis of Salisbury to head the Conservative party and the Earl of Rosebery to lead the Liberals ensured that the predominance of wealth and aristocratic connection in the ranks of the country's rulers changed little. Political history has largely been written round the policies and tactics of these national figures, on the assumption that they were leaders of national parties reflecting the wishes or interests of the electorate. However, from the ordinary voter's point of view the world of politics probably looked somewhat different. At the grass roots, local and regional personalities loomed large and political issues were perceived through the dark glass of prevalent social and cultural assumptions. For instance, party allegiance was closely related to religious denomination, with the nonconformists supporting Liberalism and the Church of England the Tories. The issues and vocabulary of politics at the popular level were often religious. Ethnic feeling, such as anti-Irish sentiment in the north-west of England, could easily be translated into a political issue. The centrality of the workplace in the lives of the mass of voters (and non-voters) suggests the possibility of influences or pressure being exerted from that quarter. A recent study has shown how in Lancashire the factory was at the centre of political life, and how employers' power and influence was exercised.[5] Industrial paternalism and deference, class feeling and protest, were the realities which underpinned popular politics. It seems clear that many cultural and community influences will have to be taken into account before we can properly distinguish the real world of the voters from the political myths propagated at the time and subsequently.

II

Social Structure

2

The Elite

For many hundreds of years Britain had been ruled by a tiny elite who owned most of the wealth, made all the important decisions and exercised exclusive class power. It was not to be expected that this privileged position would be surrendered easily, and despite the industrial revolution and the widening of the franchise the aristocracy continued to dominate political and social life until the end of the nineteenth century. Radicals like Joseph Chamberlain might thunder against the Conservative leader, Lord Salisbury, that he spoke only for a class 'who toil not, neither do they spin' (30 March 1883), but that class demonstrated great resilience and powers of survival in claiming to represent the national interest. It was a ruling class which was landed, hereditary, wealthy and leisured; it was also very small, interrelated, and exclusive. Yet it could be entered or joined by outsiders under certain conditions. It maintained values and codes of behaviour which were envied and emulated; it was the arbiter of taste, manners and refined living. Nothing is more remarkable than the way in which this aristocracy, belonging almost completely to a pre-industrial, even feudal, age, not only survived but continued to flourish in the vastly altered conditions of the late nineteenth and early twentieth centuries.

The basis of the aristocracy's power was land. They simply owned the greater part of Britain. In 1873 the first (and last) return of owners of land since the Domesday survey of 1086, showed that four-fifths of the land of the United Kingdom was owned by less than 7000 persons, out of a total population of some 31 million. In England 360 persons had estates of more than 10,000 acres, and of these about 2–300 constituted the aristocracy, having both hereditary titles and large estates. Below these ranked the gentry, the greater of whom, numbering about

1000, had estates of between 3000 and 10,000 acres. The lesser gentry, or squires, had estates of 1–3000 acres, and there were about 2000 of them. Burke's *Landed Gentry*, covering the whole of the United Kingdom, for the same date had about 4000 entries. The lower income limit for the gentry was £1000 per year and the upper limit around £10,000. Among the aristocracy incomes ranged from the Duke of Bedford's £141,793 (plus another £102,296 from his London property) to the Earl of Clarendon's modest £3,741 per annum. (At this time an agricultural labourer's weekly wage was 12–14s, and a skilled artisan could hope to earn 28s to £2 per week).

With such economic strength the traditional ruling classes were able to withstand challenges to their hegemony for a long time. But in addition they had one inestimable advantage: their rivals aspired not to overthrow but to join them. As a mildly critical contemporary put it, 'men who have made their fortunes in trade are . . . covetous of land, which for them is the one sure passport to social consideration'.[1] The prestige of land ownership was so great that new aspirants to power wished usually to set themselves up as country gentlemen. What Trollope's Archdeacon Grantley had said somewhat earlier remained true until the end of the nineteenth century: 'land gives so much more than the rent. It gives position and influence and political power, to say nothing about the game.'[2] The aristocracy and gentry were by no means adverse to new wealth acquired through banking, business and industry, provided it was transmuted in approved fashion. It was a traditional saying that 'gentry is but ancient riches'. Some landowners moreover had recent riches as well, acquired from the exploitation of minerals, notably coal, beneath their land, or from the development of urban building sites. Economically land was a declining asset in the later years of the nineteenth century as agriculture suffered in the Great Depression and rents fell drastically. Without some fresh influx of wealth the nobility as a class would have been hard pressed. But from the 1880s new peerages were granted to men whose fortunes had been made in trade and industry: the Allsopps, Basses and Guinnesses in brewing; Cunliffe-Lister in textiles; Armstrong in engineering and armaments. In the decade before 1886 only 4 peerages were granted to men from commerce and industry; in the ten years from 1886 the number was 18. There was also an increase in the number of new baronetcies and knighthoods, most of which went to businessmen and manufacturers. The top echelons of industry and commerce were thus assimilated into the ruling elite, and second and third generation brewers or millowners graduated easily via the public schools and the Universities of Oxford and Cambridge into high society. A shrewd contemporary observer, the literary journalist Thomas Escott, ascribed the strength of English society to a blending of 'the three rival elements – the aristocratic, the plutocratic and the democratic'; and was in no doubt that 'the aristocratic principle is still paramount, forms the foundation of our social structure, and has been strengthened and extended in its operation by the plutocratic.'[3] This fusion of old and new wealth consolidated the power of the aristocracy while at the same time modifying the nature of the ruling class.

The political power of the aristocracy was still visibly dominant in late Victorian Britain. Despite the entry of 'new men' from business, the law and the professions into politics after 1868, those who held high office, and who therefore made the most important decisions, were still likely to be members of the aristocracy. Curiously, the two greatest leaders of the Conservative and Liberal parties, Disraeli and Gladstone, were outsiders in aristocratic England and had to integrate themselves in different ways into 'Society'. But the class structure of cabinets in the late nineteenth century (as shown in the table on p. 32) tells its own story.[4]

The representative strength of the aristocracy and landed interest in the cabinet was relatively greater than the group's membership of the House of Commons. In 1868 nearly two-thirds of all MPs were members of landed families; by 1886 this figure had declined to a half; and in 1900 to less than a third.

The tone of aristocratic politics was reflected in the behaviour of the leaders of the Conservative party, which was in office for most of the period 1874–1906. The third Marquess of Salisbury, head of the great house of Cecil, was prime minister for a total of thirteen and a half years, and was succeeded by his nephew, Arthur J. Balfour. Their style was that of the great aristocrat who

Cabinet Personnel, 1868–1914

Administration	Year	Aristo-crats	Middle Class	Working Class	Total
1. Gladstone	1868	7	8	–	15
2. Disraeli	1874	7	5	–	12
3. Gladstone	1880	8	6	–	14
4. Salisbury	1885	11	5	–	16
5. Gladstone	1886	9	6	–	15
6. Salisbury	1886	10	5	–	15
7. Gladstone	1892	9	8	–	17
8. Salisbury	1895	8	11	–	19
9. Balfour	1902	9	10	–	19
10. Campbell-Bannerman	1906	7	11	1	19
11. Asquith	1914	6	12	1	19

felt obligated to do his duty of governing the country but found it all rather a bore. Politics was a game, to be played by those who were the natural rulers of the country. Affairs of state were to be conducted according to the conveniences of country house living:

> During the months that Lord Salisbury's household was in residence at Hatfield [records his daughter] the interviews at the Foreign Office were limited by the necessity of his catching a seven-o'clock train from King's Cross. He prided himself on wasting no time over this operation, and a regular drill established itself. One Foreign Office messenger stood outside the door of his room with his greatcoat ready, while another was on the watch at the foot of the private staircase which led from it to the Parade, where a single-horsed brougham stood waiting. His duty was to throw open the brougham door as soon as the Prime Minister's footstep was heard on the stairs, and the horse was trained to start at full speed the instant that it clashed to behind him. It is a measure of the changed conditions of traffic that the speed was maintained throughout the journey: under the Horse

Guards' Arch, along Whitehall, across Trafalgar Square, up Charing Cross Avenue, and amidst the intricacies of Bloomsbury, any momentary stoppage being made up for by the horse being whipped into a small gallop at the next stretch of clear going. Seventeen minutes, carefully timed by his watch, was the period which Lord Salisbury allowed from the moment of leaving his room in Downing Street to that of arriving at King's Cross. If the limit had been exceeded by a minute, he would report it as depressedly as a player who has taken a stroke beyond his established form in getting round the golf-course. The daily challenge to London traffic was his outlet for the sporting instinct, universal in mankind.[5]

The gap between Salisbury, the political leader of his country, and the mass of post–1884 voters whom he supposedly led, could hardly have been greater. He was in fact disdainful of attempts to appeal to the voters. Typically he was prepared to express sympathy for working-class people but bleakly assured them that they could never realise their hopes of social betterment through legislation:

> We must learn this rule, that no men and no class of men ever rise to any permanent improvement in their condition of body or mind except by relying upon their own personal efforts. The wealth with which the rich man is surrounded is constantly tempting him to forget that truth . . . The poor man, especially in these days, may have a similar temptation offered to him by legislation, but the same inexorable rule will work. The only true lasting benefit which the statesman can give to the poor man is so to shape matters that the greatest possible liberty for the exercise of his own moral and intellectual qualities should be offered to him by law . . .[6]

When the Tories fell briefly from power in 1892 the succeeding Liberal Government was led at first by the aged Mr Gladstone, but from 1894 onwards by the Earl of Rosebery, another great magnate, who resembled Salisbury in background and outlook.

Politics were only one aspect of the life of the ruling elite and were not expected to interfere with such things as sport, travel or social activities.

Aristocratic life was predicated on the assumption of ample leisure. What distinguished the aristocracy and to some extent the gentry from other classes was that they enjoyed a substantial income without having to spend the greater part of their time earning it. This left them free for a great variety of other activities, some of which were perhaps little more than an escape from boredom. The figure who best typified the life style of gentlemanly leisure was the Prince of Wales, later King Edward VII. He and his circle of 'fast' friends seemed to enjoy an endless round of pleasure: gambling, horse racing, yachting, shooting, womanizing, visits to music hall, Paris, Biarritz and German spas. Luxury and conspicuous consumption were much to the taste of the heir to the throne, and rumour and scandal were seldom absent from his immediate circle. His name was linked with the *demi-mondaines*, actresses and aristocratic women who were his companions and mistresses. 'He preferred men to books and women to either,' commented his private secretary, Sir Frederick Ponsonby. All this was much disapproved of by his mother, Queen Victoria, whose court was a model of respectable bourgeois morality. Nevertheless, as the first gentleman of the land Edward's tastes and habits, including his liking for the *nouveaux riches*, set the tone in high aristocratic circles. He did not invent the conventions of life among the most privileged sections of society but he approved and encouraged those aspects which he found most congenial. Among these were the enjoyments of country house living.

Set in the midst of skilfully landscaped parks and carefully tended gardens the great country houses are today perhaps the best-known surviving monuments to aristocratic life (indeed, they have been subtly but dubiously insinuated into our consciousness as comprising part of our National Heritage). Many of these mansions dated from Tudor, Stuart and Georgian times, but others were nineteenth-century creations in the fashionable Gothic or baronial style. Splendour and ostentation were the keynotes of such aristocratic building, reflecting the dignity and wealth of their owners. Designed for public rather than domestic life, the great country house was used for entertainment and hospitality, providing opportunities for blood sports and social intercourse of all kinds. Country house parties also served other purposes, as the following rather idealised picture suggests:

> In a gathering of people selected by a really clever hostess, there might be one or two Cabinet Ministers who welcomed the opportunity of quiet conversation, or there might be a Viceroy or high official from a far-off corner of the Empire, anxious to make someone in the government of the day realise a little more the difficulties of a particular experiment that Britain had delegated to him to carry out. These parties often included a diplomat home on leave, a painter, and almost certainly a musician who played to some of the company in the evenings. Beside these eminent people there were usually a sprinkling of women famous for their beauty or wit or both, who either gave the conversation a sparkling turn, or were wise enough not to interrupt good talk, and who accordingly sat looking statuesque or flowerlike.[7]

The country house was, as Escott put it, 'an institution situated in that extensive borderland where politics and society meet'.

The aristocracy usually spent only part of the year on their country estates; the rest of the time they were in London – or abroad. During the London 'Season', from the late spring to August, they lived in their town houses, large elegant dwellings in the West End, whence they continued their round of social and political activities: balls, dinners, banquets, garden parties, receptions, opera, theatre, lectures, croquet, lawn tennis, the Henley Regatta, Ascot, Bisley, Eton, Harrow, Lords. In the mornings one rode in Rotten Row, in the afternoons one went for a drive in the park, always to see and be seen. One woman, who was at the centre of this charmed circle, Frances Greville (later Countess of Warwick, and also for some years mistress of the Prince of Wales), described how it was:

> When we spoke of 'The Park' it was always Hyde Park near the Corner. If you entered by the Albert Memorial or Marble

Arch you were certain to be making for that select spot lying between Albert and Grosvenor Gates. Here the small circle of Society with the big 'S' was sure of meeting all its members on morning ride or drive, or in the late afternoon between tea and dinner, in what was practically a daily Society Garden Party! . . . My memory [flies] back to the noon daily drive of my phaeton with high-stepping chestnuts, or browns, or bays, eagerly recognised by admiring friends who crowded round on horseback or on foot when one pulled up at the entrance to the Row and chatted of the social round – of future meetings, of dances, lunches, and dinners within 'the Circle'. My horses were so well known that they always made a stir. One 'booked' friends for luncheon, and perhaps drove them down Piccadilly prancing on the wide sweep of pavement, glancing up at the Turf Club window as a possible place to find an extra man for a dinner-party . . .

Late afternoon in Hyde Park meant state carriages and barouches with beautifully dressed occupants pulled up under the trees. It was not etiquette to handle the reins oneself in the afternoons, so we sat on rows of chairs chatting and behaving as if the world we knew bounded by the Smart Set was a fixed orbit, as if London – our London – was a place of select social enjoyment for the Circle, as if nothing could change in this best of delightful worlds. Then there would be clatter of faster horses, and down this mile of drive came the well-known Royal carriage with the beautiful Alexandra, Princess of Wales, bowing right and left as only she could bow, and hats were raised and knees curtsied before seats were resumed and interrupted chatter continued.[8]

The London season came to an end in August, with an exodus to the grouse moors of the North in time for 'the Glorious Twelfth', or yachting at Cowes; and the shutters were put up and the dust sheets brought out in the great houses of Belgravia and Mayfair.

Escott was at pains to point out that this picture (which he called the popular notion) was not the whole story and that duties as well as enjoyment were the lot of the aristocracy.

Whether as many of them as he claimed actually concerned themselves with the management of their estates seems doubtful. The details of estate management were in any case best left to stewards and bailiffs. The main impact of the landed aristocracy lay elsewhere, in the undisputed leadership of county society, as the visible apex of the social system. The great house, with its 40 or 50 domestic servants and an equal number of estate workers, was a whole community in itself, a symbol and reminder of the grandeur of its titled owner. A visit by the Prince of Wales, who loved to spend time with his friends (the Dukes of Devonshire, Richmond and Hamilton, Lords Savile, Carrington, Crewe, Rosebery, Iveagh, Londonderry and others) set the seal on this social magnificence, but imposed a formidable burden on the host and his wife. Not only did the royal visitor bring his own retinue of servants who had to be accommodated, but he expected to be entertained continuously. Gargantuan meals with many courses and types of wine, elaborate wardrobes and frequent changes of costume (Edward had a passion for ceremonial and dressing up), enormous *battues* in which hundreds of gamebirds (grouse, pheasant, partridge, snipe) would be slaughtered in a single day's shooting, were requirements for such visits. An immense amount of organisation and an army of retainers were involved. The evil spirit of boredom had to be exorcised at any cost. Even so, for the women the exorcism was not always successful. Lady Warwick explains:

We began the day by breakfasting at ten o'clock. This meal consisted of many courses in silver dishes on the side-table. There was enough food to last a group of well-regulated digestions for the whole day. The men went out shooting after breakfast and then came the emptiness of the long morning from which I suffered silently. I can remember the groups of women sitting discussing their neighbours or writing letters at impossible little ornamental tables. I never could enjoy writing at spindly-legged tables. I like plenty of elbow room and a broad expanse. We were not all women. There were a few unsporting men asked – 'darlings'. These men of witty and amusing conversation were always asked

as extras everywhere to help to entertain the women; otherwise we should have been left high and dry. The 'ladies' then
were not like the women of today. They rarely took part in
the shoot, not even going out to join the shooters until
luncheon time. Then, dressed in tweeds and trying to look
as sportsman-like as the clothes of the day allowed, we went
out together to some rendezvous of the shooters. A woman
who was very bloodthirsty and sporting might go and cower
behind some man and watch his prowess among the
pheasants. But there were very few even of those brave ones.
After a large luncheon, finishing up with coffee and liqueurs,
the women preferred to wend their way back to the house.
They would spend the intervening time until the men returned for tea once more, changing their clothes. This time
they got into lovely tea-gowns. The tea-gowns of that day
were far more beautiful than the evening gowns worn for
dinner. We changed our clothes four times a day at least.
This kept our maids and ourselves extraordinarily busy . . .

When I think of all these gorgeous gowns round a tea-table
I fancy we must have looked like a group of enormous dolls.
Conversation at tea was slumberous. Nobody woke up to
be witty until dinner time with its accompanying good wines.
The men discussed the bags of the day and the women did
the admiring. With the coming of bridge in later years the
hours between tea and dinner were relieved of their tedium.
It used often to be sheer boredom until seven when we went
off to dress for dinner. [9]

Life among the landed gentry was much more modest, though
patterned upon the same basic premises of an assured income
and leisure. The squire who divided his time between the hunting
field and the local magistrates' bench was a familiar enough
figure at any time before 1914, and indeed later. He and his
family were the backbone of county society, on terms of easy
familiarity with the aristocracy, whose leadership they normally
accepted as part of the natural order of things. Because they spent
more of their time in the country and often could not afford
extended visits to Town, the squirearchy were the day-to-day

rulers of the shires. It was they who enforced the game laws, their wives and daughters who visited the village sick and aged, and their families who filled the assembly rooms of the county town at that annual highlight, the Hunt Ball. Hunting was the gentlemanly activity *par excellence*. The horse, with all that went with it (stables, grooms, carriages) was a symbol of social standing; and fox hunting was the sport which unified aristocracy, gentry, farmers and some city people under a blanket of patronage and deference. A rough equality in the field extended even to women, a minority of whom were keen hunters. Large landowners regarded it as their duty to keep a pack of hounds, and to be a great MFH (Master of Fox Hounds) was a highly regarded distinction.

The gentlemanly Siegfried Sassoon, born in 1886, recalled his youthful passion for fox hunting:

The meet was at 'The Five Bells', a wayside inn close to Basset Wood, which was the chief stronghold of fox-preservation in that part of the Ringwell country. There was never any doubt about finding a fox at Basset. Almost a mile square, it was well-ridden and easy to get about in, though none too easy to get a fox away from . . . Memories within memories; those red and black and brown coated riders return to me now without any beckoning, bringing along with them the wintry smelling freshness of the woods and fields. And how could I forget them, those evergreen country characters whom I once learnt to know by heart, and to whom I have long since waved my last farewell (as though at the end of a rattling good day). Sober faced squires, with their civil greetings and knowing eyes for the run of a fox; the landscape belonged to them and they to the homely landscape. Weather-beaten farmers, for whom the activities of the Hunt were genial interludes in the stubborn succession of good or bad seasons out of which they made a living on their low-lying clay or wind-swept downland acres. These people were the pillars of the Hunt – the landowners and the farmers. The remainder were merely subscribers; and a rich-flavoured collection of characters they were, although I only half-recognized them as such while I was with them.[10]

The more serious side of a squire's life is indicated in the following recollections of a boyhood spent in the 1890s by Sir Lawrence Jones. His father was a Norfolk baronet of modest means:

> On most days of the week the dog-cart whisked him away after breakfast, to the Board of Guardians, to Petty Sessions, to the County Council . . . Having succeeded my grandfather at the age of twenty-seven, after two years at the Bar during which his total earnings amounted to a small silver clock given to him by a QC for whom he devilled, he commenced Squire with an overdraft, mortgages, jointures, a strong sense of duty, and a slight sense of grievance because his younger brother, who became a Bishop, had snatched up my grandfather's gold watch and chain, after the funeral, from under his elder brother's nose. His own father's prolonged reign as Chairman of Quarter Sessions ensured his welcome into county affairs; and his rather lordly manners rescued his personal prestige among his own tenants and retainers from the damage which it might so easily have suffered from his extreme affability and friendliness. When two Cambridge friends hired the partridge-shooting and lodged at the Home Farm, they spoke to the bailiff's wife of their longstanding friendship with her employer. 'Ah well,' said Mrs Olley, 'Sir Lawrence never were partic'lar who he took up with.'[11]

Servants, and the attitude towards them, were central to the ruling-class consciousness. Even the impecunious Joneses 'made do' with: 'a butler, house-keeper, footman, cook and kitchen-maid, three housemaids, two laundry-maids, two nurses, a coach-man and groom, four gardeners, two game-keepers, two woodmen and two estate carpenters'. Servants were expected to be extremely deferential. As Sassoon, describing his aunt's groom with whom he spent much time in childhood, put it: 'he was what I afterwards learnt to call "a perfect gentleman's servant", he never allowed me to forget my position as "a little gentleman": he always knew exactly when to become discreetly respectful. In fact, he "knew his place".' The earliest childhood memories of many members of the upper classes were connected with the servants – nurses, maids, grooms – who looked after them, and towards whom they developed feelings of both affection and patronage. For the landowning classes, the deference of servants provided a daily reinforcement of their self-assurance, superiority and self-perception as natural leaders. The world was quite simply divided into those who led and those who were fit only to be led, or as Lady Warwick put it, rural society was 'a small select aristocracy born booted and spurred to ride, and a large dim mass born saddled and bridled to be ridden'.

This expected subservience was extended to all who belonged to the 'lower orders', and especially to dependents in the village or estate. Although the landed classes habitually thought of the villagers as 'our' people, in fact they had little knowledge of labouring life, which was totally outside their experience. The sensitive Sir Lawrence Jones reflected:

We were not class-conscious, because class was something that was there, like the rest of the phenomenal world; moreover, they were all our respected friends, who simply happened to be 'the poor', and consequently could not expect to dine, like ourselves, off turkey and plum-pudding. When we visited them in their homes, we were prone to envy them for their warmth and cosiness, the shell-boxes, the grandfather clocks, the china dogs upon the mantelpiece, rather than to compare their cramped dwellings unfavourably with our own. Nobody told us that the widow Grimmer was bringing up two boys on five shillings a week from the parish, and lighting in her grate, from time to time, a piece of brown paper, in order that she and the children might warm their hands, for three or four fleeting seconds, when the paper flamed and roared in the draught of the crooked chimney. Did my father, the kindest of men, know this? He was paying his farm-labourers, married men with families, fourteen shillings a week. But they were lucky, for they got free milk and butter from Mrs Olley's dairy. Did my father know that young Willy Woodhouse, aged seventeen, who worked in the carpenter's shop, walked seven miles in the morning, with his tool-bag on his back, to repair the barn at Kettlestone, and seven miles home again at night? Old John Basham, the head-carpenter, drove there in his cart, to keep an eye on the work. My father swore by old John Basham, and selected, for old John's tombstone, after much thought, the text: 'The path of the just is as a shining light, that shineth more and more unto the perfect day'. But if John Basham was about to return from Kettlestone half an hour before knocking-off time, not once did it occur to his just mind to wait and give his workmen, or at worst their heavy tools, a lift home in his pony-cart. He rode the path of the just behind his pony, and Sam and young Willy trudged again the seven miles of dusty lanes.[12]

It is characteristic of elites that they seek to preserve and justify their position through certain styles of living and codes of behaviour. The preeminence of the gentlemanly ideal was widely acknowledged by the Victorians, though they found exact definition difficult. As Anthony Trollope, the novelist, said in his *Autobiography* (1883): if a man tried to define the term he would fail but everyone would know what he meant. By the later nineteenth century gentility had been extended beyond its chivalrous and honorific origins to include a whole set of assumptions and attitudes as to how a gentleman and a lady should behave. They were expected to be honest, dignified, courteous, considerate and socially at ease; to be disdainful of trade and money-grabbing; and to uphold the tenets of *noblesse oblige*. A gentleman paid his gambling debts, did not cheat at cards, and was honourable towards ladies – though he might not always show the same consideration for his tradesmen's debts or the reputations of female servants and village girls. The man who offended against the rules was a cad, a bounder, an upstart. The gentlemanly virtues were ascribed to 'good breeding'. The well-bred, claimed Lady Warwick, 'have an air! The middle classes may have manners but they have no manner.'

The mechanism through which elite society was controlled was Society. Sociologically Society 'can be seen as a system of quasi-kinship relationships which was used to "place" mobile individuals during the period of structural differentiation fostered by industrialisation and urbanisation'.[13] The crucial problem of access to membership of the elite was resolved through a strict system of social ritual and etiquette, largely enforced by the upper-class wives. An elaborate code governed introductions, calling and dining. The leaving of cards, for instance, was explained in *The Lady* (9 February 1893):

> There is very strict etiquette in this matter of cards and calls and there is one essential difference between *calling* and *leaving cards*. It is usual on paying a first visit merely to leave cards without inquiring if the mistress of the house is at home. Thus Mrs A. leaves her own card and two of her husband's cards upon Mrs B. Within a week, if possible, certainly within ten days Mrs B. should return the visit and leave cards upon Mrs A. Should Mrs A., however, have 'called' upon Mrs B. and the latter returned it by merely leaving cards this would be taken as a sign that the latter did not desire the acquaintance to ripen into friendship. Strict etiquette demands that a call should be returned by a call and a card by a card.[14]

The apparent triviality of this etiquette should not be allowed to mask the real power of social endorsement or exclusion which it contained. If after an introduction a superior person did not wish to continue the relationship she 'cut', usually by ignoring the person concerned if they happened to see each other. A *Punch* cartoon of 23 January 1892 shows two young ladies and their mother walking past three similarly well-dressed ladies in the park, with the accompanying dialogue:

> There go the Spicer Wilcoxes, Mamma! I'm told they're dying to know us. Hadn't we better call?
>
> Certainly not, Dear. If they're dying to know us, they're not worth knowing. The only people worth *our* knowing are the people who *don't* want to know us!

In Victorian usage it was possible to meet someone but not to 'know' (i.e. recognise) her.

Access to the ranks of the elite was also controlled through marriage. It was obviously desirable that young people should meet only partners deemed suitable by their parents, and the Season provided an elaborate ritual for the girls of 'coming out', presentation at court, chaperonage, balls and dances – organised by the matrons and dowagers of Society. Lady Warwick again:

I 'came out' in the season of 1880, and my engagement to Lord Brooke was announced in June of that year. I was that rare thing – as rare as any *oiseau bleu* – a great heiress, for America may scarcely be said as yet to have assaulted the fastnesses of English society. I was a 'beauty', and only those who were alive then know the magic that word held for the period. I was physically fit, eighteen, unspoilt, and I adored dancing. My stepfather and mother rented 7 Carlton Gardens for the year; the house belonged to the then Earl of Warwick, father of the man I was destined to marry. I was married from that house. We lived there afterwards, and one of my children was born there . . . Many balls were given specially for me. In those days men gave balls; the balls of the Blues and the Life Guards were noted for their excellent dancing, and the Bachelors' Ball of that season was one of the great successes . . . I was feted, feasted, courted, and adored, in one continual round of gaiety, and I lived in and for the moment. Nor was I a mere fool. My reason and my mentors whispered to me sometimes that my money and estates were perhaps more important than my person to some of my thronging admirers.[15]

And so to the 'brilliant society wedding' in Westminster Abbey in April 1881, with the Prince and Princess of Wales among the guests.

Ritualized behaviour for men was exercised through the institution of the Gentleman's Club. Membership was selective and so conferred social acceptability in the circles for which the club catered. The club also provided a home in Pall Mall, Piccadilly, or St James's for single men or gentlemen up from the country, a place where they could feel at ease with others of their own kind. The names of the Bath, the Turf, Boodles, the Reform, the Carlton, and the Athenaeum conjure up visions of genteel leisure, good dining, and informal political influence.

The Elite

The gentlemanly pattern of life in what G. M. Young called 'the late Victorian age and its flash Edwardian epilogue' is beautifully encapsulated in Vita Sackville-West's novel, *The Edwardians*. A critic tells Sebastian, the hero:

My dear boy, your life was mapped out for you from the moment you were born. You went to a preparatory school; you went to Eton; you are now at Oxford; you will go into the Guards; you will have various love-affairs, mostly with fashionable married women; you will frequent wealthy and fashionable houses; you will attend Court functions; you will wear a white-and-scarlet uniform – and look very handsome in it, too – you will be flattered and persecuted by every mother in London; you will eventually become engaged to a suitable young lady; you will marry her in the chapel here and the local bishop will officiate; you will beget an heir and several other children, who ought to have been painted by Hoppner; you will then acquire the habit of being unfaithful to your wife and she to you; you will both know it and both, out of sheer good manners and the force of civilisation, will tacitly agree to ignore your mutual infidelities; you will sometimes make a speech in the House of Lords; you will be given the Garter; you will send your sons to a preparatory school, Eton, Oxford, and into the Guards; after dinner you will talk about socialism and the growth of democracy; you will be worried but not seriously disturbed; on the twelfth of August you will go north to shoot grouse, on the first of September you will return south to shoot partridges, on the first of October you will shoot pheasants; your photograph will appear in the illustrated papers, propped on a shooting-stick with two dogs and a loader; you will celebrate your golden wedding; you will carry a spur or a helmet at the next coronation; you will begin to wonder if your son (aged fifty-one) wants you to die; you will oblige him by dying at last, and your coffin will be borne to the family vault on a farm cart accompanied by a procession of your employees and your tenants.[16]

How far indolence and extravagance were typical of the aristocracy as a whole is hard to say. The Prince of Wales's 'Marlborough House set' was a very small group, and, although it set a certain tone for high society, was not representative of the bulk of the landed classes. Popular perceptions of aristocracy may not accord with the objective reality but are nevertheless important in assessing the cultural role of the elite. Every dominant and privileged class seeks to legitimize itself by securing assent to its beliefs on the part of the unprivileged, and popular notions of gentlemanly life reflect to some extent the success or otherwise of such efforts. Among the most widely read novelists in the late nineteenth century was Ouida (Marie Louise de la Ramée). Her novel, *Under Two Flags*, is a romance of aristocratic life set in the 1860s. The Honourable Bertie Cecil, second son of Viscount Royallieu, is an officer in the 1st Life Guards. After a youth and early manhood of aristocratic luxury and indulgence he is compelled to flee to North Africa and join the French Army of Africa as a *chasseur d'Afrique* in order to preserve the honour and good name of a lady friend and also to cover up a fraudulent act by his beloved younger brother. After twelve years of incredible hardship in the ranks Cecil is able to return home, but only after his life has been saved by Cigarette, a camp follower who secretly loves him. Her anti-aristocratic feelings are finally overcome by her recognition of Cecil's noble qualities, and she sacrifices herself by throwing herself between him and the firing squad just in time for the reprieve. The novel is full of stereotypes and clichés about the aristocracy. Bertie's valet declares:

> He's a true gentleman, Mr Cecil; never grudge a guinea, or a fiver to you; never out of temper either, always have a kind word for you if you want – thoro'bred every inch of him; see him bring down a rocketter, or lift his horse over the Broad Water! He's a gentleman – not like your snobs that have nothing sound about 'em but their cash, and swept out their shops before they bought their fine feathers! – and I'll be d – d if I care what I do for him.

The hero's father, Viscount Royallieu, is 'the haughtiest of haughty nobles'; the ladies are all 'high bred'; and honour is the virtue that comes above all else. Although the Royallieu peerage is one of the most impoverished but ancient in the kingdom, Bertie manages to live at the level expected of a nobleman:

A Guardsman at home is always, if anything, rather more luxuriously accommodated than a young Duchess, and Bertie Cecil was never behind his fellows in anything; besides, he was one of the cracks of the Household . . . Though his debts were considerable, and he was literally as penniless as a man can be to stay in the Guards at all, he had never in any shape realised the want of money. He might not be able to raise a guinea to go towards that long-standing account, his army tailor's bill, and post obits had long ago forestalled the few hundreds a year that, under his mother's settlements, would come to him at the Viscount's death; but Cecil had never known in his life what it was not to have a first-rate stud, not to live as luxuriously as a duke, not to order the costliest dinners at the clubs, and be among the first to lead all the splendid entertainments and extravagances of the Household; he had never been without his Highland shooting, his Baden gaming, his prize-winning schooner among the R. V. Y. Squadron, his September *battues,* his Pytchley hunting, his pretty expensive Zu-Zus and other toys, his drag for Epsom, and his trap and hack for the Park, his crowd of engagements through the season, and his bevy of fair leaders of the fashion to smile on him, and shower their invitation-cards on him, like a rain of rose-leaves, as one of their 'best men'.[17]

The significance of such a passage lies not in its hard evidence of aristocratic life so much as in its revelation of what ordinary people expected that life to be like. The values and assumptions implicit in the novel testify to the popular sensibilities of the age.

In the same way the popular interest in *causes célèbres* reveals a view of the elite from below. The Victorian age was rich in scandal, fraud and crime in high as well as low society, all avidly followed in the press. Echoes of the Tichborne case (1867–75) were still present in the 1880s, though the claimant (who pretended to be the baronet Sir Roger Tichborne) was discredited and in gaol. In 1875 Valentine Baker, an army colonel who had served with the cavalry in the Crimea, South Africa and India, figured in a colourful case of indecent assault on a young lady in a train. She managed to escape from his clutches only by hanging on the outside footboard of the carriage as it sped towards Waterloo. In the Dysart peerage case of 1881, Elizabeth Acford said that she had been seduced by Lord Huntingtower, son of Lady Dysart, in whose service she had been working. She claimed that a 'Scotch marriage' had taken place in 1844 in front of a servant, that three children were born, that Lord Huntingtower had deserted her and she was left on the parish. Such *causes célèbres* provided not only salacious details or the excitement of murder and violence, but also fascinating glimpses of upper-class life. Despite some populist overtones the *causes célèbres* served not to discredit the aristocracy but to provide elements of theatre. The revelation that high-born people also had their faults and limitations could be comforting, an assurance that 'they' were not really all that different from 'us'.

Yet like all stereotypes the popular view of the elite probably failed to take sufficient account of the changes which were taking place after 1880. The familiar outward façade concealed a transformation of the ruling class. While the old nobility continued to dominate Society, their ranks were being infiltrated by the plutocracy. At the same time the agricultural depression weakened the power of the landed interest, so that the traditional ruling classes were challenged from both within and without. Nevertheless, they manifested a high degree of resilience and flexibility over the next few decades. Through the admission of new blood to the peerage, and a new readiness to accept non-landed income, they consolidated their position as social leaders and retained much of their grip on the life of the nation.

3

Comfortable England

Despite the continuing existence of an aristocratic elite most late Victorians no longer thought of themselves as living in a primarily aristocractic nation. From the Widow at Windsor to the respectable lower orders, the tone of society was unmistakably bourgeois. Many years previously Engels had complained that even the working class was bourgeois in this most bourgeois of nations. By the later years of the century the values, attitudes and assumptions of the middle classes had become endemic in the national life. It is significant that in one of the severest critiques of Victorianism, *The Way of All Flesh*, Samuel Butler retained great respect for the power of money. Happiness for all, he suggested, would be attained if only we could be buried like wasps' eggs in neat little cells with ten or twenty thousand pounds in Bank of England notes wrapped round each of us and could wake up, like the wasp, completely free to enjoy this ample provision.[1]

Power can be exercised in many ways; and bourgeois hegemony in the nineteenth century was exerted through economic, religious and cultural institutions before the middle class assumed the reins of politics. One of the misleading impressions left by an older historiography is that in 1832 the middle class suddenly took over political power from the aristocracy and became the *de facto* ruling class. In fact for many years the new voters were content to share political power with the representatives of the landed classes while concentrating their main energies elsewhere in commerce and industry. Only gradually and step by step, as the franchise was widened and the political nation extended, did the middle classes play an increasingly active part in politics; until by the final decades of the century it was taken for granted that power was in the hands of the middle class and that the challenge of the day was from the working class who were demanding full political emancipation.

Like the gap between the popular image and the reality of the aristocracy, the concept of the bourgeoisie was not wholly in accord with the realities of middle-class life. For one thing the middle class was far from homogeneous, stretching from rich *rentiers* who hobnobbed with royalty to modest clerks and shopmen who shaded off into the elite of the working class. To talk of the bourgeoisie is not to employ a precise description so much as to imply a certain status or quality common to all those who ranked between the gentry and the working class in the social hierarchy. The determinants of membership of the middle class were still essentially the same as they had been earlier in the Queen's reign: an income above a certain minimum, a particular occupation or calling, education beyond simple literacy, recognised religious affiliations, a certain style of home, and the employment of at least one servant – in short, the wherewithal to lead a comfortable life. It was a main feature of late Victorian society that the middle classes were more numerous and more prosperous in Britain than in any other country, with the possible exception of the USA. In this sense we can speak of the Age of the Bourgeoisie or bourgeois England. But for purposes of analysis it is convenient to differentiate between the various sections or layers of the middle class.

The very top level of the middle class, the *haute bourgeoisie*, lived on terms of familiarity with the aristocracy and they intermarried. London bankers and City merchants were amongst the wealthiest people in the country. The three largest personal fortunes left by millionaires who died between 1880 and 1909 were those of Charles Morrison (d.1909), warehouseman and merchant banker, who left £10.9 million; Herman, Baron de Stern (d.1887), merchant banker, £3.5 million; and Wentworth Beaumont, first Baron Allendale (d.1907), landowner, £3.2 million.[2] Most of the largest fortunes, such as those of the Rothschilds, Morrisons, Barings or Sassoons, came from commerce or finance, and not from manufacturing or industry. Factory owners were usually wealthy but not immensely wealthy. The upper middle class was in fact divided into two fairly distinct

groups: the financiers and merchants of London, and the manufacturers of the North and Midlands. The former were generally
wealthier, of higher social status and closer to the landed aristocracy than the industrialists. By late Victorian times (and perhaps
earlier) Britain was as much the Clearing House of the World as
the Workshop of the World.

The social intercourse between members of the upper classes,
whether of commercial, professional, industrial or landed background, was admirably recorded by Beatrice Webb. She was one
of the nine daughters of Richard Potter, a rich railway promoter
and timber merchant. He had a country house in Gloucestershire
and a fashionable mansion in Kensington, whence Beatrice was
able to observe London Society in the 1880s:

> The bulk of the shifting mass of wealthy persons who were
> conscious of belonging to London Society, who practised its
> rites and followed its fashions, were, in the last quarter
> of the nineteenth century, professional profit-makers: the
> old-established families of bankers and brewers, often of
> Quaker descent, coming easily first in social precedence;
> then one or two great publishers and, at a distance, ship-
> owners, the chairmen of railway and some other great cor-
> porations, the largest of the merchant bankers – but as yet
> no retailers. Scattered in this pudding-stone of men of rank
> and men of property were jewels of intellect and character;
> cultivated diplomatists from all the countries of the world,
> great lawyers, editors of powerful newspapers, scholarly
> ecclesiastics of the Anglican and Roman Catholic com-
> munions; the more 'stylish' of the permanent heads of
> Government departments, and here and there a star person-
> age from the world of science, literature or art, who hap-
> pened to combine delight in luxurious living and the
> company of great personages with social gifts and a fairly
> respectable character.[3]

Although the amalgam of London Society and country-house life
lacked fixed caste barriers and seemed to Beatrice to be remark-
ably open, she shrewdly divined that the unstated qualification
for membership of this governing class was the possession of

some form of power over other people. The most obvious and easily measurable form of power was wealth. However, the often subconscious pursuit of power could be manifested in various forms. For instance, 'the conventional requirements with regard to personal morality, sexual or financial, were graded with almost meticulous exactitude to the degree of social, political or industrial power exercised by the person concerned'. Thus a duchess could safely indulge in sexual adventures which for plain Mrs Smith would have resulted in complete social ostracism. Similarly the past iniquities of a multi-millionaire, whose millions were secure, were discreetly forgotten, whereas the bankruptcy of a lesser man led to his complete exclusion. 'There seemed in fact to be a sort of invisible stock exchange in constant communication with the leading hostesses in London and in the country; the stock being social reputations and the reason for appreciation or depreciation being worldly success or failure however obtained.'

A middle-class family of more modest means than the Potters, though still well within Beatrice Webb's definition of the middle class as the class that habitually gave orders, was the Darwins of Cambridge. They are delightfully portrayed in the 1880s and 1890s through the childhood eyes of Gwen Raverat, a granddaughter of the great Charles Darwin. Her father was a university professor and fellow of Trinity College and the family lived at Newnham Grange, a rambling eighteenth-century house on the river. There was no London season for them and they did not keep a carriage. Nevertheless a comfortable home life was enjoyed thanks to the usual establishment of servants: housekeeper, cook, housemaid, nursery maid, nanny and gardener. In the house next door a rich widow had eight servants, a little dog, two horses, a carriage, a coachman and a footman. In later life Gwen Raverat remembered how dependent the whole family was on the servants:

> Even when I first married it would never have occurred to me that I could possibly be the cook myself, or that I could care for my baby alone, though we were not at all well off at that time. It was not that I was too proud to work – it

was simply that I had not the faintest idea how to begin to run a house by myself, and would not have thought it possible that I could do it, in spite of all my mother's efforts to train us in housework. The children were always looked after by the nanny: I can never remember being bathed by my mother, or even having my hair brushed by her, and I should not at all have liked it if she had done anything of the kind. We did not feel it was her place to do such things.

Echoing Beatrice Webb, Gwen Raverat concluded:

Ladies were ladies in those days; they did not do things themselves, they told other people what to do and how to do it. My mother would have told anybody how to do anything . . . She would cheerfully have told an engine driver how to drive his engine, and he would have taken it quite naturally, and have answered: 'Yes, ma'am, Very good ma'am, Quite right ma'am,' and then would have gone on driving his engine exactly as before, with hardly even an inward grin at the vagaries of the upper classes.[4]

Social life in Cambridge revolved round the university. When the Darwins gave a formal dinner party they invited twelve to fourteen people, and everybody of dinner-party status was invited strictly in turn:

The guests were seated according to the Protocol, the Heads of Houses ranking by the dates of the foundations of their colleges, except that the Vice-Chancellor would come first of all. After the Masters came the Regius Professors in the order of their subjects, Divinity first; and then the other Professors according to the dates of the foundations of their chairs, and so on down all the steps of the hierarchy. It was better not to invite too many important people at the same time, or the complications became insoluble to hosts of only ordinary culture. How could they tell if Hebrew or Greek took precedence, of two professorships founded in the same year? And some of the grandees were very touchy about their rights, and their wives were even more easily offended.

Dinner was at 7.45 p.m. and there were eight or even ten courses. The menu for a rather grand dinner in 1885 was:

> Clear Soup
> Brill and Lobster Sauce
> Chicken Cutlets and Rice Balls
> Oyster Patties
> Mutton, Potatoes, Artichokes, Beets
> Partridges and Salad
> { Caramel pudding   }
> { Pears and Whipped Cream }
> { Cheese Ramequins   }
> { Cheese Straws   }
> Ice
> Grapes, Walnuts, Chocolates and Pears

Even when there were only four people to dinner they had:

> Tomato Soup
> Fried Smelts and Drawn Butter Sauce
> Mushrooms on Toast
> Roast Beef, Cauliflower and Potatoes
> Apple Charlotte
> Toasted Cheese
> Dessert: Candied Peel, Oranges, Peanuts
> Raisins and Ginger

The Victorian rules of propriety, so often derided by later generations, were fully observed in the Darwin circle. Gwen Raverat was frequently used as a chaperon to courting couples and she records the lengths to which maintaining appearances was carried. When her uncle, Francis Darwin, was engaged to Miss Ellen Crofts (his second wife, whom he married in 1883) he was thirty-five and she was twenty-seven and a Fellow and lecturer at Newnham College. Yet, while Miss Clough, the principal of Newnham, was away for a few weeks Uncle Frank was not able to call on his betrothed because Miss Clough insisted that she alone would do as chaperon. There could be no question of the pair meeting in each other's rooms in college. Propriety assumed many other forms in middle-class life. For instance, one of the hazards of a picnic on the river in summer was having to pass bathing places where naked boys were playing. To avoid embarrassment each lady unfurled her parasol and like an ostrich buried her head in it until the crisis was past and the river decent again. Female modesty extended even to the same sex. 'You could see a friend in her petticoat,' recalled Gwen Raverat, 'but nothing below that was considered decent. At school, the sight of a person in her white frilly drawers caused shrieks of outraged virtue; and I should have thought it impossible to be seen downstairs in my dressing-gown.' A young lady with whom she shared a room one night wore no less than fourteen items of clothing:

1 Thick, long-legged, long-sleeved woollen combinations.
2 Over them, white cotton combinations, with plenty of buttons and frills.
3 Very serious, bony, grey stays, with suspenders.
4 Black woollen stockings.
5 White cotton drawers, with buttons and frills.
6 White cotton 'petticoat-bodice', with embroidery, buttons and frills.
7 Rather short, white flannel petticoat.
8 Long alpaca petticoat, with a flounce round the bottom.
9 Pink flannel blouse.
10 High starched, white collar, fastened on with studs.
11 Navy-blue tie.
12 Blue skirt, touching the ground, and fastened tightly to the blouse with a safety-pin behind.
13 Leather belt, very tight.
14 High button boots.

Beyond the university circles, but to some extent overlapping them, was another professional middle-class group with a distinctive life-style, the Anglican clergy. The comfortable, closed world of Trollope's Barsetshire clergy continued in some rural areas until the end of the century. But the faded photographs of family groups taken outside the vicarage's front door or images of tea on the rectory lawn are only part of the story. In contrast to

Gwen Raverat's light-hearted account of a Cambridge childhood, Flora Mayor's novel, *The Rector's Daughter*, presents a sombre picture of middle-class life in a country rectory at the turn of the century. In an insignificant village in the Eastern counties, the quiet, inner life of a shy, dowdy spinster unfolds. Her one admirer marries someone else, and she is left as the dutiful companion of her adored but austerely learned father, the rector. This semi-autobiographical novel is valuable as historical evidence for the sensitive way it presents the plight of the single woman deprived of sexual or occupational fulfilment, and also for the incidental details which convey the tone of life in a late Victorian context. The rectory household consisted of Canon Jocelyn, his daughter Mary, a cook, housemaid and gardener.

Mary Jocelyn was one of that army of one and a quarter million unmarried women between 20 and 44 who figured in the decennial censuses of 1881–1901. She spent her days ministering to the wants of the villagers, with whom she was more at ease than with her own class. There were new mothers to be reassured and old people to be comforted, the day school to be visited, and jobs in service to be found for the village girls when they left school. She superintended the Sunday school, trained the choir, had a boys' bible class and a mothers' meeting, and patched up 'those differences among the various layers of society which make the excitement of village life'. It was a life set within narrow bounds:

> The year went round with its accustomed routine: Advent Sunday, Carols, the Christmas treat, Ash Wednesday, and a hope that people *will* come to Church this Lent (never realised); the Confirmation, with occasionally the Bishop to lunch; summer treats; garden- and tennis-parties, their own among the number; the Clerical Book Club Tea, with peaches on the lawn; the Harvest Festival, with the preacher to supper afterwards; and the Diocese and Government Inspectors. If they were gentlemen, and in addition classical gentlemen, Canon Jocelyn would enjoy himself, and make them enjoy themselves. If they were neither, Canon Jocelyn would get further and further into his shell.[5]

Canon Jocelyn, aged 82, had been rector of the parish for the past forty-three years. He spent most of his time in his study reading the classics and remembering the Cambridge days of his youth: 'I have always said there is nothing like a first-rate Cambridge man.' His values were those of a previous generation. He thought trade was so inextricably connected with fraud that anyone engaged in it must not be expected to be treated on a level with gentlemen. 'He looked on rich tradesmen with more contempt, supposing that the poor tradesman had remained more honest.' His gallantry and courtesy were by this time old-fashioned, as was noted during one of the rare visits by Mary's old friend, Dora:

> The evening was just a repetition of the visit Dora had paid the Rectory twenty years ago; for the Rectory life was like a chapter of history, twenty years did not count for much with it. Canon Jocelyn offered his arm to form the procession to the dining-room. There was grace before and after meals, proposed by Canon Jocelyn with 'Shall we ask a blessing?' Tea, cake, and bread and butter were brought into the dining-room at nine. Then Canon Jocelyn read Shakespeare and Milton aloud, those fireside bulwarks of the old-fashioned home evenings . . . There were prayers at ten, with verses of the psalms read by the family and servants in turn. Then came bedtime. A hip-bath was prepared before the fire in the spare room. The four-post bedstead with crimson canopies and tassels, so high that it had to be climbed into by steps, the lamp and candle-light were all relics of the past.

For all the families so far mentioned the keeping of several domestic servants was taken for granted. Indeed, when Seebohm Rowntree carried out his survey of working-class poverty in York in 1899 he took the keeping or not of domestic servants as marking the division between the working and middle classes. The middle class was defined essentially as the servant-keeping class, which in York comprised some 30 per cent of the population. A lavish use of domestic service was one of the means by which the middle class used their income to increase their comfort and status. The number and types of domestic servants (who lived in the house and received board and lodging as well as wages) were regulated according to income. There was general agreement in the domestic manuals that a complete household required the employment of at least three female servants. Below this level, it was argued, the wife and daughters would be too involved in housework to cultivate those aspects of gentility to which they rightly aspired. Menservants (butlers, footmen, coachmen, grooms) were usually regarded as something of a luxury, though for 'carriage people' they were hardly avoidable. A young man of the middle classes, unlike a labouring man, could reasonably expect his income to increase as he grew older, and therewith his social expectations. At the beginning of his married life he might be able to afford only a modest villa and one maidservant. But as he prospered his household would grow larger and more elaborate, and an increasingly large proportion of his income would be spent on domestic service. Such was the case with Molly Vivian Hughes and her husband when they married in 1897. She was a teacher and he a newly-qualified barrister, living in a flat in Ladbroke Grove, London. They engaged an eighteen-year-old country girl from Norfolk as maid: 'Emma was a treasure,' being apparently a demon for work. Later, when their family grew, they moved out to Barnet.[6]

Among the lower middle classes the 'servant problem' was reduced to the employment of a single person. She might be a young girl of twelve or thirteen who made the fires and helped with the washing, or only a daily charwoman. H. G. Wells, whose parents kept a china shop in the High Street in Bromley, Kent, remembered such a character: 'The only domestic help I ever knew [my mother] to have was a garrulous old woman of the quality of Sairey Gamp, a certain Betsy Finch. In opulent times Betsy would come in to char . . .' But his mother was ashamed of this situation and was determined to keep up appearances at all costs: 'She believed that it was a secret to all the world that she had no servant and did all the household drudgery herself. I was enjoined never to ask questions about it or let it out when I went abroad.'[7]

Wells came from the lower middle class, and it was there that the 'paraphernalia of gentility' (type of home, servants, expenditure on dress, education, holidays) grew notably in the later years of the century.[8] Two main groups made up the bulk of the lower middle class: first, shopkeepers and small businessmen; and second, white-collar employees such as teachers and, especially, clerks. To these should be added managers, commercial travellers and minor professional people. Earnings were around £150 per annum for clerks and small shopkeepers, and up to £300 for small businessmen. Below this were poorer clerks who had to struggle hard to maintain their respectability, and above it were the substantial middle class. Structural changes towards a larger tertiary or services sector in the late Victorian economy resulted in a growth in the number of clerical and administrative employees. This is shown clearly in the case of clerks, who were perhaps the most representative of all the lower middle-class groups. In 1861 they numbered nearly 92,000, virtually all men; by 1891 there were 370,000 men and 19,000 women; and in 1911 they totalled 561,000 men and 125,000 women. Clerks in banking, insurance, and top mercantile firms were of semi-professional standing; but the lower clerks earning around 30s a week were little different in income and prospects from the better-off skilled working men.

It was the peculiar fate of the lower middle class to be caught between the upper and nether millstones of the British class system. While sharing the aspirations and values of the class above them, the lower middle class were under constant pressure to differentiate themselves from the working class whose way of life they rejected. There was an unresolved tension between the need to maintain the symbols of status and the constraints of economic reality.

> Be our ideas ever so humble, it was still necessary to keep a certain standard of life. It would never do to let Mrs Brown think that we dined on lentils and porridge ... and how might Nell go forth shopping if the perambulator had a shabby hood?

asked Robert Thorne in Shan Bullock's novel about a London clerk.[9]

This status-consciousness and the striving for respectability were well depicted in the writings of H. G. Wells, George Gissing, Arnold Bennett, and forgotten novelists like Pett Ridge. Even more tellingly, and with gentle humour, George and Weedon Grossmith brilliantly portrayed lower middle-class life in the 1890s in their minor classic, *The Diary of a Nobody*. Charles Pooter is a clerk in the City and sets down his thoughts in diary form. He and his 'dear wife Carrie' have just been a week in their new home, 'The Laurels', Brickfield Terrace, Holloway:

a nice six-roomed residence, not counting basement, with a front breakfast-parlour. We have a little front garden; and there is a flight of ten steps up to the front door, which, by-the-way, we keep locked with the chain up. Cummings, Gowing, and our other intimate friends always come to the little side entrance, which saves the servant the trouble of going up to the front door, thereby taking her from her work. We have a nice little back garden which runs down to the railway. We were rather afraid of the noise of the trains at first, but the landlord said we should not notice them after a bit, and took £2 off the rent. He was certainly right; and beyond the cracking of the garden wall at the bottom, we have suffered no inconvenience.

After my work in the City, I like to be at home. What's the good of a home, if you are never in it? 'Home, Sweet Home', that's my motto. I am always in of an evening . . . There is always something to be done: a tin-tack here, a Venetian blind to put straight, a fan to nail up, or part of a carpet to nail down – all of which I can do with my pipe in my mouth; while Carrie is not above putting a button on a shirt, mending a pillow-case, or practising the 'Sylvia Ga-votte' on our new cottage piano (on the three years' system), manufactured by W. Bilkson (in small letters), from Collard and Collard (in very large letters).

Pooter's attitude towards the tradesmen, and their response, is revealing:

April 3. Tradesmen called for custom, and I promised Farmerson, the ironmonger, to give him a turn if I wanted any nails or tools. By-the-by, that reminds me there is no key to our bedroom door, and the bells must be seen to. The parlour bell is broken, and the front door rings up in the servant's bedroom, which is ridiculous. Dear friend Gowing dropped in, but wouldn't stay, saying there was an infernal smell of paint.

April 4. Tradesmen still calling: Carrie being out, I arranged to deal with Horwin, who seemed a civil butcher with a nice clean shop. Ordered a shoulder of mutton for to-morrow, to give him a trial. Carrie arranged with Borset, the butterman, and ordered a pound of fresh butter, and a pound and a half of salt ditto for kitchen, and a shilling's worth of eggs.

April 6. Eggs for breakfast simply shocking; sent them back to Borset with my compliments, and he needn't call any more for orders . . . In the evening, hearing someone talking in a loud voice to the servant in the downstairs hall, I went out to see who it was, and was surprised to find it was Borset, the butterman, who was both drunk and offensive. Borset, on seeing me, said he would be hanged if he would ever serve City clerks any more – the game wasn't worth the candle. I restrained my feelings, and quietly remarked that I thought it was *possible* for a City clerk to be a *gentleman*. He replied he was very glad to hear it, and wanted to know whether I had ever come across one, for *he* hadn't. He left the house, slamming the door after him, which nearly broke the fanlight . . . When he had gone, I thought of a splendid answer I ought to have given him. However, I will keep it for another occasion. [The next day Borset came round to offer his apologies and a pound of fresh butter.]

Pooter and his wife were thrilled to receive an invitation from the Lord and Lady Mayoress to dinner at the Mansion House:

May 1. Carrie said 'I should like to send mother the invitation to look at.' I consented, as soon as I had answered it. I told Mr Perkupp, at the office, with a feeling of pride, that we had received an invitation to the Mansion House; and he said, to my astonishment, that he himself gave in my name to the Lord Mayor's secretary. I felt this rather discounted the value of the invitation, but thanked him; and in reply to me, he described how I was to answer it. I felt the reply was too simple; but of course Mr Perkupp knows best.

May 2. Sent my dress-coat and trousers to the little tailor's round the corner, to have the creases taken out. Told Gowing not to call next Monday, as we were going to the Mansion House. Sent similar note to Cummings.

May 3. Carrie went to Mrs James, at Sutton, to consult about her dress for next Monday. While speaking incidentally to Spotch, one of our head clerks, about the Mansion House, he said: 'Oh, I'm asked, but don't think I shall go.' When a vulgar man like Spotch is asked I feel my invitation is considerably discounted. In the evening, while I was out, the little tailor brought round my coat and trousers, and because Sarah [the maid] had not a shilling to pay for the pressing, he took them away again.

May 4. Carrie's mother returned the Lord Mayor's invitation, which was sent to her to look at, with apologies for having upset a glass of port over it. I was too angry to say anything.

May 5. Bought a pair of lavender kid-gloves for next Monday, and two white ties, in case one got spoiled in the tying.

May 6, Sunday. A very dull sermon, during which, I regret to say, I twice thought of the Mansion House reception to-morrow.

The petty vanities and ambitions of the lower middle class are laid bare: 'He [the curate] wants me to take round the plate, which I think a great compliment.' And the Pooters' taste in home furnishings is not spared: 'I bought a pair of stags' heads made of plaster-of-Paris and coloured brown. They will look just the thing for our little hall, and give it style.' It was not difficult to lampoon the social mores of the lower middle class (the *Diary* appeared originally in *Punch*) and there was (still is) a long tradition of this vein of English humour. The significance of the

Pooters, however, is not as objects of ridicule but as very real human beings in a specific social situation in late Victorian Britain. Here we have the home-centredness, the localness and individualism of the lower middle class. Although clerks, drapers' assistants and school teachers were not gentlemen they were expected to be gentlemanly, for they were in direct contact with the established middle class whose businesses and customers and children they dealt with.[11] Respectability in manner, dress and associations were essential for that upward mobility which was the goal of all who received a 'salary' rather than a wage.

The Pooters' house was in Holloway, but it might just as easily have been in West Hampstead, Kilburn, Peckham or Camberwell. In north and south London, as also in Liverpool, Manchester, Birmingham and other large cities, the growth of the suburbs was a main feature of the last thirty years of the nineteenth century. Fuelled by the massive growth of urban population, and facilitated by the provision of new railways, omnibuses and tramways for the journey to work, whole new areas of terraced houses, semi-detacheds and villas appeared. These were single-family dwellings, satisfying a desire for social exclusiveness. The new suburbia was more than bricks and mortar. It was a middle-class state of existence, a romantic ideal of what the Englishman's home should be like – no less than a practical solution to urban housing problems. For the inhabitants of 'Homelea', 'Belle Vue', 'Sunnyhurst' or 'The Laurels' their homes were not just houses in a street, but also the embodiment of attitudes of mind and social behaviour. The right address was a sign, almost a guarantee, of respectability. Suburbia has usually been scorned by writers and intellectuals, who have seen in it nothing but cultural poverty, banality and pretentiousness. Even those who, like C. F. G. Masterman, were prepared to acknowledge the basic decency, honesty, and family affection hidden behind the aspidistra and carefully draped curtains, complained about the narrowness and triviality of suburban life. Masterman's image was also of middle-class 'suburbans' fearful of the working classes, whose territory they had to cross daily by train or underground on the way to work:

He [the suburban] would never be surprised to find the crowd behind the red flag, surging up his little pleasant pathways, tearing down the railings, trampling the little garden; the 'letting in of the jungle' upon the patch of fertile ground which has been redeemed from the wilderness.[12]

Ironically the poorer members of the lower middle class were in many ways no better off than the working class whom they so feared. For young unmarried clerks and shop assistants life was anything but genteel. Living in shabby lodgings or above the shop, with a low income and long hours of work, they were unconstrained by family or neighbourhood pressures. They experienced to the full the problem of maintaining their status in the face of economic marginality. H. G. Wells began his adolescent life as a draper's assistant in Southsea in 1881. Typically, this position was obtained for him by his mother through personal contacts and a recommendation to the proprietor of the Southsea Drapery Emporium. Wells hated it:

We apprentices were roused from our beds at seven, peremptorily, by one of the assistants . . . We flung on old suits, tucking our nightgowns into our trousers, and were down in the shop in a quarter of an hour, to clean windows, unwrapper goods and fixtures, dust generally, before eight. At eight we raced upstairs to get first go at the wash basins, dressed for the day and at half-past eight partook of a bread and butter breakfast before descending again. Then came window dressing and dressing out the shop. I had to fetch goods for the window dresser and arrange patterns or pieces of fabric on the brass line above the counter. Every day or so the costume window had to be rearranged and I had to go in the costume room and fetch those headless effigies on which costumes are displayed and carry them the length of the shop, to the window dresser, avoiding gas brackets, chairs and my fellow creatures en route. Then I had to see to the replenishing of the pin bowls and the smoothing out and stringing up of paper for small parcels . . . There were a hundred small fussy things to do, straightening up, putting away, fetching and carrying. It was not excessively laborious but it was indescribably tedious. If there was nothing else to do I had to stand to attention at the counter, as though ready for a customer, though at first I was not competent to serve ... Half an hour before closing time we began to put away for the last time and 'wrapper up', provided no customer lingered in the department. And as soon as the doors were shut and the last customer gone, the assistants departed and we junior apprentices rushed from behind the counters, scattered wet sawdust out of pails over the floor and swept it up again with great zest and speed, the last rite of the day. By half-past eight we were upstairs and free, supping on bread and butter, cheese and small beer. That was the ritual for every day of the week, thirteen hours of it, except that on Wednesday, Early Closing Day, the shop closed at five.[13]

Although this type of work was unstable in some respects it nevertheless provided more security than was the lot of most manual workers. It was usually better paid, offered some prospect of promotion, and was not dependent on the weather or the seasons. The unemployed clerk or the draper's assistant who lost his 'crib' could of course be plunged into destitution; but poverty was not endemic in lower middle-class life. Jerome K. Jerome shrewdly observed that for the lower middle class 'being poor is a mere trifle. It is being known to be poor that is the sting.'[14]

It was the obsession with keeping up appearances at all cost that led the children and grandchildren of the late Victorians to accuse them of hypocrisy. But this was not the only or perhaps the most abiding character trait of the middle classes. Their search was for security, comfort and peace of mind – above all for that social acceptance and approval denoted by respectability. These were not perhaps very noble strivings, especially when pursued in a competitive and individualist spirit. Materialism in an undisguised form seldom appears very attractive. Henry James wrote a story, *The Spoils of Poynton* (1897) about a middle-class woman who identified her whole life with objects in her home: 'the things in the house . . . were our religion, they were our life, they were *us*.' This was what William Morris called the Tyranny of Things.

Late Victorian Britain

In retrospect the years 1890–1914 have come to seem like a golden age of the middle classes. Masterman regarded their way of life in the suburbs as a distinct civilization – 'detached, self-centred, unostentatious'. It was a basically conservative civilization, alternately complacent and fearful, whose favourite (or only) reading was the *Daily Mail* (1896) and its imitators. Yet it should not be forgotten that criticism of the middle class was largely endogenous. The brilliant collection of writers, intellectuals, socialists and feminists who exposed and attacked bourgeois civilization in the 1880s and 1890s were for the most part themselves raised within it. But the result was scarcely nemesis.

4

Labouring Life

Although the middle class and aristocracy set the tone and fashion of the later nineteenth century, about 75 per cent of the population belonged to the working class; and for many of them their priorities of life were different from those of their social superiors. The business of making a living was for thousands of craftsmen, tradesmen, labourers, farm servants, factory hands, miners, engineers, mill and foundry workers, shipbuilders, railwaymen, laundresses, domestic servants and a host of others the central experience of life. Perversely these are the people usually left out of history. They have been largely ignored because it was thought they did not matter, since they did not make important national decisions. But for that very reason they are the ones who experienced the true values of late Victorian society, not its pretensions.

In the second half of the nineteenth century the size of the labour force continued to grow in line with the increase in population, reaching some 16.2 million, of whom 4.7 million were women, in 1901. This was about 45 per cent of the total population – broadly the same ratio as today. However, in other respects the late Victorian labour force was different from today's. First, a greater proportion of the male population aged fifteen and over was at work, and far fewer of them either lived long enough, or had pensions on which to enjoy retirement. Manual workers had to keep on working as long as they could. Ageing was accompanied by failing strength, reduced earnings and fear of the workhouse. Secondly, although the proportion of women in paid employment resembled today's – 35 per cent compared with 38 per cent in 1986 – the number of married women so employed was far fewer. Thirdly, the number of children between the ages of 10 and 15 at work was still considerable, despite the introduction of mass education after 1870. In the textile-producing districts many children of 12 and 13 spent half their time in the mill and half at school. Elsewhere, although the general school-leaving age was raised to 14, about a third of the children left school at 12 or 13 under local by-laws, and children in full-time attendance often worked after school.

The trend of wages was favourable to the working classes. Real wages rose during the period 1850 to 1896, perhaps by as much as 70 or 80 per cent. An 'average operative' who was earning 20s a week in 1850 would expect about 35s in 1900. In our day, inured as we are to steady inflation and rising standards, this may not seem very much. But in comparison with all previous periods it was a massive improvement, comparable only with the rise in real wages during the sixty or seventy years after the Black Death in the fourteenth century. Around 1900 this improvement came to an end, and until 1914 real wages were stationary or declined. This was not a reversal of the gains made in the previous half-century, nor did it affect all workers equally. For many working people the combination of steady earnings and falling prices between 1873 and 1896 meant a period of modest comfort. Virtually all working men who recorded their memoirs in the 1880s and 1890s were in no doubt that working people were better off than ever before, and certainly much better off than when they were children fifty years earlier. To this extent the working classes participated in the gains of late Victorian prosperity. It is well known, however, that Mr Average does not exist; and so great was the diversity of jobs and work experience in the late nineteenth century that generalization about working-class living standards is hazardous. Despite the undeniable gains of the preceding fifty years, the research of Charles Booth and of Seebohm Rowntree at the end of the century revealed poverty on a scale which jolted contemporary optimism. Working-class incomes in 1900 seldom exceeded £100 per annum and most were considerably less. At the bottom of the scale were the agricultural labourers with about 14s 6d a week, and at the top skilled men, like compositors, engineers and iron-founders, who could make 39s to 42s a week. In between were the majority of skilled and semi-skilled workers and that great army of working-class families who had to live on 'round about a pound a week'.[1]

Some clues as to what life at this level was really like can be gleaned from the diets and housing affordable on these incomes. Food was the main item of working-class expenditure, accounting for a half to three-quarters of total earnings. Bread, followed by potatoes, were the mainstay of the diet, with meat (commonly bacon or pork) when possible. Agricultural labourers and poor urban workers lived – as they had done earlier – on bread (usually white), potatoes, tea, butter, cheese and sugar, with meat several times a week. But for better-off workers there were significant changes in eating habits after 1870. The consumption of meat increased with the importation of refrigerated beef from the Argentine, mutton and lamb from Australia and New Zealand, and pork from the USA. Cheap jam, fruit, fish and margarine appeared on working-class tables; and that most English of working-class institutions, the fish-and-chip shop, spread rapidly from its original home in Lancashire.

A typical menu of meals for a York carter (lorry driver), earning 20s a week in 1901, and with a family of wife and two children aged 5 and 2, was as appears on p. 70.[2]

This may be compared with the diet of a more comfortably-off worker in York at about the same time. He was a foreman, with a wife and six children, and wages of 38s a week (see p. 71).

Like their diets, the homes of these two families differed considerably. Here is the investigator's description of the carter's house:

Although the house in which the family live contains only three rooms, it is three storeys high. From the living room you go upstairs straight into the bedroom, and from that by means of a ladder into the attic. The only place for keeping food is in an unventilated cupboard under the stairs. There is a water-tap in the living room, in a corner behind the entrance door, but as there is no sink or drain the droppings from the tap fall on the floor, which consists of red bricks, badly broken and uneven. The floor is partly covered with a piece of linoleum, in addition to which there are several woollen rag mats about. The fireplace is usually untidy. A

MENU FOR MEALS PROVIDED DURING WEEK ENDING
FEBRUARY 22, 1901

	Breakfast	*Dinner*	*Tea*	*Supper*
Friday	Bread, butter, tea.	Bread, butter, toast, tea.	Bread, butter, tea	
Saturday	Bread, bacon, coffee.	Bacon, potatoes, pudding, tea.	Bread, butter, shortcake, tea.	Tea, bread, kippers.
Sunday	Bread, butter, shortcake, coffee.	Pork, onions, potatoes, Yorkshire pudding.	Bread, butter, shortcake, tea.	Bread and meat.
Monday	Bread, bacon, butter, tea.	Pork, potatoes, pudding, tea.	Bread, butter, tea.	One cup of tea.
Tuesday	Bread, bacon, butter, coffee.	Pork, bread, tea.	Bread, butter, boiled eggs, tea.	Bread, bacon, butter, tea.
Wenesday	Bread, bacon, butter, tea.	Bacon and eggs, potatoes, bread tea.	Bread, butter, tea.	
Thursday	Bread, butter, coffee.	Bread, bacon, tea.	Bread, butter, tea.	

square table (generally covered with dirty cups, saucers, plates, etc.) occupies the centre of the room, around the sides of which there are two wooden easy-chairs, a sofa covered with American cloth, and a large chest of drawers. Under the window stands a table on which many household treasures are displayed – fancy vases, glass slippers, photographs, etc. There are several framed photographs on the wall, and an unframed almanac or two. The house is situated down a narrow cobbled thoroughfare, and being faced by a high brick wall it gets very little sun. The rent is 3s per week.

In contrast the foreman's house 'contains four rooms, the front door opening straight into the parlour. The yard and sanitary convenience at the back are shared with one other house, but there is a water-tap and sink in the kitchen. The rent is 4s per week.'

The vast majority of working-class families in Britain lived in

MENU OF MEALS PROVIDED DURING WEEK ENDING
SEPTEMBER 30, 1898

	Breakfast	Dinner	Tea	Supper
Friday	Toast, tea.	Soup, dumplings, meat, bread, tea.	Sardines, bread, milk, tea.	Bread, cheese, cocoa
Saturday	Bacon, bread, toast, tea.	Meat and potato pie, 2 bottles ginger ale.	Bread, butter, pastry, tea.	Bread and milk, meat, ginger ale.
Sunday	Ham, bacon, mushrooms, porridge, bread, coffee.	Roast beef, Yorkshire pudding, potatoes, beer.	Bread, butter, pastry, tea.	Bread and milk, meat, fried potatoes.
Monday	Fried bacon, bread, porridge, tea.	Cold meat, potatoes, rice pudding, tea, ginger ale.	Bread, butter, pastry.	Bread, butter, pastry, cocoa.
Tuesday	Bacon, bread, porridge, tea.	Hashed beef, potatoes, rice pudding.	Bread, butter, pastry, tea.	Bread and milk, fried fish, potatoes.
Wednesday	Bacon, bread, tea, porridge.	Meat, soup, bread, dumplings, tea.	Bread, butter, cheese, pastry, tea.	Bread and milk, fish, bread, beer.
Thursday	Bacon, bread, butter, mushrooms, tea.	Meat, potatoes, soup, cheese, bread, rice pudding.	Bread, butter, pastry, tea.	Sheeps 'reed' with sage and onions, potatoes.

rented accommodation, usually houses, or parts of houses, in courts or terraces, sometimes of the back-to-back variety. Less than six per cent of working-class families in York owned or were buying their homes. Seebohm Rowntree described the houses occupied by 'those in receipt of moderate but regular wages', some 62 per cent of working-class families in York:

> The great majority of houses ... have an average frontage of about 12 feet 6 inches. The street door opens straight into the living-room. This room combines the uses of parlour and kitchen. It is fitted with open range and oven, and all

the cooking is done here. The floor is either of tiles or boards covered with linoleum. A table, two or three chairs, a wooden easy-chair, and perhaps a couch, covered with American cloth, complete the furniture of the room. The walls are papered, and decorated with coloured almanacs and pictures, often including some coloured plates from the *Graphic* or other Christmas Supplement. From the living-room a door leads into the scullery, a small room about 9 feet by 12. It is fitted up with a sink and a 'copper' used for washing clothes. In some houses a portion of the scullery is partitioned off for a pantry, in others the space under the stairs is made to serve for that purpose. Sometimes a small pantry is erected in the yard. From the scullery a door leads into the yard . . . Occasionally there is no back way, and all ashes and refuse from the midden privy have to be removed through the living-room. Under existing bye-laws, however, a back entrance to every house is insisted upon. Upstairs there are two bedrooms, reached by stairs leading in some cases from the kitchen, in others from the scullery. Many houses approximating more or less closely to this type are being erected at the present time. The rents vary from 4s to 5s weekly, the landlord paying the rates, which average about 1s per week. It is to be regretted that many houses . . . are jerry-built, with thin walls of porous and damp-absorbing bricks, put together with inferior mortar, and with wood so 'green' that after a short time floors, window-frames, and doors shrink, and admit draughts and dust. Such houses will soon tend to degenerate into slums.

In the country as a whole few working-class homes had water closets at the end of the century: pails and ashpits (midden privies), often shared with several other families, were usual. The water supply was also shared in poorer homes. Lighting was by candle and oil lamp, in contrast to middle-class houses where gas-lighting had been common since mid-century. In rural areas the agricultural worker's cottage was usually devoid of any sanitation or indoor water supply, and often without any means of cooking except an open fire. Many cottages were old, damp and picturesque and not infrequently had only one bedroom for parents and grown-up children. Rents were comparatively low – normally 1s 6d a week. Unlike better-off town workers the farm labourer was left with no margin out of his wages after provision for the basic necessities of food, rent and clothing; though this was mitigated to some extent by opportunities for gardening and keeping a pig and chickens.

One of the darker shadows over late Victorian working-class life was the almost total lack of security. Unemployment had long been endemic in many trades affected by the weather, the seasons or fashion. Wet days deprived thousands of building workers, painters and agricultural labourers of their means of livelihood. The seasons created brisk and slack periods for brick-layers, dressmakers and printers. Longer-term fluctuations in the demand for labour came from the trade cycle, resulting in alter-nate periods of boom and slump – peak activity in 1873, 1883, 1890, 1900, and troughs in between. But unemployment was not limited to periods of economic depression. In some parts of the economy there was a continual state of semi-employment or concealed unemployment: they worked on jobs which fluctuated from day to day, and there were gaps between one job and the next. Best known of these workers on short engagements were the building labourers and, above all, the dockers, whose conditions were well publicized in the great dock strike of 1889. On the fringe of the skilled trades were also many casuals who were underemployed. "To go in" for one half-a-day, one day, two, three, four, or five days out of the five and a half is common to bootmaking, coopering, galvanising, tank-making, oil pressing, sugar boiling, piano-making, as it is to dock labouring, stevedor-ing, crane lifting, building."[3] It was on these men that unemploy-ment fell heaviest in bad times. Dismissal could be at the end of the week or the day, with no notice given. Overall the rate of unemployment among wage earners varied from under 3 per cent in a good year like 1899 to over 10 per cent in a bad year like 1886. But almost all workers were liable to be unemployed at some time. Even among such aristocrats of labour as the London compositors, whose average rate of unemployment was under 5 per cent, more than 20 per cent were without work at least once in any one year.

When a worker fell out of work the only public provision for his support was the Poor Law, which treated him as an able-bodied pauper. Before accepting this humiliation the skilled man would fall back on his savings, his friendly society or trade union, and credit with the local shopkeepers. The unskilled man had no such support, and once he had exhausted local charity and his credit at the pawnshop he had no alternative to workhouse relief. In practice the strict workhouse test was unworkable, and various forms of out-relief and municipal relief works were instituted.

If a labouring man and his wife survived the hazards of unemployment – and even if they did not – there were two further ways in which they might suffer: through sickness and in old age. The risk of injury at work was high. Miners, navvies, dock workers and building trades labourers could expect to become casualties in the industrial army any day. Aches and pains, bronchitis and rheumatism afflicted agricultural labourers, whose clothes were often soaked through for days on end. Accidents might be accepted as a risk of the job, but it was doubly hard that the family should have to suffer too. Only a minority of well-paid artisans were in a position to put anything by 'for a rainy day'. They alone had the support of sickness and unemployment benefit from their trade unions.

Finally, when a labouring man turned fifty (and in heavier jobs much earlier) his strength and quickness began to desert him. The most he could then hope for were a few more years in a lighter but less well-paid job. Old age was anything but a pleasant anticipation of retirement. With no provision for an income, unable to continue at work, and in failing health, all he could look forward to for himself and his wife was a corner by the fireside in his children's home in return for such odd jobs and baby minding as they could manage. If this were not available the only place for them to go was the workhouse. The last indignity, to be avoided at almost any cost by respectable folk, was a pauper burial. Funerals were important social occasions and the burial club was a ubiquitous part of working-class culture. 'Burying him with ham' or 'a slow walk and a cup of tea' were common northern expressions signifying the ultimate respectability. 'I put him away splendid' said a Middlesborough widow proudly at the turn of the century.[4]

In the past historians have relied mainly on the evidence of middle-class investigators like Lady Bell, Seebohm Rowntree, Charles Booth and Sidney and Beatrice Webb for accounts of working-class life in the late nineteenth and early twentieth centuries. Indispensable as these surveys still are for the vast amount of information they contain, they are nevertheless the views of outsiders, and are not necessarily the same as those of working people themselves. In recent years, however, many more autobiographies, memoirs and diaries of the common people have come to light.[5] By means of oral history we also have been able to record the accounts of old people whose memories reach back to the 1890s. From these and older sources it is now possible to recapture a good deal more of the experiences, perceptions and expectations of labouring men and women than was previously thought possible. Something of the rich diversity of labouring life may be indicated in the extracts that follow. They are, of course, but a fragment of the material available and cannot hope, in the space of a few pages, to cover all that wide variety of types of job by which the English working classes earned their livings.

We may begin with that upper 10 to 15 per cent of the working class who formed an aristocracy of labour: engineers, masons, carpenters, compositors, cotton spinners, and other artisan tradesmen. They enjoyed a combination of good wages, steady employment and craft skill that secured their independence and respect from those above and below them. It has been suggested that in their pursuit of respectability this elite accepted middle-class standards and values, and mediated them to the working class as a whole. Indeed, the labour aristocracy has been presented as an instrument of bourgeois hegemony, a mechanism by which the ruling classes maintain their supremacy less through force than by diffusing their ideology throughout all sections of society, who are thus persuaded to accept the status quo. Support for this view comes from the observation that at various points working-class culture converged with that of the bourgeoisie, which it would seem was imposed on the former. But this is not how the issue was seen by class-conscious artisans, who thought of their culture as indigenous and separate, though not necessarily always in conflict with middle-class aims and intentions. Despite a hunger for respectability, which they shared with the lower middle classes (and also with some sections of the 'deserving' poor), the labour aristocracy regarded themselves as part of the working classes, with their own standards of respectability.

Alfred Williams worked as a forgehand and hammerman in the Great Western Railway workshops at Swindon from 1892 to 1914 and his account of life there has unusual poetic qualities:[6]

> Arrived in the shed the workmen remove their coats and hang them up under the wall, or behind the forges . . . A terrible din, that could be heard in the yard long before you came to the doors of the shed, is already awaiting. Here ten gigantic boilers, which for several hours have been steadily accumulating steam for the hammers and engines, packed with terrific high pressure, are roaring off their surplus energy with indescribable noise and fury, making the earth and roof tremble and quiver around you, as though they were in the grip of an iron-handed monster. The white steam fills the shed with a dense, humid cloud like a thick fog, and the heat is already overpowering. The blast roars loudly underground and in the boxes of the forges, and the wheels and shafting whirl round in the roof and under the wall. The huge engines, that supply the hydraulic machines with pressure, are chu-chu-ing above the roof outside; everything is in a state of the utmost animation . . . The furious toil proceeds hour by hour. Bang bang, bang. Pum-tchu, pum-tchu, ping-tchu, ping-tchu. Cling-clang, cling-clang. Boom, boom, boom. Flip-flap, flip-flap. Hoo-oo-oo-oo-oo. Rattle, rattle, rattle. Click, click, click. Bump, bump. Scrir-r-r-r-r-r. Hiss-s-s-s-s-s-s. Tchi-tchu, tchi-tchu, tchi-tchu. Clank, clank, clank, clank, clank. The noise of the steam and machinery drown everything else.

Williams describes the smith, amongst the elite of the workforce:

> He is at all times steady and cool, and he seems never to be in a hurry. At the anvil he gives one the same impression, so

that a stranger might even think him to be sluggish and dilatory, but he is in everything sure and unerring, never too soon or too late. Every action is well-timed; nothing is either over- or under-done. He performs all his heats with a minimum amount of labour. Where a nervous or spasmodical person would require forty or fifty blows to shape a piece of metal he will accomplish it with about twenty-five. His masterly eye and calculating brain are ever watchful and alert. He understands the effect of every blow given . . . He moves always at the same pace, and his work is of a uniformly superlative character.

Life for the twelve thousand workers in the railway workshops had its own yearly, weekly and daily rhythms. The factory year was divided into three periods: Christmas to Easter, Easter to 'Trip' (held in July), and Trip to Christmas; and there were the additional one-day bank holidays of Whitsuntide and August. From Christmas to Easter was a period of hope and rising spirits, looking forward to brighter days, longer evenings, and time spent in the garden. After Easter all thoughts were directed toward the Trip, or annual holiday. Trip Day was the most important day in the calendar of the railway town. For several months preceding it 'fathers and mothers of families, young unmarried men, and juveniles' had been saving up for the outing. Whatever new clothes were bought for the summer were usually worn for the first time at Trip. The trade of the town was at its zenith during the week before the holiday. A general exodus from the town took place, and some twenty-five thousand people were hurried off by early morning trains to London, Weymouth, and other resort towns. About half of the trippers returned the same night; the others stayed for a week. Return to work after Trip was painful; and after the August bank holiday there was nothing to break the monotony of labour until Christmas.

The week too had its characteristic pattern for the workmen. Monday was always a 'flat, stale day', especially up to dinner time. 'Everyone seems surley and out of sorts.' Tuesday was the 'strong day', when the most and best work was done. 'The men come to work like lions.' Wednesday was similar to Tuesday, though the pace was not quite as brisk. Thursday was 'humdrum day', when the men began to look 'tired and haggard', and more effort was required to maintain production. By Friday morning 'the barometer will have risen considerably'. Despite tiredness, the men were more cheerful because it was pay-day and the last whole day to be worked before the weekend. Saturday was 'the day of final victory', when the week's battle was almost finished. Sunday was a day of complete inactivity with most workmen; and Williams hazarded the opinion that it was 'possibly the weakest and the least enjoyed of all'. If the weather was dull and wet a great number stayed in bed till dinner-time, and sometimes till Monday morning – when they would be all the more refreshed for the 'toil and battle' of the coming week.

Williams was convinced that exploitation of the workers had increased during this period in the workshops. 'The speeding up of late years has been general and insistent.' The output in some instances was increased tenfold, and the exertions of the workman were doubled or trebled; yet he received scarcely any more in wages. Again, the balance between day wages and piecework was altered to the detriment of the workers. 'On the hammers under my charge during the last ten years the day wages of assistants – owing to their being retained on the job up to a greater age – had doubled, and the piecework prices had been cut by one half. As a result the gang lost about £80 in a year.' Fear of illness and old age was greater among workmen than previously because of the management's ruthless policy of getting rid of anyone who was not one hundred per cent fit. The views of workers, even respected and experienced men, were rarely sought: 'If offered, they are belittled and rejected.' If a workman had a grievance it was useless for him to complain to an overseer (who was usually the cause of it); 'and if he takes it upon himself to go and see the manager he gets no redress. The manager always supports the foreman whether he has acted rightly or wrongly, and the man is remembered and branded as a malcontent.'

The conviction that the pace of work had been increasing was also borne out by the experience of workers in the cotton industry, who complained of 'the driving system'. The Lancashire mill and its operatives was the archetype of capitalist factory production, for cotton had powered the first industrial revolution. By the second half of the century the work-force was a mature industrial proletariat – though it is well to remember that only about 10 per cent of all occupied persons in the country worked in textiles in 1881, and by 1911 this had fallen to 7.8 per cent. Cotton was unusual among manufacturing industries for the high proportion of women employed, some 57 per cent of all textile workers in 1881. In Lancashire the male operatives preserved a monopoly on mule-spinning, but most weaving, except on heavy looms, was done by women. In Oldham and Bolton spinners' wages were 35–38s a week, female weavers and cardroom hands 14–18s, piecers 10–17s, and half-timers 2s 6d–5s.

Allen Clarke, a Bolton operative and journalist, described the conditions of work in the 1890s[7]:

The spinners (males) are clad only in shirt, with sleeves rolled up, and a pair of thin white drawers, reaching to the ankles, and are bare-footed (for shoes or clogs would slip on the oil-saturated wooden floor); the female weavers and card-room lasses wear a short skirt, having taken off their shawls and dresses and hats. The hair is also tied up, as there is a danger of it catching in the machinery. The 'piecers' (boys and youths) are dressed as lightly as the men, and are also in bare feet. The factories start at 6 o'clock a.m., and stop at 8 till 8.30 for breakfast, which is generally taken in the mill as the time is too brief for the operatives to put on their clothes and go home. Then the machinery rattles away again till 12.30, when an hour is allowed for dinner. Those who do not live far go home to dinner; but many are forced to have this meal also in the mill. At 1.30 the engine starts again, and does not stop till 5.30, when the day's work is done. On Saturday the work finishes at 1 o'clock, giving the operatives Saturday afternoon for holiday ... The male spinner [stands] in the midst of 2500 whirling spindles, every thread of which must be incessantly watched by himself and two assistants, so that it may be instantly 'pieced up' if it breaks, in a hot room, amid machinery roaring so loudly that one can only converse with those close at hand, and only then at the top of one's voice, amid whizzing wheels, and bands, and swift-straps, which could snatch off a limb for a second's carelessness; all this in hot air, so hot that in summer a great thirst scorches the throat; and for the same length of time the female weaver has been encircled by four clattering looms, with shuttles making 200 or more picks per minute, in a 'steamed' atmosphere; and a din even worse than that of the spinning-room, and in which a deaf and dumb method of communication has to be used; while at any instant a rebellious shuttle may shoot forth and knock an eye out (I have myself frequently met young women who were thus blinded at their work), or a loose skirt may be seized by wheel or strap, and then – horror!

And all these hours – ten hours a day – spinner and weaver are on their feet: no sitting down; no resting; one must keep up to the machinery though agonised with headache, or troubled by any other complaint. While the engine runs the workers must stand: the machinery cares nought for fatigue, weakness, ailment, sorrow, anxiety for sick husband, wife, or child, at home; grief for a dear one's recent death, maybe the night before; with the motion of the spindles and shuttles no human pain or woe must interfere.

Clarke, who was a socialist, was concerned to emphasise the inhumanity of the factory-work system. More recently we have been shown the extent to which the culture of the factory in a broader sense dominated the world of the operative in the late nineteenth century.[8] Cotton necessitated not only a certain type of work; it also produced a whole urban civilization, a way of thinking about the world in general. The 'rule of the tall chimneys' was absolute. Not everyone in a northern mill town worked in a factory; but everyone's place in the society was affected by the dominant mode of production. Clarke postulated a three-class model for a factory town such as Bolton or Oldham:

The first caste, consisting of employers, clergymen, solicitors, physicians, tradesmen on a large scale, dwells in wide sub-urban streets, made respectably natural with a few trees, inhabiting villas, semi-detached and single, shopping at the big stores (in the daytime, having first choice of everything), drinking at the grand hotels, occupying the front seats at the more select concerts, the boxes, and stalls, and dress circle of the theatre, front cushioned seats nearest the pulpit at church or chapel, buying magazines in addition to newspapers, and having pictures, book-cases, and wine-cellars of their own, and often private carriages. The second caste is composed of the best paid clerks, book-keepers, managers, and the better sort of working folks; they live in streets narrower than those of caste one, have no trees, drink their beer at smaller hotels, buy food and clothes at the smaller stores (or maybe the Co-operative Society), use the pit of the theatre, the middle and rear pews of the church, buy a newspaper or two, have a few cheap pictures on their walls (the inevitable oil portrait of the head of the family and his spouse), get books from the public library, perhaps buy a few of their own, and walk, or use tram.

The third caste is made up of 'labourers' and poorer workmen; they live in small houses – all joined and jammed together to save space and make more rents for the landlord – in narrow streets; they shop at the smallest and dirtiest shops, they drink in low taverns, we find pawnshops numerous in their localities, they get their music in hideous singing-rooms, they sit in the gallery at the theatre, they have no books, no church, no art.[9]

Although textiles employed large numbers of women, the biggest category of female employment was domestic service. The number of indoor domestic servants reached a peak of over 2 million in 1891, which was almost one in three of all girls between the ages of 15 and 20. By comparison textiles employed less than half this number. Forty per cent of this huge army of female indoor domestic servants were under the age of twenty. They were the daughters of working-class parents, and, as they had to earn their living as soon as possible, respectable service in a middle-class home was considered a desirable occupation for girls until they were married. Conditions of work varied enormously, from households where only one servant was kept to wealthy homes with a full panoply of housekeeper, cook, housemaids, nursemaid, groom and coachman. But everywhere the amount of hard physical labour involved was great, for the object of keeping servants was the comfort and convenience of the middle-class family, who had little interest in 'labour-saving' devices as long as cheap labour was available. Because domestic service provided accommodation and board the actual cash wages were relatively modest. A single servant to a provincial shopkeeper or a farmer might earn £10 a year; but a cook in an upper-class household in London would get at least £20. Taking the board, lodging, and various perquisites such as cast-off clothing into account, domestic servants were fairly well paid in comparison with other women workers.

There is no lack of testimony as to both the good and bad sides of life as a servant at the turn of the century. A woman interviewed in the 1970s recalled her life as a servant in a large house in Lancaster in the 1890s.[10] She was a country girl and started work at the age of thirteen as a kitchen maid, cleaning pans and getting up at 4 a.m. to prepare the cooking range. In due course she was promoted to more congenial work as a housemaid. She remembered many things with pleasure:

the elegance of the house, the kindness of the mistress, the new uniforms the maids were given for a family wedding:
   'We were all dressed in grey, lovely silver grey, shiny like alpaca, in them days, nice plain pinnies, no lace, but happen a lot of tucks round the bottom.' The food was good and plentiful. She particularly enjoyed the annual visit made by the whole household to the family's country house in North Wales: 'Well everybody mucked in up there, you weren't as strict like, you could muck about and go out on the hills and sing ... or have a cup of tea ...' [She] frequently mentioned her friendship and feeling of companionship with the other girls; there was none of the feeling of loneliness and isolation sometimes complained about by domestic servants in small households where they might be the only servant.

A less rosy picture was painted by another Lancashire woman who came from a very poor family, and who at the age of thirteen worked as a domestic servant for a farmer. She was engaged in 1905 at Ulverston hiring fair, where both men and women seeking farm work waited to be hired by local farmers for a six month period.

> We went to farm service and we used to walk from here to Ulverston, wait till eleven o'clock till they started. The old farmers used to come up King Street and say, 'Is tha for hiring lass?' I used to say, 'Aye.' He'd say, 'What's tha asking?' We used to say, 'What are you going to give us?' 'I'll give you four pound ten.' We'd say, 'No thank you.' We used to walk on a bit farther down King Street and another farmer would come up and say, 'Is tha for hiring lass?' Perhaps we'd get five pound ten off him for the six months. He used to say, 'Can you wash, can you bake, can you scrub?'

She received board and lodging but no wages until the end of the six months. Her reminiscences were somewhat rueful:

> One Christmas I was at Longridge and Christmas Day come and I was a bit homesick, you know, and had our Christmas Day's dinner, I washed up and all that, and she said, 'Has tha finished now?' I said, 'Yes madam,' so she said, 'Well if thou get all that paper there, you'll see a lot of paper there and there's a big needle there and a ball of string, if you go down to the paddock [that was the toilet], sit there and take the scissors and cut some paper up and thread it for the lavatory.' And I sat there on Christmas Day and I think I cried a bucketful of tears. Christmas afternoon and I was sat … sitting cutting bits of paper, bits of paper like that and getting this big needle, threading them and tying knots in them and tying them on these hoops, till about half past four when I went in for m' tea. Sitting there on the lavatory seat.

Another large employer of women was the millinery and dress-making trade. An interview with a woman who was apprenticed to a dressmaker in Barrow in 1898 when she was thirteen went like this:

I served two years with a lady who was m' Sunday school teacher. And I was so timid in those days that that was the only reason I went to work for her because I would have been afraid of anybody else.

When you went to work, what hours did you work?

From half past eight in a morning to eight o'clock at night ... with an hour for dinner and half an hour for tea ... I used to go home for dinner and I'd run home for m' tea. We never had Saturday, we had Thursday afternoon. We'd all the work to finish on a Saturday to be sent out.

What would your first wage be?

Ten shillings a week. It was an average wage. In the workroom where I'd served my time we had twelve or sometimes fourteen apprentices all working for nothing, and one paid hand and she got ten shillings a week.

But you weren't paid as an apprentice?

Oh no. I served two and half years before I got my ten shillings. I've often thought about it after, when I grew up. This one was responsible for everything going out perfect for ten bob a week.

Were you paid for holidays?

We never had any holidays.

Not a fortnight in summer or anything?

Oh no. You had Bank holidays, of course.

Did you do it all by hand, or by sewing-machine?

Sewing-machine. But more was done by hand then. All the finishing work was done by hand. There was a lot of hand-work and in those days linings were all tacked in and seamed in. We'd a lot of tacking and that carry-on to do. All skirts had braid and binding in them. Sometimes we'd four times to go round a skirt — the hem and then there was a binding. You ran that on all the way round the skirt and then turned it over to hem it in. That was three times round the skirt. Then they used to be six or seven yards wide a skirt, so you'd a bit of sewing to do.

I suppose you all did a different bit, or did one person work on one dress?

No, you got different bits to do. The things that you learned when you went was to do over-casting. All seams in skirts, all seams in bodices were over-sewn and you learned to do that. You learned to tidy the workroom every morning. The youngest apprentices did that. Look after the fire. One week it was your fire week another one it was your iron week, keeping the irons hot. Then you'd learn to tack skirts out, tack them onto the lining and cut lining to match and then you learnt to put them into the belts and turn the bottoms up. I went on through stage and stage. It took two and half years to learn it all.

After that there was a very high class dressmaker and m' father got me in as an improver . . . He used to deliver to this shop and it was a shop that had nothing in the window but a piece of material and perhaps a pair of gloves, it was a very posh shop . . . Madam had worked for Worths in Paris. She came from London and brought her milliner with her . . . I learnt tailoring and to work with fur.

For the majority of women, however, work meant the unpaid work of running their home. They got little, if any, help in the house from their menfolk, and it was a common but true saying that 'a woman's work is never done'. Cleaning, washing up, mending, cooking, shopping, bringing up the children, and managing on a meagre budget were the lot of the wives of working men. 'Women wore their lives away washing clothes in heavy, iron-hooped tubs, scrubbing wood and stone, polishing furniture and fire-irons . . . Only too well known was the Saturday morning custom . . . of cleaning and colour-stoning the doorstep and then the pavement.' [11] Almost all reminiscences by working-class women have something to say about the labour of the Monday wash day, which

was a whole day's work. First of all you sorted out your whites from your coloureds and put them all in to soak. Then you gave everything a good scrub with a brush on a washboard, especially the collars and cuffs. Then you boiled up the whites in the copper, poking them down all the time with a wooden stick and plenty of soap – pieces cut off a big block. After that you rinsed and blued them – you put a 'bluebag' into the water to bring the whites up white. Then the coloureds had to be done, everything rinsed and put through the mangle. Then out on the line to dry. Then you had to clean out the copper and scrub it ready for next time.[12]

In addition to their household chores country women frequently worked in the fields. It comes as something of a surprise to realise just how many people in the most urbanized and industrial of nations still worked in agriculture. There had of course been a massive decline from 1851 when farming accounted for over a quarter of the male labour force. But in 1901 agriculture employed 1.3 million men, or 12 per cent of male workers. Labouring life in the countryside was bound by the same seasonal rhythms and basic demands of husbandry as it had been in previous centuries. There was the same need for a great variety of aptitudes and skills (all too often glossed over in outsiders' descriptions of Hodge) and the continuation of local and regional variations in the organisation of work. It is impossible to generalize the experience of agricultural labour from, say, the work of a Wiltshire shepherd, a Norfolk horseman, a Yorkshire cowman, and a Warwickshire hedger and ditcher. But to recapture something of the feel of work in the fields we can turn to haymaking and harvest, the great peak of the agricultural year which drew in all who worked on the land, no matter what their normal job might be. In all parts of the country, as the time of the harvest approached, plans were made for the hectic work of getting in the crops. This was the time when the labourer did not have to beg for work, but for once was able to bargain freely with the farmer. The harvest contract was negotiated from a position of relative strength:

We were allus hired by the week . . . except at harvest. Then it was piece-wukk. I dessay your've heard of the 'lord', as we used to call 'im? Sometimes he was the horseman at the farm, but he might be anybody. His job was to act as a sort of foreman to the team of reapers – there was often as many as ten or a dozen of us – and he looked after the hours and wages and such-like. He set the pace, too. His first man was sometimes called the 'lady'. Well, when harvest was gettin' close, the 'lord' 'ld call his team together and goo an' argue it out with the farmer. They'd run over all the fields that had got to be harvested and wukk it out at so much the acre. If same as there was a field badly laid with the wather, of course the 'lord' would ask a higher price for that. 'Now there's Penny Fields,' he'd say – or maybe Gilbert's Field – or whatever it was; 'that's laid somethin' terrible,' he'd say. 'What about that, farmer?' And when the price was named he would talk it over with his team to see whether they'd agree. The argument was washed down with plenty of beer, like as not drunk out of little ol' bullocks' horns; and when it was all finished, and the price accepted all round, 'Now I'll bind you,' the farmer 'ld say, and give each man a shilling.[13]

Work in the harvest fields was very hard, for the weather was hot and the pace relentless.

Women were an essential part of the harvest team. But their work was not limited to the special effort required at that time of the year. They worked in the fields at gleaning, potato gathering ('tatering'), turnip pulling, hoeing, weeding, thinning, hop-binding, and in all kinds of fruit and vegetable picking. In some jobs the children worked alongside their mothers. The reality of fieldwork is vividly portrayed in Thomas Hardy's great novel, *Tess of the D'Urbervilles* (1891):

The swede-field in which [Tess] and her companion were set hacking was a stretch of a hundred odd acres, in one patch, on the highest ground of the farm, rising above stony lanchets or lynchets . . . The upper half of each turnip had been eaten off by the live-stock, and it was the business of the two women to grub up the lower or earthy half of the root with a hooked fork called a hacker, that it might be eaten also . . . They worked on hour after hour, unconscious of the forlorn aspect they bore in the landscape, not thinking of the justice or injustice of their lot . . . In the afternoon the rain came on again, and Marian said that they need not work any more. But if they did not work they would not be paid; so they worked on. It was so high a situation, this field, that the rain had no occasion to fall, but raced along horizontally upon the yelling wind, sticking into them like glass splinters till they were wet through. Tess had not known till now what was really meant by that. There are degrees of dampness, and a very little is called being wet through in common talk. But to stand working slowly in a field, and feel the creep of rain-water, first in legs and shoulders, then on hips and head, then at back, front, and sides, and yet to work on till the leaden light diminishes and marks that the sun is down, demands a distinct modicum of stoicism, even of valour.[14]

At the bottom of the social pile, below the respectable working class, was a large, amorphous group of labouring poor, living in rookeries and hovels and existing from meal to meal. Allen Clarke described them in the factory towns as a fourth caste who could not be classified and who were buried in common graves in the cemetery. They were not confined to the metropolis or the big towns but were found also in cathedral cities and picturesque villages. With little schooling, irregular work and large families, they lived off their wits and local charity. One of the most remarkable accounts of life in this sub-stratum of society is by George Hewins, whose story was taken down orally in the 1970s.[15] George was born in 1879, an illegitimate child, and brought up by a great-aunt in Stratford-upon-Avon. His family tree (see p. 92) – showing the amount of illegitimacy, the gaps in remembered history, the large number of children and the typical names (abbreviated in family usage) – encapsulates a forgotten world of the casual poor. After a succession of childhood jobs as a barber's lather boy, tailor's errand boy, and bakery helper, he became a bricklayer, learning from his grandfather who did odd jobs in pub yards and farms, 'general knocking about':

It was sixpence an hour for a good bricklayer then, and we worked fifty-six hours and a half when the weather

was fine, from six in the morning to half-past five o'
nights. The only summer holidays we had was when it
rained a quarter and you went in the shed to dry. He'd
book it, and then when you stopped again for another
quarter he'd stop you half-an-hour. We had no holidays
with pay, no tea breaks. If you had a bit o' food you ate
it as you went along, kept putting it in your mouth.
Sat'day was pay day. We didn't get our money afore one
o'clock, and if the job was in Stratford the gaffer would
likely keep you waiting at his house. Sometimes we had
to wait an hour or so whiles he finished his dinner. We
didn't get paid for that! ... Often you felt like telling a
gaffer what to do with his job, but at that time o' day it
was always the other way round. You worked for him
and *he* ended it. He simply said on Sat'day when he paid
you: 'Well, I shan't want you no more.' There was no
money, no cards. If you hadn't got fixed up your heart
sank. There was no union to back you up: if you got
dismissed nobody took no notice.

Hewins was frequently out of work, and then he lived on
whatever he could get, 'selling sticks at the door, doing odd
jobs for folks', snow sweeping in the streets, delivering the
Christmas mail, peapicking, or simply stealing:

Everybody pinched. You had to pinch to make up your
money. Going to gaol, that was a risk you had to take. I
was careful, I was getting to be crafty. I'd had some good
lessons off my Grandad: he was the craftiest chap I
knowed. You didn't pinch off neighbours, but the farmers,
the shopkeepers, they could afford it! I was building their
new houses for them: every modern fol-de-rol, 'no expense
spared' –'cept on our pay! I never pinched nothing 'cept
food and firing.

George married a domestic servant and their first child was
born four months later. After that the 'babbies kep coming
fast', despite crude attempts at abortion. From the start of
their married life the couple had to live with his mother-in-law,

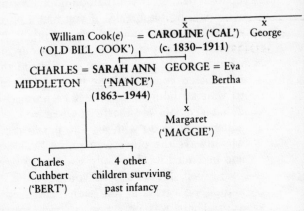

```
                              x                    x
        William Cook(e)   = CAROLINE ('CAL')   George
        ('OLD BILL COOK')    (c. 1830–1911)

        CHARLES = SARAH ANN   GEORGE = Eva
        MIDDLETON  ('NANCE')            Bertha
                   (1863–1944)
                                      |
                                      x
                                  Margaret
                                  ('MAGGIE')

        Charles        4 other
        Cuthbert     children surviving
        ('BERT')       past infancy
```

KEY—X illegitimate (in the case of a married person, not by spouse)
—(X) oral sources throw doubt on recorded legitimacy

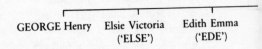

```
        GEORGE Henry    Elsie Victoria    Edith Emma
                           ('ELSE')        ('EDE')
```

A working-class genealogy: the Hewins family.
(from George Hewins, *The Dillen*: *Memories of a Man of Stratford-upon-Avon*, 1981/Reproduced by kind permission of the publishers, Oxford University Press.)

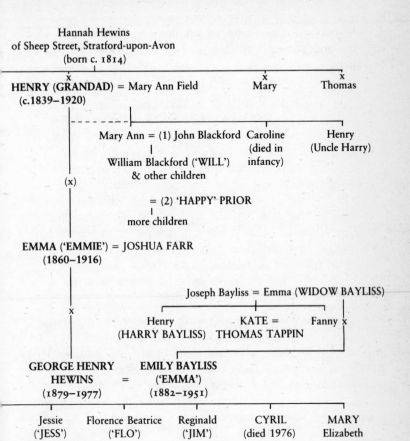

Hannah Hewins
of Sheep Street, Stratford-upon-Avon
(born c. 1814)

```
                    x                              x            x
HENRY (GRANDAD) = Mary Ann Field            Mary         Thomas
(c.1839–1920)
         |- - - - - - -|
              Mary Ann = (1) John Blackford   Caroline      Henry
                    |                         (died in   (Uncle Harry)
              William Blackford ('WILL')      infancy)
                  & other children
       (x)
                      = (2) 'HAPPY' PRIOR
                         |
                    more children

EMMA ('EMMIE') = JOSHUA FARR
(1860–1916)
                           Joseph Bayliss = Emma (WIDOW BAYLISS)
          x               |                                   |
                      Henry           KATE =        Fanny x
                 (HARRY BAYLISS)   THOMAS TAPPIN

  GEORGE HENRY        EMILY BAYLISS
     HEWINS       =      ('EMMA')
  (1879–1977)          (1882–1951)

   Jessie    Florence Beatrice  Reginald      CYRIL        MARY
   ('JESS')       ('FLO')        ('JIM')   (died 1976)   Elizabeth
  (died 1932)
```

a widow who had a tiny cottage in Pimm's Court. 'We had to share a bed with her mother. There was us at one end, and her mother's feet a-sticking in our faces! But I was lucky – the old lady generally dropped off fast enough after a day's charring and a couple o' stouts.' The cottage was old, dark and dirty.

> However much the missus scrubbed the flags, however much I limed the walls we couldn't keep it clean! Bugs and fleas, it was one long battle, and we was on the losing side. Those we catched was splattered on the wall, blood and all, like pressed flowers. There was one room downstairs with an open fire, where the missus did the cooking and the washing and the ironing, two tiny rooms upstairs – the one we slept in was over the passage. Outside in the yard was the well, and a double-handled pump. When we wanted our side we pulled the handle; the neighbours pulled it back when they wanted it. A score o' folks or more used that pump – men, women and kiddies – and the earth closet. I always went for a crap in the fields on my way to work.

The family, the community and work (or lack of it) dominated George Hewins' world. Life was for him a continual struggle to exist, and for this one needed to be 'crafty'. His grandfather put the matter thus: 'There's one law for them and one law for us, allus was and allus will be while they's makin' 'em, stands to reason. Some day ... us'll make the laws.' In the meantime, he advised, 'Lay low, that's my motto.'

III

Perceptions and Values

5

Certainties

I

Every age has certain ideas that are absolutely basic to it. The Cambridge philosopher, T. E. Hulme, explained the matter thus:

> There are certain doctrines which for a particular period seem not doctrines but inevitable categories of the human mind. Men do not look upon them merely as correct opinions, for they have become so much a part of the mind, and lie so far back, that they are never really conscious of them at all. They do not see them, but other things through them. It is these abstract ideas at the centre, the things which they take for granted, that characterise a period.[1]

Throughout the nineteenth century the combination of Malthusianism with the doctrines of political economy and philosophic radicalism provided one of the most compelling interpretations of the modern world, the obvious and 'natural' way of looking at society for most thinking people. It was a way of seeing – and also of course a way of not seeing certain things which are not visible to us. Contemporaries saw but did not take in those aspects of their society which did not fit in with their assumptions. The Victorians were not so much wilfully blind to other theories or philosophies as simply unable to see that serious alternatives existed. When critics suggested other ways of looking at things they were dismissed as hopelessly impractical and out of line with what everyone knew was normal.

Central to these certainties were the doctrines of economic liberalism. In its popularly accepted form (free from the theoretical refinements of the classical political economists) these included the belief that the economy was regulated by the law of supply and demand, that its mainspring was the motive of private profit, and that the pursuit of individual self-interest would result in the general good. The operation of a free market economy was to be interfered with as little as possible. *Laissez faire*, or the 'leave alone' principle was the guiding rule for politicians. Individualism, competition, self-help, private enterprise, and private property were the key concepts in orthodox Victorian social philosophy. How these beliefs ruled the conduct of everyday life is admirably illustrated by Beatrice Webb's account of her mother's housekeeping:

> Tested by economy in money and time she was an admirable expenditor of the family income: she never visited the servants' quarters and seldom spoke to any servant other than her own maid. She acted by deputy, training each daughter to carry out a carefully thought-out plan of the most economical supply of the best regulated demand. Her intellect told her that to pay more than the market rate, to exact fewer than the customary hours or insist on less than the usual strain – even if it could be proved that these conditions were injurious to the health and happiness of the persons concerned – was an act of self-indulgence, a defiance of nature's laws which would bring disaster on the individual and the community. Similarly, it was the bounden duty of every citizen to better his social status; to ignore those beneath him, and to aim steadily at the top rung of the social ladder. Only by this persistent pursuit by each individual of his own and his family's interest would the highest general level of civilisation be attained ... No one of the present generation realises with what sincerity and fervour these doctrines were held by the representative men and women of the mid-Victorian middle class.[2]

Looking back on her youth in the early 1880s Beatrice Webb marvelled at the way in which the commercial spirit dominated her home life. From her father's business acquaintances as well as from a wide selection of professional, political and intellectual friends and relatives she became habituated to a view of the world in which capital and labour were taken as eternal verities. 'Water plentiful and labour docile', 'The wages of labour are falling to their natural level', she read in the journals and company reports which lay on the library table and which she heard constantly in her father's conversation.

The doctrines of political economy had all the force of laws of nature. To seek to raise wages artificially – for example by trade union action – was as futile as trying to make water run uphill. 'The labour of the economic thinker is only successful when he explains the real working of natural forces,' explained the *Economist* in 1879. Giving evidence before the Royal Commission on Labour (1894), Hugh Bell, the Middlesbrough ironmaster, repeated several times that his views on industrial relations were simply 'in the nature of things'.[3] Darwinism too was harnessed to strengthen the ideology of competitive capitalism. The principle of the survival of the fittest could easily be popularized to justify the workings of the economic system and give it an aura of scientific authority. Not only was economic liberalism natural, reasonable, and just plain common sense, it was also scientific. Beatrice Webb noted the idolization of science:

It is hard to understand the naive belief of the most original and vigorous minds of the 'seventies and 'eighties that it was by science, and by science alone, that all human misery would be ultimately swept away. This almost fanatical faith was perhaps partly due to hero-worship. For who will deny that the men of science were the leading British intellectuals of that period? . . . Nor was the cult of the scientific method confined to intellectuals. 'Halls of Science' were springing up in crowded working-class districts; and Bradlaugh, the fearless exponent of scientific materialism and the 'Fruits of Philosophy', was the most popular demagogue of the hour.[4]

Science seemed to offer unlimited progress. In a popular work, first published in 1872 and reprinted many times, Winwood Reade promised that

When we have ascertained, by means of science, the methods of Nature's operation, we shall be able to take her place to perform them for ourselves . . . men will master the forces of Nature; they will become themselves architects of systems, manufacturers of worlds. Man will then be perfect; he will be a creator; he will therefore be what the vulgar worship as God.[5]

The strength of political economy, or economics as it was called later in the century, was that its doctrines were not felt to be doctrines but facts, part of the ordinary, everyday business of living. Political economy, wrote Walter Bagehot, the editor of *The Economist*, is simply 'the science of business ... It is an analysis of that world so familiar to many Englishmen – the "great commerce" by which England has become rich.'[6] Or, as the Professor of Political Economy at Cambridge, Alfred Marshall, said in his definitive *Principles of Economics* (1890), 'Economics is a study of men as they live and move and think in the ordinary business of life.'[7]

The point to be made is that these ideas were not simply the theories of intellectuals but were the widely-held assumptions of ordinary people and coloured their thinking about virtually all aspects of life in the late nineteenth century. There had of course been powerful critics of economic liberalism from the 1830s onwards, and the founding fathers of political economy had always recognised certain political and social limitations to individualism and *laissez faire*. The writings of Thomas Carlyle and John Ruskin, reinforced by the attacks of Matthew Arnold, were a constant inspiration to reformers. But it would be unwise to suppose that their views, despite the articulacy with which they were delivered, were shared by more than a small minority of Victorians. Comparatively few people in any generation possess a mastery of economic theory; but the diffusion of the ideas of economic liberalism can be seen in attitudes to life in other spheres. Views about poverty, unemployment, personal responsibility, and the class structure reflected the assumptions of the political economists, backed up by that moral certainty so characteristic of the respectable classes. Two examples illustrate the all-embracing nature of the ideology of liberalism.

First is the survival into the twentieth century of the principles of the 1834 Poor Law. The workhouse test, conditions of 'less eligibility', and the moral obloquy of receiving relief were written deep into people's consciousness. Administrative meanness, feelings of shame, the distinction between the 'deserving' and 'undeserving' poor followed from adherence to belief in the beneficent effects of the operation of 'scientific' laws and non-interference in the labour market. Seventy years later these were still the principles and sentiments which informed English poor law policy, and indeed most social policy.

The second, and perhaps more surprising, example is the absorption of the principles of competitive capitalism by some of the very institutions which were set up to oppose or drastically modify that system, namely the trade unions. Under the sliding scale agreements of the 1870s and 1880s the ironworkers and miners of the North agreed that their wages should be determined by the selling price of iron and coal. As the price of the product (fixed by a competitive market) rose, so did the rate of wages; and conversely wage rates were reduced when prices fell. This was tantamount to acceptance of the employers' argument that wages like prices should be determined by supply and demand. The price of labour was to be determined by what Adam Smith called 'the higgling of the market'. In a wider sense this higgling and bargaining provided the very *raison d'être* for trade unionism, which grew strongly in the last two decades of the century. The most powerful indigenous institution of the working classes operated on the assumption of a market economy, where questions of work and wages were to be settled on the basis of market prices and the capitalists' profits ('the state of the industry'). The ideology of organized labour was thus firmly rooted in the world of economic liberalism.

In the later years of the nineteenth century the orthodoxies of bourgeois liberalism were to be increasingly challenged, and eventually undermined. John Stuart Mill (the most widely recognised mid-Victorian exponent of economic liberalism) in the later edition of his *Political Economy* modified his earlier enthusiasm for the free market economy. The trade unions had second thoughts about the sliding scale, and few unions advocated such agreements after the late 1880s. From this decade too a whole generation of socialists took up the critiques of Carlyle and Ruskin and demanded that capitalism should be either abolished completely or reformed out of all recognition. With hindsight we can see that these challenges pointed the way to future changes. However, for the time being, the dissidents and reformers were a minority. In any case there is little evidence that ideas quickly motivate a majority of the people. It is by deeper and more persistent beliefs that ordinary people are guided throughout their lives. These basic certainties are abandoned only slowly and such change is reflected in generations rather than decades. As long as the 'science of political economy' seemed to be a common-sense explanation of business and British commercial success it was unlikely to be given up lightly. The entrepreneurial ideal, as it has been called,[8] was acceptable as long as the Victorian economy appeared to offer prosperity and 'progress' to a sufficient number of people.

> Whatever may be said as to the ideal perfection or imperfection of the present economic *regime*, the fact of so great an advance having been possible for the masses of the people in the last half-century is encouraging. [Sir Robert Giffen told the Statistical Society in 1883] . . .
> Surely the lesson is that the nation ought to go on improving on the same lines, relaxing none of the efforts which have been so successful. Steady progress in the direction maintained for the last fifty years must soon make the English people vastly superior to what they are now.[9]

But when the gap between ideal and reality became too great, as it did after the 1880s, the values of the entrepreneurial society began to be called in question. Until the early twentieth century, however, the orthodoxies easily held their own.

II

Alfred Marshall, the most influential political economist of his time, was of the opinion that economics and religion were 'the two great forming agencies of the world's history'. For a late Victorian this was not a surprising view, for the age was not only dominated by energetic economic enterprise, it was also religious. This does not mean that everyone, or even a majority of the population, went to church or occupied their minds with religious thoughts; but that religion was assumed to be relevant to all aspects of the national life. Religious ways of thinking about life and its problems were taken as the norm, even though there were many exceptions and deviations. Religion was central, not marginal as it is today; it provided a range of certainties and satisfactions – to be examined in the remainder of this chapter.

First-hand evidence about beliefs and personal convictions is notoriously difficult to find for any period, especially in respect of ordinary people who left few records. In the absence of anything better we have to make do with such evidence as is available, notably forms and patterns of behaviour, from which we might infer something about beliefs and values. In this respect statistics of religious activities provide a possible clue (to say no more) to late Victorian religious belief. It is unlikely that the vast amount of religious observance – publicly in church attendance and mission work, and privately in prayer and bible reading at home – was entirely social and outward, and quite unconnected with personal beliefs and hopes. People do not, as a rule, regularly and voluntarily attend institutions, religious or otherwise, without absorbing or approving at least some of the ideas and values associated with those institutions, particularly when, as in the case of the churches, the promulgation of certain doctrines was their primary objective. We do not have to disregard the social and respectable aspect of religion to appreciate its spiritual and moral content and its likely impact on the way people thought of themselves and their world. Much of this thinking was no doubt vague and inconsistent, a jumble of childhood teaching, later haphazard experience, and accumulated prejudice. Incomplete, unorthodox and heretical by theological or church standards, it nevertheless provided a religious form for some of the certainties of life.

The most obvious outward sign of Christian belief was attendance at a place of worship. Several surveys of church and chapel attendances were made between 1881 and 1903, though none on the national scale of the unique 1851 census. An average attendance at church and chapel of 38 per cent of the total population was recorded for a selection of English cities in 1881; though this masked variations from 19.9 per cent in Liverpool to

52.7 per cent in Hastings. At York in 1901 Seebohm Rowntree's survey showed that between 28 and 35 per cent of the adult population went to church or chapel. In London in 1903 attendances were 19–22 per cent, though again there were great regional variations, from 47.4 per cent of the adult population in Ealing to 11.8 per cent in Fulham. Until about 1886 overall attendances increased in proportion to the rising population; but thereafter a relative decline set in, despite the continuance of what today would be regarded as high absolute levels of attendance. Contemporary commentators, almost without exception, were concerned with the non-attenders, especially the absence of the working classes. The close correlation between attendance and social class was everywhere remarked upon. Equally important were the differences between town and country and between north and south. The general picture that emerges is of a nation in which the middle and upper working classes accepted the idea of Sunday worship and in which the influence of the churches reached outwards beyond their members through Sunday schools and other agencies, so that a significant proportion of the population were at some time in their lives touched directly by Christian doctrine.

The map of religion was very much as it had been earlier. After the middle of the century no new sect or denomination of any great national significance, with the exception of the Salvation Army, appeared; and religious allegiances hardened along the lines already laid down. The central ground was occupied by the Church of England, the established, official religion of the land. It had many more churches, schools, full-time clergy, and greater financial resources than any other religious body; and could rely on the support of the aristocracy, the landed interest and the richer classes generally. In some villages the traditional structure of squire and parson remained unchanged at the end of the century, and it was the ideal of the rural parish that still conditioned much Anglican thinking. In the towns the Church of England had a much harder struggle to maintain its influence. Doctrinally tolerant, it found a place (though not always very comfortably) for everyone from High Churchmen with ritualistic and 'Romish' tendencies to evangelical Low Churchmen who were virtually indistinguishable from Methodists, as well as liberal-minded Broad Churchmen. Its claim to be the church of the overwhelming majority of the English people had received a rude shock in the 1851 religious census which revealed that only a minority of the population attended its services and that the Nonconformists were almost equally strong nationally, and in some places were the majority. Nor had this position changed subsequently; though socially the 'best' people were still assumed to be Church of England. The York survey showed that 43 per cent of the worshippers attended Church of England services, as against 38 per cent Nonconformist, 14 per cent Roman Catholic and 5 per cent Salvation Army.

Nonconformity too embraced a number of doctrinal and cultural positions, from the various Methodist connections to the Old Dissent of the Congregationalists (Independents), Baptists, Presbyterians, Quakers and Unitarians, together with independent chapels of all shades of Protestant sectarianism. Deriving their support from the middle and respectable working classes, the Nonconformists were strongest in the towns, especially in the North, with some Primitive Methodist and Baptist chapels in rural areas, notably East Anglia, Yorkshire, the West Midlands, Lincolnshire and Buckinghamshire. In some parts of the North and in Cornwall and most of Wales Nonconformity was the dominant form of religion.

At the other end of the doctrinal spectrum were the Roman Catholics, whose numbers in England grew steadily in the second half of the century, reaching an estimated 1.3 million, of whom perhaps 726,000 attended mass in 1891. Despite the prestige of a few famous converts like J. H. Newman and H. E. Manning earlier, and the existence of some old Catholic families among the aristocracy and gentry in the northern counties, the Roman Catholic church remained marginal to the mainstream of English life. Anglicans for long obstinately persisted in classifying it as a sect. By most people it was regarded, with justice, as the church of poor Irish immigrants in large towns, especially London, Liverpool and Birmingham.

A wide variety of patterns and styles of worship resulted from this free trade in religion. Something of this diversity is indicated in the following vignettes, chosen almost at random from the very large number of examples available. The first is a description, from Charles Booth's massive survey of religious life in London, of High Church practices in Holborn:

> *St Alban's* is a large handsome church, with a great hanging rood – a huge gilt cross bearing the figure of Christ, and at either side a saint standing – suspended in front of the chancel. Round the church are the Stations of the Cross for processional use. There is a good deal of painted glass, and an elaborate altar-piece in metal, the enclosing doors of which open out into a triptych. In front of this hang lighted lamps. The service is of the highest; High Mass in fact. The priests, all three officiating, wore embroidered vestments, and the sacrifice of the Mass was made just as in Roman Catholic churches. There seemed to be as many men as women present: the men sat to the right, the women to the left. Almost all knelt through the service, and many crossed themselves at the proper time, and a considerable portion made all the requisite responses, following the order of the service exactly. There could be no question as to the feeling of devotion shown. They were men and women kneeling in the presence of their God. The service was beautifully given.[10]

In contrast comes the account of a service taken by a popular Congregationalist preacher, Campbell Morgan, at his church, New Court, Upper Holloway, in 1897:

> The church to my mind more than 'looked full', it was practically full; I doubt if more than another hundred could have been crowded in. They were almost exclusively, as Mr M. says, middle-class. I watched them streaming in for five to ten minutes, and only saw one who looked like a working man. There was a sprinkling of young people, but on the whole they were an elderly lot; and in no church have I seen so small a proportion of the congregation under eighteen; few of the parents seem to bring their elder children. The service lasted for eighty minutes of which forty-five were

given up to the sermon; prayer and praise take a very subordinate place, and even at that led up to the culminating glory of the sermon, the hymns, lessons, etc., all being chosen with reference to it. The singing of the hymns and anthems was hearty and congregational, but there is no attraction to the music. One felt indeed all through that the people in the main had come not to worship, but to listen to a sermon. Mr M. preached the first of a series of three sermons on Sin, taking as his text the sin of Achan ... I thought him a preacher of extraordinary eloquence ... He completely held his audience; and in spite of the damp and cold not a word was lost through coughing.[11]

Turning to rural religion, Flora Thompson gives an endearing account of a village church in north Oxfordshire in the 1880s:

Every Sunday, morning and afternoon, the two cracked, flat-toned bells at the church in the mother village called the faithful to worship. *Ding-dong, Ding-dong, Ding-dong*, they went, and, when they heard them, the hamlet churchgoers hurried across fields and over stiles, for the Parish Clerk was always threatening to lock the church door when the bells stopped and those outside might stop outside for all he cared ... The congregation averaged about thirty. Even with this small number, the church was fairly well filled, for it was a tiny place, about the size of a barn, with nave and chancel only, no side aisles. The interior was almost as bare as a barn, with its grey, roughcast walls, plain-glass windows, and flagstone floor. The cold, damp, earthy odour common to old and unheated churches pervaded the atmosphere, with occasional whiffs of a more unpleasant nature said to proceed from the stacks of mouldering bones in the vault beneath ... The church, like the village, was old and forgotten, and those buried in the vault, who must have once been people of importance, had not left even a name. Only the stained glass window over the altar, glowing jewel-like amidst the cold greyness, the broken piscina within the altar rails, and a tall broken shaft of what had been a cross in the churchyard, remained to witness mutely to what once had been.

The Squire's and clergyman's families had pews in the chancel, with backs to the wall on either side, and between them stood two long benches for the school-children, well under the eyes of authority. Below the steps down into the nave stood the harmonium, played by the clergyman's daughter, and round it was ranged the choir of small school-girls. Then came the rank and file of the congregation, nicely graded, with the farmer's family in the front row, then the Squire's gardener and coachman, the schoolmistress, the maidservants, and the cottagers, with the Parish Clerk at the back to keep order.[12]

Flora Thompson also describes a handful of Primitive Methodists who met in a cottage on Sunday evenings. They sang, prayed, testified and listened to a travelling preacher:

Methodism, as known and practised there, was a poor people's religion, simple and crude; but its adherents brought to it more fervour than was shown by the church congregation, and appeared to obtain more comfort and support from it than the church could give. Their lives were exemplary.

The same was true of Methodism in an industrial setting. The *Primitive Methodist Magazine* for 1896 painted a picture of a service in a northern mining village. Although the account is somewhat overdone, it does attempt to convey the atmosphere of a Primitive Methodist meeting:

It is to the chapel we are going – the gathering place for worship, the house of God. It is a plain, unpretentious building, commodious enough, but lacking both in beauty and comfort. In the pulpit is a tall, spare man, with a face in which mysticism and intelligence are strangely blended. We learn that he is a miner from a neighbouring colliery . . . Never shall I forget the singing of that service. There was a little scraping and twanging of fiddle-strings before all the stringed instruments – of which there were a dozen – were brought into accord with the organ, but then such a glorious outburst of music as could not fail to help the spirit of devotion. How these North folks sing . . . We felt the Divine enchantment of the hour. The glory of the Lord was in His sanctuary. Forgotten in the ecstatic bliss of mystic communion with heaven were the bare, unsightly walls, the hard seats, the dreary pit, perhaps beneath our very feet, in which men crawl like beasts for six days in the week, heaving coals, naked to the waist . . . the vision of God and the Celestial City are seen by these men in that outburst of song in which the soul was finding expression . . . After the first hymn came the prayer . . . There are men who have what the old Methodists called the 'gift of prayer', and the preacher had that gift . . . The pitman preacher talked with God with the familiarity which comes of frequent communion, and yet, withal, with a reverence that moved even the restless youths sitting near the pulpit . . . And the preacher carried his congregation along on the strong pinions of his own faith, until a low rumbling of murmured responses broke forth in loud 'Amens'. Suddenly one man sprang to his feet, and, with a loud shout of 'Praise the Lord', jumped into the air. Few observed it, or if they observed it, took any notice, so absorbed were they in their own devotions. 'Make the place of Thy feet glorious,' exclaimed the preacher, and with outcries of 'He does it', 'He does it now', the petition came to a close. The reading of the Scriptures was interspersed with a few remarks here and there more or less appropriate – generally less – and the service would not have suffered by their omission. But the Sermon – who shall describe it? It was a Sermon to be heard, not to be reported. What a mixture of humour, passionate appeal, thrilling exhortations and apposite illustrations it was . . . Laughter and tears this preacher commanded at will, and when he closed with heartsearching appeals to the unconverted to fly to the Cross for pardon, one almost wondered that men and women did not spring to their feet and rush somewhere – anywhere, exclaiming with Bunyan's Pilgrim, 'Life, Life, Eternal Life'![13]

A more unusual experience is recorded by the sculptor, Eric Gill. His father was an assistant minister at a chapel of the Countess of Huntingdon's Connection in North Street, Brighton, in the 1890s. This small sect had seceded from the Church of England in 1790 and was in effect 'a kind of combination of Congregationalism ... and "Low" Church of England'. The congregation was evangelical and from the comfortable middle classes. Gill remembered how

> The service was read with great care and expression and the choir sang at the proper times, but the sermon was the chief thing and, for this, the preacher put on a special black gown, very noble and voluminous. The sermon, always entirely over our heads, lasted forty minutes or an hour, so, with 'Morning Prayer' as well, the whole 'service' lasted a good hour and a half ... It will not be difficult ... for the reader to guess what sort of religion we learned. They had 'the Communion' once a month and a very large proportion of the congregation took the Bread and Wine. 'Do this in remembrance of Me' ... I haven't the faintest idea what they preached about. The religion we got was out of the Prayer Book and from the lessons and hymns, from the Sunday school and from our father and mother at home. We didn't attempt, at least I didn't, to follow the sermons – that was for the grownups as I supposed.[14]

But in 1897 Gill's father left the Connection and became an Anglican, and the family then attended Church of England services:

> At the north end of Preston Park hidden in the trees is the old parish church of Preston – just on the outskirts of Brighton. Here we now went to church. I forget all about the doings there – whether they were 'High' or 'Low' or, more probably, 'Broad'. I only remember, but I remember very well, that it was a treat to go there, as church-going had never been before. We had always had the Church of England Book of Common Prayer, and, as I have said, we got religion from it and not at all or very little from sermons.

It would be true therefore to say that the practice and even the idea of liturgical worship was not a new thing to us. But, in spite of our inattention to sermons, the liturgy at North Street was heavily overpowered by worship of the preacher. The liturgy was there but it was at the foot of the pulpit, in the lower place, and the table of the Holy Supper was in the background.

We were too young and too uneducated in religious matters to know what the great difference was, and perhaps I should now speak only for myself, but I, at any rate, was aware of a great change in the idea of religion and, to some extent, I was aware of the nature of it.

Between the various churches there was little love lost. Enthusiasm for ecumenism was still far in the future. Yet from today's perspective we are struck by how much they had in common. For most people in late Victorian Britain religion meant evangelical religion. This was as true for members of the Church of England as for the Nonconformists. Much of the Calvinist rigidity and dogmatism of earlier evangelicalism had been modified, but its basic doctrines and pieties remained the norm for the majority of practising Christians. The classic accounts of evangelical religion – Samuel Butler's *Way of All Flesh*, Edmund Gosse's *Father and Son*, John Ruskin's *Praeterita*, Mark Rutherford's *Autobiography* – written in the late nineteenth and early twentieth centuries, were all set in the earlier years of the century and were written by authors who were deeply critical. They imply that such religion is now, or should be, a thing of the past; yet a little probing soon unearths examples which suggest a time-lag of at least two generations. The beliefs and practices of evangelicalism were too strong to suddenly disappear.

The Christian hopes and understanding of ordinary church members differed relatively little between denominations. They believed in a personal God who was a stern and yet loving father to his children; in heaven as a state of future bliss; and (more controversially) in a hell to which the wicked would be consigned after death. Man, it was held, is of his nature innately sinful, but can be redeemed if he will accept God's saving grace, made available to all men through Christ's death on the cross. Atonement is made possible through the sacrifice of Christ's blood. The words of the Reverend Augustus Toplady's great evangelical hymn, so beloved by Victorian congregations, enshrined this faith:

> Rock of ages, cleft for me,
> Let me hide myself in thee;
> Let the Water and the Blood,
> From they riven side which flowed,
> Be of sin the double cure,
> Cleanse me from its guilt and power.

The search for salvation and the experience of finding it in the act of conversion is the central concern of the faithful Christian, but man alone cannot succeed in his endeavour:

> Not the labours of my hands
> Can fulfil thy law's demands;
> Could my zeal no respite know,
> Could my tears for ever flow,
> All for sin could not atone;
> Thou must save, and thou alone.

Life, in the immortal words of John Bunyan (another favourite of the Victorians) is a 'pilgrim's progress from this world to that which is to come'. Only after crossing the River of Death will it be completed:

> While I draw this fleeting breath,
> When mine eyes are closed in death,
> When I soar through tracts unknown,
> See thee on thy judgement throne;
> Rock of ages, cleft for me,
> Let me hide myself in thee.

It was through the language of theology that Christian teaching was conveyed in sermons, prayers and above all in hymns; so that phrases such as 'before the throne of grace', 'washed in the blood of the lamb', or 'a green hill far away' were familiar to all regular church goers. The imagery of this type of religion was extraordinarily vivid, especially to children. It coloured the thinking about, or at least the expression of deeply-felt emotions or beliefs. But to be assimilated it had to be translated into categories which ordinary people could recognise, and those were moral, ethical and practical. What most late Victorians were looking for was not a set of credal beliefs but rather rules to guide them in leading a 'good' (meaning usually also a happy) life.

The practices of evangelical religion were not confined to one particular section of the community. Sabbatarianism, for instance, was virtually universal among the middle and upper classes, and family prayers and grace before meals were widespread. Even those who did not subscribe to such observances, such as working men who preferred to lie in bed on Sunday mornings and spend the rest of the day in the pub or on an 'outing', could hardly escape the impact of social restrictions imposed by religious pressure. Other members of the working class, like domestic servants, were willy-nilly implicated in the full rigour of the evangelicalism of their employers. Religion in the home was the natural consequence of a conviction that prayer, meditation and daily bible-reading were necessary if one were to 'know Christ' and lead a truly God-guided life. There are many accounts of this experience, but none more telling than those through the eyes of childhood, when the mysteries of faith are but dimly perceived and the petty rituals of social conformity loom large. Lawrence Jones describes how it was in one Norfolk manor house in the 1890s:

My grandfather's portrait hung in the Inner Hall, a room lighted, like a ship's saloon, by a sky-light. It had six doors, and a harmonium, and there family prayers were held. It was the thing to look as grave as possible during prayers, and my grandfather looked very grave indeed, book in hand ... The gardeners ... brought in to family prayers a faint, and the stable-men a stronger, whiff of manure, and sat on slender benches behind the maids. A marble angel, restraining a child from treading upon a serpent, presided, very white, over the shadowy space where the household sat. Our own little wicker chairs, that creaked if we fidgeted, faced the servants; and at the words 'Let us pray' we all rose, turned round, and aimed our rumps at one another, family against domestics, like the children defying the wolves in *Peter Pan*. This manoeuvre seemed to us to be entirely proper, natural, and religious. I do not think it could have occurred to any of the Christians kneeling in that Inner Hall that it would be possible to pray to God standing up, as the Presbyterians do. Made in His Image, as we were (except Mrs Pleasance, the laundrywoman, who was made in the image of a cottage-loaf), we did not, it must be admitted, make the best of our divine shapes when praying. It was the fault, no doubt, of the benches, and of our small chairs, for being so low; but to One looking down from Above through the sky-light, the spectacle must have been, even if endearingly, ridiculous.

Family prayers consisted, naturally, of 'repetitions'; whether they were vain repetitions cannot certainly be known. It demands an unusual gift of concentration to throw heart and mind, dynamically, behind an over-familiar form of words, spoken by a third person; we children did not attempt it but caught each other's eyes when a word like 'study' occurred in a collect, to remind us of our father's study. I cannot answer for the cook and the maids, or even for Dockerell, the butler (our warm friend 'Docker', who wore black side-whiskers); but it seems not unlikely that, at that early hour of the day, with so much to be done, there were scattered thoughts beneath the trim lace caps, and that much, if not all, of those incomparable cadences carried no further than the range of my father's carrying voice. Indeed, there came a day when the out-door men begged off; so much cleaning up, they said, spoilt the morning, and my father readily agreed that, if praying spoilt the morning, the morning must come first.[15]

More privately, children learnt to pray at their mother's knee, nightly lisping

> Jesus, tender shepherd, hear me,
> Bless thy little lambs tonight,

> Through the darkness be thou near me,
> Keep me safe till morning light.

They heard stories from the bible, some favourites, others more frightening; and observed their parents living the seasons of the Christian year from Advent to Easter. They took part in the joyfulness of Christmas and the sadness of Good Friday. The images of the Christian faith were implanted into their consciousness. Much has been written about the gloom and severity of evangelical childhood, though many of the well-known accounts relate to the earlier Victorian period. To counter the terrors of hell and God's punishment of sinners there was also the picture of Jesus as a loving friend, gently leading his little lambs.

On one issue, however, there was almost universal agreement in childhood memories: the gloom of Sunday. The Victorian sabbath made an impact on children which lasted throughout their lives. It was a day set apart, quite different from the rest of the week; a day in which special things were done, like going to church and Sunday school, and other things were not done, like going to work and playing with toys. Molly Vivian Hughes, whose parents were by no means extreme, recalled the late Victorian Sunday of her middle-class childhood in London:

The mere word 'Sunday' is apt to give a mental shiver to people of long memories. The outer world closed down. It was wrong to travel except for dire necessity, and then very difficult. It was wrong to work, and wrong to play . . . However, we did the best we could with the day, and it had the advantage of my father being with us all the time. He didn't take religion *too* seriously, and left it to mother to enforce all her superstitious restrictions that she had imbibed in her Cornish home. She for her part put all the cheerfulness she could into the food, against which there seemed to be no Biblical taboo. Instead of the daily tea for breakfast we had coffee – lashings of real strong coffee, with a great jug of hot milk . . . But while these appetizing smells were around us we had to learn the Collect and get it 'heard' before breakfast . . . Even now a Collect smells to me of coffee. Breakfast over, the whole family walked in detachments to St Paul's Cathedral ... Dinner-time on Sunday was the occasion for us all to compare notes and criticisms of the voices of canon, minor canon, and preacher, and the shade of ritualism of the stranger. Whether he stood at the north end of the altar, or in the middle – it was a burning question in those days, when clergymen were being imprisoned for Romish practices. We had no feelings in the matter, but we loved to see some one sailing near the wind.

The afternoons hung heavy. It seemed to be always 3 o'clock. All amusements, as well as work, were forbidden. It was a real privation not to be allowed to draw and paint. However, an exception was made in favour of illuminated texts, and we rivalled the old monks in our zeal for copying Scripture, with the same kind of worldly decorations that they devised.

Naturally our main stand-by was reading, but here again our field was limited by mother's notions of what was appropriate for Sunday. *Tom Brown*, *Robinson Crusoe*, Hans Andersen's *Tales*, and *Pilgrim's Progress* were permitted, but not the *Arabian Nights*, or Walter Scott, or indeed any novel. We had to fall back on bound volumes of *Good Words for the Young*, which were not so bad as the title suggests, and contained plenty of stories ... Sunday newspapers did exist, but were not respectable. How horrified my father was on discovering that the servants had been reading little bits to me out of *Lloyds Weekly*! He gave me to understand that I must never read it because the small print was so bad for me.[16]

In their religious life, as in so much else, the Victorians were extremely busy people. Round each church or chapel was a penumbra of organisations, activities and causes dedicated to spreading Christian principles and providing opportunities for 'good works'. Sunday schools, bible classes, adult schools, mutual improvement societies, Bands of Hope (juvenile temperance), PSAs (Pleasant Sunday Afternoons), men's fellowships, ladies' sewing meetings, young people's guilds, choir practices, prayer meetings, and a host of week-night activities absorbed a huge amount of time and energy. The larger town churches had day schools (also in some villages), church halls and institutes attached to them. Sunday school excursions, anniversary celebrations, soirées, tea parties, cricket and sports clubs provided the social cement deemed necessary for the success of religious institutions. Missions, settlements and philanthropic agencies in the poorer urban areas were also part of the Christian endeavour of middle-class churches. 'In Darkest England and the Way Out' was the challenge set by General Booth and his Salvation Army.

William Kent, who became a clerk in the London County Council, spent his youth in the Nonconformist world of south London, and left an unforgettable portrait of lower middle-class religion in the 1890s and early 1900s. After a strongly Methodist upbringing and active involvement in all aspects of chapel life, he later lost his faith and became an atheist. At the end of his autobiography he imagined being back again in Wheatsheaf Hall, the mission in south Lambeth where he had spent so many hours as a young man:

I stood in the vestibule . . . there was the notice board, where I pinned my C.E. [Christian Endeavour] notices. I went into the small room on the right. There I attended the Rechabite meetings as a child. There later I attended the Teachers' meetings and their prayer meetings. There, met, on Sunday afternoons, the Infants they were willing to entrust to my care. Next was the kitchen, bright with huge copper boilers, all aglowing when there was a 'tea-fight' on. There I sat for a time on Saturday nights to receive Goose Club subscriptions . . . I go through the main door into the large hall . . . About half way down the right hand block of seats is where I had my Sunday School Class. Nearer the front was Mr Adams's Class – being top in point of age . . . On the left side, I could find the seat upon which I sat – a lover near his lass – on those early Sunday mornings. A little farther forward, and to the left, was where I always sat at Communion. The picture of Christ in the cornfield is still there, and also the long desk, which served as a pulpit . . . I go upstairs. There on the left, is the door leading to the gallery. I sat on the right, at the angle. This was regarded as the Young Men's Corner . . . I used to take up the collection from the few galleryites. I go up a further flight of stairs. At the top is a cupboard. Here some missionary boxes were kept . . . Opposite is the smallest room of all. It was called the vestry, but for this purpose was most inconveniently situated . . . in the vestry the Young Men's Bible Class met, when I first knew it. When it quitted for the Institute, Miss Lott and her damsels took our place . . . The next and last room would fill me with most emotion. Here my father had led his Adult Bible Class. Here both Christian Endeavour Societies met. I could find the exact spot where I rose for my first speech, and where I was, week after week, on Tuesdays; the exact place where I sat with my Juniors.[17]

The strength of ideas and beliefs in a society cannot always be measured by the number of outward adherents. In late Victorian Britain, Christian assumptions and forms of thinking were deeply embedded in certain aspects of popular culture. Rites of passage were still widely associated with the churches. Thus 65.8 per cent of all children born alive in 1902 were baptised into the Church of England, and 69.8 per cent of marriages in 1899 were Anglican. The Roman Catholic and Nonconformist churches accounted for most of the rest. Civil marriages amounted to 17.9 per cent of the total in 1904. But perhaps the most resonant form of popular religious feeling was the singing of hymns. Far more than the bible or the prayer book, certain hymns became virtually part of oral folk culture. 'Abide with me', for example, expressed sentiments that were shared by thousands who seldom attended public worship, and it could be sung as well at the Cup Final as in church. This favourite Victorian hymn, written by the Reverend Henry Francis Lyte, vicar of Brixham, Devon, shortly before his death in 1847, has an elemental religious appeal. It deals with the commonest, inescapable facts of life, and the simple tune is hardly more than a series of scales. The fear of growing old and the need for comfort and help are its basic theme:

> Abide with me; fast falls the eventide;
> The darkness deepens; Lord, with me abide!

> When other helpers fail, and comforts flee,
> Help of the helpless, O abide with me.

The realisation that life is short and that death will soon be upon us adds urgency to the plea for help:

> Swift to its close ebbs out life's little day;
> Earth's joys grow dim, its glories pass away;
> Change and decay in all around I see;
> O thou who changest not, abide with me.

Assurance comes from St Paul's triumphant challenge:

> Where is death's sting? Where, grave thy victory?
> I triumph still, if thou abide with me.

Finally there is the glorious hope of resurrection:

> Heaven's morning breaks, and earth's vain shadows
>   flee;
> In life, in death, O Lord, abide with me!

The popularity of 'Abide with me' perhaps tells us more about the nature of belief of ordinary people than church leaders were prepared to recognise. The hymn struck a chord of sentimentality very dear to the Victorians, and it implied no particular creed or dogma. It offered assurance where most needed, without making any demands.

In these respects it harmonized with other vestigial Christian beliefs among the non-churchgoing majority of the population. Middle-class missionaries and investigators reported very little professed atheism. The chaplain at a hospital in inner London found that nearly all the working-class patients believed in God:

> In a vague and hazy way most of them may be described as Christians; that is, there is a general tendency to 'suppose that it is all true', but those who have thought the matter out, or have any definite convictions, are few and far between; they have for the most part put religion deliberately out of their lives and dislike to be reminded of it.[18]

The working-class point of view was put more forcefully in Robert Tressell's novel, *The Ragged Trousered Philanthropists*, describing a group of house painters in Hastings about 1910:

> 'Religion is a thing that don't trouble *me* much,' remarked Newman; 'and as for what happens to you after death, it's a thing I believes in leavin' till you comes to it – there's no sense in meeting' trouble 'arfway. All the things they tells us may be true or they may not, but it takes me all my time to look after *this* world. I don't believe I've been to church more than arf a dozen times since I've been married – that's over fifteen years ago now – and then it's been when the kids 'ave been christened. The old woman goes sometimes and of course the young 'uns goes; you've got to tell 'em something or other, and they might as well learn what they teaches at the Sunday School as anything else.'

These sentiments were approved by his workmates, and another painter formulated his own idea of religion:

> 'I don't see as it matters a dam wot a man believes,' said Philpot, 'so long as you don't do no 'arm to nobody. If you see a poor b—r wot's down on 'is luck, give 'im a 'elpin' 'and. Even if you ain't got no money you can say a kind word. If a man does 'is work and looks arter 'is 'ome and 'is young 'uns, and does a good turn to a fellow creature when 'e can, I reckon 'e stands as much chance of getting into 'eaven – if there *is* sich a place – as some of these 'ere Bible-busters, whether 'e ever goes to church or chapel or not.' [19]

This type of religion, untheological and severely practical as it was, nevertheless embodied a system of well-defined beliefs, the basic one being the golden rule that one should behave towards others as one would want them to behave towards oneself. 'Doing the best you can and doing nobody any harm' was a sufficient philosophy of life for many non-church goers. Flora Thompson commented similarly:

> Many in the hamlet who attended neither church nor chapel and said they had no use for religion, guided their lives by the light of a few homely precepts, such as 'Pay your way and fear nobody', 'Right's right and wrong's no man's right';

'Tell the truth and shame the devil', and 'Honesty is the best policy'.

Strick honesty was the policy of most of them; although there were a few who were said to 'find anything before 'tis lost' and to whom findings were keepings. Children were taught to 'Know it's a sin to steal a pin'.[20]

The general picture of late Victorian religion is thus one of great diversity. A large minority of the population were active Christians, and many of the remainder would have described themselves as, in some sense, believers. The churches of all denominations were confident that progress was being made towards the realisation of Christ's kingdom, with more churches, more members and more ministers – and this despite the failure to attract the working classes at large, and the relative slowing down of the rate of increase:

God is working his purpose out as year succeeds to year,
[declared a hymn writer in 1894]
God is working his purpose out and the time is drawing
  near;
Nearer and nearer draws the time, the time that shall surely
  be,
When the earth shall be filled with the glory of God as the
  waters cover the sea.

6

Doubts and Anxieties

I

Just as every age has its basic orthodoxies so also it has its doubts and difficulties, and the late Victorian period was no exception. The certainties of economic liberalism were challenged in the 1880s and 1890s by socialism and the rise of labour, to which we shall refer later. The challenge to evangelical religion was more formidable, for its doctrines were deeply embedded in much of the national life. The mood of doubt, as it has been called, which was well publicized by a succession of able writers, had its roots in the controversies of the preceding decades, and came to a head in the 1880s. It was perhaps inevitable that a religion as aggressive and dominant as evangelicalism should provoke a reaction; but the form which the revolt took was an intellectual rejection of Christian claims and not only a passive falling away.

The general opinion was that 'science' was in some way responsible for this falling away from the faith. The name of Charles Darwin was frequently taken as a symbol of, if not the actual intellectual force behind, the spread of unbelief. The celebrated debates over the *Origin of Species* belonged to the 1860s; and before the end of the century the doctrine of evolution was acceptable to clergymen as eminent as Frederick Temple who became Archbishop of Canterbury in 1896. Nevertheless there was a widespread feeling that a conflict between science and religion existed. In fact, this was probably due more to the unsettling effects of biblical criticism than to the discoveries of the natural scientists. The 1840s and 1850s had been shaken by the geologists, the 1860s by the biologists and anthropologists, and the 1870s posed the conflict between reason and religion. In the 1880s publicity centred on the struggle of Charles Bradlaugh, a declared atheist, to take his seat in the House of Commons.

Doubts and Anxieties

The cumulative effect of these challenges was felt in the later years of the century.

Evangelical religion rested firmly on the Bible, and the idea that the sacred book might not be literally true came as a shock to many believers. Educated Christians could no longer believe what the churches had for so long taught: that the world was created six thousand years ago, that the human race was descended from Adam and Eve, and that there had been a universal flood in which only Noah and his family had survived. Old Testament stories like Jonah and the whale or Balaam's speaking ass could only be accepted as legends. Miracles contradicted the scientific view of uniform natural laws; and scriptural inconsistency and obscurity further strained belief. These intellectual doubts drove some people to open scepticism. The majority of churchgoers, however, probably came to some form of mental accommodation, for their religion was not primarily intellectual but moral and ethical. They were not so likely to be susceptible to the effects of what the Victorians called 'unsettling' books, and they did not find the stereotyped images of earlier atheists and 'infidels' very attractive. Nevertheless doubt and unbelief were much more talked about in the later decades of the century than earlier, and this encouraged intelligent people to question some of the traditional certainties of religion.

Doubt sprang from a variety of sources. For some sensitive souls the narrowness, intolerance and bigotry of much chapel life, the general absence in Nonconformity of what Matthew Arnold called 'sweetness and light', proved too much. For others the comfortable complacency, not to say hypocrisy, of the Church of England seemed dead and uninspiring. Intellectual doubt soon followed from such discontents. In the 1870s a spate of books and articles criticizing orthodox Christianity appeared; and from then on agnosticism spread among the intellectual leadership of the nation. Leslie Stephen's *An Agnostic's Apology*, published in 1893 (though parts of it had appeared as an article in 1874) presented the case for unbelief with clarity and precision. Stephen had resigned his tutorship at Trinity Hall, Cambridge in 1862 because he had lost his faith. He came to the conclusion that dogmatic Christianity was unreal, in the sense that it was not provable. Christian teaching about rewards and punishments, he argued, was immoral and the doctrines of atonement, hell and immortality were unbelievable and offensive. How could a loving Father punish his children with eternal torment? How can one believe, standing by an open grave, that St Paul's promise of immortality is more than a comforting fiction? Miracles, sacraments and other dogmas of the church can no longer be accepted uncritically. In short, the bases of Christian faith are undermined.

In most cases the slide into unbelief was gradual. It was also deeply unsettling. At the personal level it raised the question of whether it was possible to lead the good life ('to live and die like a gentleman', as Leslie Stephen put it) without believing in God. The wider issue was whether the foundations of public life could be preserved without the traditional sanctions of religion. The abandonment of orthodox beliefs could bring a wonderful sense of relief and a new freedom, as portrayed in George Gissing's first novel, *Workers in the Dawn* (1880); or it could be a sad, reluctant parting, as in the moving lines from Matthew Arnold's poem, 'Dover Beach':

> The Sea of Faith
> Was once, too, at the full, and round earth's shore
> Lay like the folds of a bright girdle furl'd.
> But now I only hear
> Its melancholy long, withdrawing roar,
> Retreating to the breath
> Of the night wind, down the vast edges drear
> And naked shingles of the world.
>
> Ah, love, let us be true
> To one another! For the world, which seems
> To lie before us like a land of dreams,
> So various, so beautiful, so new,
> Hath really neither joy nor love, nor light,
> Nor certitude, nor peace, nor help for pain;
> And we are here as on a darkling plain
> Swept with confused alarms of struggle and flight,
> Where ignorant armies clash by night.

For each person the ending of belief created problems or opportunities which were handled in different ways.

The easiest way out, of course, was to keep one's doubts to oneself while outwardly conforming. Thus Leslie Stephen's brother, Sir James Fitzjames Stephen, took his children to church and had family prayers despite his scepticism. Writing in 1873 he confessed:

> As to my theological opinions . . . I do not believe the New Testament narrative to be true. To my mind, the whole history of Christ, in as far as it is supernatural, is legendary. As to Christian morals, I cannot regard them as either final or complete. As to natural religion, I think its two great doctrines – God and a future state – more probable than not; and they appear to me to make all the difference to morality. Take them away and Epicureanism seems to me the true and proper doctrine.[1]

Religion had been used as a form of social control by ruling classes for hundreds of years, and the Victorians were well aware of its power. But a cynical observance of church-going by middle-class sceptics was not enough. Society needed a value system to hold it together, and if Christianity was no longer acceptable some other form of social cement was necessary. The agnostics found an alternative in morality as the guardian of right conduct and the stability of society. The great Victorian devotion to the idea of duty remained as a legacy of the Nonconformist conscience for many agnostics. In a famous passage Frederick W. H. Myers, a Cambridge don, recalled a meeting with the novelist George Eliot in 1873:

> I remember how, at Cambridge, I walked with her once in the Fellows' Garden of Trinity, on an evening of rainy May; and she, stirred somewhat beyond her wont, and taking as her text the three words which have been used so often as the inspiring trumpet-calls of men – the words *God, Immortality, Duty* – pronounced, with terrible earnestness, how inconceivable was the *first*, how unbelievable the *second*, and yet how peremptory and absolute the *third*.

Myers was thirty and had for some time been troubled, like others of his generation at Cambridge, by doubt. George Eliot's words left him without comfort:

> I listened, and night fell; her grave, majestic countenance turned towards me like a Sibyl's in the gloom; it was as though she withdrew from my grasp, one by one, the two scrolls of promise, and left me the third scroll only, awful with inevitable fates. And when we stood at length and parted, amid that columnar circuit of the forest-trees, beneath the last twilight of starless skies, I seemed to be gazing, like Titus at Jerusalem, on vacant seats and empty halls – on a sanctuary with no Presence to hallow it, and heaven left lonely of a God.[2]

There is ample testimony from the later Victorians to the loneliness, despair, and desperate searching for alternative sources of assurance, once the old certainties had gone. The Victorian crisis of faith is nowhere treated more sensitively than in the novels of William Hale White ('Mark Rutherford'). In the *Autobiography of Mark Rutherford* (1881) and *Mark Rutherford's Deliverance* (1885) the narrowness of evangelicalism is exposed, the slow dissolution of faith is traced, and the search for alternative beliefs by which to live is begun. By doubters like William Kent, the *Autobiography* and *Deliverence* were 'eagerly embraced'.

The problem of doubt was most widely dramatized in *Robert Elsmere* (1888) by Mrs Humphry Ward. Elsmere, an earnest and hard-working country vicar, lost his faith in miracles as a result of historical study and the influence of a local secularist squire. Although he still believed in God Elsmere felt it his duty to resign from his living, despite assurances from Broad Church clergy that this was not necessary. His marriage was shaken because his wife remained a devout evangelical believer. After much agonizing Elsmere went to live in London, where he devoted himself to work among East End artisans, for whom he started a New Brotherhood of Christ. The novel was immensely popular and became a best seller in Britain and America. This is the more remarkable in that it is a very long book, drawing upon the authoress's background among Oxford academics (she was a grand-daughter of Thomas Arnold of Rugby) and in London's literary salons. It presented intellectual arguments from every side in the great debate and yet sold probably a million copies in twenty years. If ever there was a book of its time this was it. Benjamin Jowett, the Master of Balliol and Regius Professor of Greek at Oxford, writing in 1889, accurately assessed its position: 'Robert Elsmere, as the authoress tells me, has sold 60,000 in England and 400,000 in America! It has considerable merit, but its success is really due to its saying what everybody is thinking.'[3]

Robert Elsmere popularized the teaching of the Oxford Hegelian idealist philosopher T. H. Green, who appears as Mr Grey in the book; and also opened up (somewhat late in the day by European standards) the main tenets of German biblical criticism. As Gladstone, in a famous review of the novel, pointed out, the hero was really only a vehicle for the authoress's scepticism. Her doubts cut her off from the Christianity of the past but her moralism provided a religion for the future. Towards the end of the novel Elsmere's wife is reconciled to her husband's position, although she thinks her own views are unchanged:

> She was not conscious of change, but change there was. She had, in fact, undergone that dissociation of the moral judgment from a special series of religious formulae which is the crucial, the epoch-making fact of our day. 'Unbelief', says the orthodox preacher, 'is sin, and implies it': and while he speaks, the saint in the unbeliever gently smiles down his argument, and suddenly, in the rebel of yesterday men see the rightful heir of to-morrow.[4]

The late Victorians' appetite for novels of this kind was fed by many lesser efforts. Hall Caine's *The Christian* (1897) sold 50,000 copies in a month; and Marie Corelli's *The Master Christian* (1900) 260,000 over the next few years. Hall Caine's hero is a clergyman who becomes an Anglo-Catholic slum priest in the East End of London. Of gentlemanly descent and well-connected, he is torn between love of God (and celibate vows) and love for his childhood sweetheart. He revolts against the complacency of middle-class religion, turns to the social gospel, and tries unsuccessfully to live the monastic life in an Anglican brotherhood. He becomes a strange, prophetic figure who is mortally beaten up in a riot sparked by fears of divine retribution on London, and marries his sweetheart on his deathbed. *The Christian* is not a novel about doubt in the *Robert Elsmere* manner. It deals with the difficulties and problems of trying to live a Christian life, but its message, if any, is woolly and inconclusive.

In *Elsmere* and *The Christian*, as also in *Mark Rutherford's Deliverance*, a resolution of the uncertainties of doubt is found in work among the labouring poor, thus relating the crisis of faith to another great problem of the later nineteenth century, poverty and the 'social question'. For those who rejected the creeds and dogmas of the churches but who yet wished to retain some vestigial Christian belief, the syndrome of the Working Man of Galilee often proved attractive. Jesus was to be respected as a noble reformer and teacher, whose simple message of 'good will towards men' had been perverted by the rich and powerful. If Christ were to return to Victorian England what would he do and what would happen to him? In the *True History of Joshua Davidson, Christian and Communist* (1872) Eliza Lynn Linton provided an answer. Joshua (Jesus – Joshua – son of David), the son of a village carpenter, loses his faith in orthodox Anglicanism and goes to London, but is satisfied by neither the Anglo-Catholics nor the Low Churchmen. He works out for himself a programme of Christian communism and devotes his energies to rescuing the down-trodden and outcasts of society. His efforts are misunderstood by the poor as well as the rich, and when the Paris Commune is declared in 1871 he goes to Paris 'to help in the cause of humanity'. On his return he is kicked and beaten to death while defending the Commune at a public meeting. Unlike *Elsmere*, the book was ignored by the literary savants. It nevertheless went through six editions between 1872 and 1874 and remained in print until 1916. Eliza Lynn Linton was the estranged wife of William James Linton, a republican and Chartist, and the novel draws upon her acquaintance with his agnostic friends. As such it spoke to the condition of self-educated artisans and radicals. The message was put clearly after Joshua's death by his friend John:

The death of my friend has left me not only desolate, but uncertain . . . Is the Christian world all wrong, or is practical Christianity impossible? I see men simply and sincerely devoted to the cause of Humanity, and I hear the world's verdict on them. I hear others, earnest for the dogma of Christianity, rabid against its acted doctrines. They do not care to destroy the causes of misery by any change in social relations; they only attack the sinners for whose sin society is originally responsible. They maintain the unrighteous distinctions of caste as a religion; and they denounce as delusion, or impiety, the doctrine of universal brotherhood which Christ and His apostles preached and died for . . . If the doctrines of Political Economy are true, if the law of the struggle for existence and the survival of the fittest applies absolutely to human society as well as to plants and fishes, let us then be frank, and candidly admit that Christianity, in its help to the poor and weak and in its patience with the sinner, is a craze; and let us abolish the presence of a faith which influences neither our political institutions nor our social arrangements; and which ought not to influence them. If Christ was right, modern Christianity is wrong; but if sociology is a scientific truth, then Jesus of Nazareth preached and practised not only in vain, but against unchangeable Law.

Like Joshua in early days, my heart burns within me and my mind is unpiloted and unanchored. I cannot, being a Christian, accept the inhumanity of political economy and the obliteration of the individual in averages; yet I cannot reconcile modern science with Christ. Everywhere I see the sifting of competition, and nowhere Christian protection of weakness; everywhere dogma adored, and nowhere Christ realised. And again I ask, which is true – modern society in its class strife and consequent elimination of its weaker elements, or the brotherhood and communism taught by the Jewish carpenter of Nazareth?[5]

Views such as these confirmed the worst fears of the upholders of orthodoxy: once admit religious doubt and the floodgates would be open to every kind of radicalism and communism. Beyond the respectable agnosticism of the upper classes were altogether tougher and more uncompromising movements of unbelief, drawing support from lower middle-class and artisan radicals. It did not go unnoticed that Charles Bradlaugh, the leader and hero of the secularists in the 1880s was also a republican and advocate of birth control. In the pages of his *National Reformer* first appeared (1874) that strange monument to Victorian pessimism, 'The City of Dreadful Night' by the poet James Thomson ('B.V.'), which was admired and quoted in popular freethought circles:

> And now at last authentic word I bring,
> Witnessed by every dead and living thing;
> Good tidings of great joy for you, for all:
> There is no God; no Fiend with names divine
> Made us and tortures us; if we must pine,
> It is to satiate no Being's gall . . .

> This little life is all we must endure,
> The grave's most holy peace is ever sure,
> We fall asleep and never wake again;
> Nothing is of us but the mouldering flesh,
> Whose elements dissolve and merge afresh
> In earth, air, water, plants, and other men.[6]

Another favourite of late Victorian sceptics was Winwood Reade's *The Martyrdom of Man*, whose extravagant claims for science were quoted in the previous chapter. As Sherlock Holmes went off to investigate the *Sign of Four* (1889) he gave Watson a book, 'one of the most remarkable ever penned. It is Winwood Reade's *Martyrdom of Man*.'[7] Cecil Rhodes, Sir Harry Johnson (the African explorer), as well as Conan Doyle: all admired it; and it later served as the model for H. G. Wells's *Outline of History*. The *Martyrdom* is a panoramic view of world history, drawing upon Reade's African travels as well as his reading in history, anthropology and Darwinism. It charts the progress of mankind from barbarism to civilization, with plenty of emphasis on the cruelty and delusions of religion. From these investigations he concludes emphatically that supernatural Christianity is false, prayer is useless, the soul is not immortal and there are no future rewards and punishments. In each generation the human race has been martyred that their children might profit by their woes. Present prosperity is founded on the misery and suffering of the past, for this is the way in which progress is made in accordance with the evolutionary laws of social Darwinism. In our day we are called upon for new sacrifices:

> Famine, pestilence and war are no longer essential for the advancement of the human race. But a season of mental anguish is at hand, and through this we must pass in order that our posterity may rise. The soul must be sacrificed; the hope in immortality must die. A sweet and charming illusion must be taken from the human race, as youth and beauty vanish never to return.[8]

Works like the *Martyrdom of Man*, which went through twenty-four English editions by 1926 and eighteen American by 1910, helped to promote a general feeling that intelligent, progressively-minded people could no longer accept traditional religious beliefs and practices. The churches seemed old-fashioned and Christianity increasingly irrelevant to many of the late Victorian and Edwardian younger generation. The young Eric Gill, serving his apprenticeship in a London architect's office, read H. G. Wells, Omar Khayyàm, R. L. Stevenson and Thomas Carlyle, and then moved on to the sixpenny booklets of the Rationalist Press Association (founded by Charles Watts in 1899), Fabian tracts, John Ruskin and William Morris. Such a diet of agnostic socialism only confirmed in words 'what was everywhere visible to the naked eye',[9] namely that religion was in decline. The working classes in general remained obdurately outside the mainstream churches; and the relative decline in middle- and upper-class church-going after the 1880s indicated that the ebb tide had begun.

> The meaning is gone from phrases which are still repeated, whose significance is becoming historical merely, [declared Charles Masterman in 1909] ... The drift is towards a

non-dogmatic affirmation of general kindliness and good
fellowship, with an emphasis rather on the services of man
than the fulfilment of the will of God. [10]

Like Masterman, many Christians were perplexed that ethical
advance seemed to be accompanied by spiritual decline, that
morality was present without faith.

To explain this decline of religious institutions and ideas two
theories have been advanced. The first attributes the decline of
the churches to intellectual change, notably the ethical revolt
against Christian teaching and the diffusion of Darwinian ideas.
The second, and more usual, is the theory of secularization.
Modern industrial society with its increasing relative affluence,
it is argued, undermined the values and attitudes inherited from
a world in which scarcity and insecurity had been dominant in
most people's lives. Science, technology and rationalization –
basic to a maturing industrial economy – produced a popular
consciousness inimical to traditional religious ways of thinking
and conducive to demystification. Although more people attended church in 1901 than ever before, the proportion of atten-
ders to total population was smaller than when the Queen came
to the throne, and the total number of non-attenders was also
higher than in 1837. In this sense England in late Victorian times
was more secular than previously.

II

How far the mood of religious and intellectual doubt extended
beyond a minority of upper-class agnostics and seriously-minded
clerks and artisans is hard to determine. For most of the population the worries and anxieties of their time probably lay elsewhere. Exactly where we do not know, for as with other beliefs
and values first-hand evidence is scarce. Ordinary people seldom
left records of their intimate worries, though from working-
and lower middle-class autobiographies it is possible to glimpse
pictures of misfortune, sorrow and want. Over the ordinary joys
and hopes of daily life from time to time fell the shadow of
the unknown future. The insecurity of life was nothing new.

Generations of English people had been reminded by the psalmist that 'the days of man are but as grass' and that even for those who reach fourscore years their strength is 'but labour and sorrow'. Inevitability, however, does little to allay fear. The late Victorians, from their own experiences, had ample grounds for anxiety about poverty, status, health, accidents, old age and death.

Basic to practically all working-class life was the fact of economic insecurity. Making a living was beset with hazards; and those who failed found themselves face to face with want. The fear of simply not having enough to eat, not being able to pay the rent, and not having the wherewithal to live decently haunted thousands of families. The nature and extent of poverty will be examined later. Here we make the point that inadequate means was a cause of aggravation of anxieties about other things such as disease, accidents and old age. It was the irregularity of work, even for many skilled and relatively well-paid men, that generated anxiety. Laid off because of bad weather, economic crisis or the casual nature of the labour market, a working man with a family to support immediately found himself in debt. Friendly societies and other forms of thrift provided but feeble defences against the results of unemployment. The private charity of the churches and the Charity Organisation Society offered palliatives which were often felt to be demeaning and acceptable only as a last resort. Lady Bell observed:

> We forget how terribly near the margin of disaster the man, even the thrifty man, walks, who has, in ordinary normal conditions, but just enough to keep himself on. The spectre of illness and disability is always confronting the working-man; the possibility of being from one day to the other plunged into actual want is always confronting his family.[11]

For those a little higher in the social scale economic misfortune also meant loss of status. Fear of 'what the neighbours would think' was ever present among the lower middle class. The novels of the time (amply confirmed in autobiographies) are full of examples of anxiety about maintaining the family's social standing. Respectability exacted a psychic (perhaps neurotic) cost which has not as yet been fully explored.

Next to anxiety about an adequate income – and often closely connected with it – was concern for health. One did not have to be hypochondriac to be frightened by the spectre of disease. Certainly the great killers and disablers of the mid-nineteenth century – scarlet fever, diphtheria, measles, cholera, typhus, typhoid, tuberculosis – declined in the later Victorian years, some dramatically so. But influenza baffled the doctors and the diagnosis of heart disease and cancer was erratic. The incidence of reported blindness fell sharply after 1871; for lesser forms of impaired sight there was little improvement in treatment. The biggest gain in Victorian Britain was the reduction in the number of deaths from infectious diseases. Nevertheless sudden and disabling illness and death remained as ever present fears.

It is difficult to assess what expectations people had in regard to their health, or indeed if they gave the matter any thought at all until they were struck down by illness. Probably the general state of most people's health at the end of the century – given a poorer diet, harsher social conditions, and less medical care – was lower than it is today, in that they suffered from more physical infirmities and had a shorter average life span than we do. But they were healthier than their parents and grandparents. Evidence of the general state of health of the population is scattered and incomplete. However, the provision of regular schooling for all the population after the 1870 Education Act led to the collection of statistics about the condition of children in Board schools in various parts of the kingdom. These inspections showed considerable numbers of children with poor teeth, defective eyesight, bad hearing and catarrhal afflictions. There were also significant class differentials, with middle-class children being taller and heavier than their working-class equivalents of the same age.

National concern for health was awakened by army recruitment during the Boer War which showed the poor physical condition of working men in the towns. At Manchester in 1899 three out of every five volunteers were rejected as physically unfit. Seebohm Rowntree in his study of poverty noted that of 3,600 recruits seeking enlistment at York, Leeds and Sheffield between 1897 and 1900, 26.5 per cent were rejected as unfit and a further

29 per cent were only accepted as 'specials', in the hope that a few months of army life would bring them up to standard – and this at a time when, in order to obtain the required number of men, the army standards of health and physical development had been repeatedly lowered. These findings were confirmed by an interdepartmental Committee on Physical Deterioration which reported in 1904, and sparked off a good deal of talk about the 'decline of the race' and the need for reforms along eugenicist and social Darwinist lines. National efficiency and Britain's imperialist future were alleged to be in jeopardy. In the popular consciousness the army medical examinations meant simply that many unsuspecting young working men were found to be suffering from diseases of the heart, veins and lungs, as well as from haemorrhoids, venereal disease and nervous debilities. The implications for the rest of the population were scarcely encouraging, for these recruits were drawn from the potentially fittest section of the people and had only been sent for medical examination if there was 'a reasonable probability of passing'. If they suffered so many infirmities it is hardly likely that the health of the people as a whole was much better. That daily aches and pains, some serious, others inconvenient, were a cause of anxiety is suggested by the large sales of patent medicines, the frequency of home treatments, and resort to the services of herbalists, wise men and women, and unorthodox healers of all kinds.

Apart from worries about health in general there was always the danger of accidents in the day's work – on the railway, in the steelworks, down the mine, with horses, on the scaffolding of buildings, in collapsing excavations. George Sturt recounted a typical case in Surrey:

> In a cottage near to where I am writing a young labourer died last summer – a young unmarried man, whose mother was living with him, and had long depended on his support. Eighteen months earlier he had been disabled for a week or two by the kick of a horse, and a heart-disease of long standing was so aggravated by the accident that he was never again able to do much work. There came months of unemployment, and as a consequence he was in extreme

poverty when he died. His mother was already reduced to parish relief; it was only by the help of his two sisters – young women out at service, who managed to pay for a coffin for him – that a pauper's funeral was avoided.[12]

Coalmining was one of the most dangerous occupations and the coal industry employed 750,000 workers in 1901, rising to over 1 million by 1911. Scarcely a year passed without a 'disaster' in some mine, resulting in the deaths of scores and sometimes hundreds of miners. 'Waiting for news' was a common theme of photographs and drawings depicting crowds of wives and relatives standing around the pithead. The total number killed annually in the mines for the period 1880–1910 was for most years between 1,000 and 1,500. The number of non-fatal accidents in the years 1908–1913 varied between 140,000 and 180,000 annually, which amounted to 14–15 per cent of the total number employed, and a considerably higher percentage of underground workers. The families of miners lived always in the shadow of calamity, great or small. When the man went off to the pit in the morning his wife and children could never escape the fear that before evening he might be brought home dead or injured. The same shadow hung over the families of other workers in heavy industry. Lady Bell, in her account of the lives of Middlesbrough ironworkers, noted:

> A widow whose eldest son, her remaining support, had been killed at twenty-two, said that whenever the men came in late for a meal, she always thought, according to the current phrase, that they had 'happened an accident'.[13]

For women there was the added anxiety of maternity. At the end of the century childbirth was still dangerous for both mothers and babies. In 1901 deaths in childbirth were reported as high as 4,400 in England and Wales and this figure almost certainly under-represented the true number. Maternal mortality remained at around 4.8 per thousand live births, and only began to decline slowly after 1903. It did not fall below 1 per thousand until 1944–5. The death rate for infants under one year reached a peak of 163 per thousand in 1899 (compared with 9.4 per thousand in 1985). Translated into actual deaths this meant for example 140,000 bereavements in 1901. These are average figures for England and Wales, and take no account of under-reporting or variations between large towns. From the experience of relatives and neighbours every woman pregnant for the first time knew that she faced a dangerous, painful and generally unpleasant time. The absence of ante-natal care or the precautions of Victorian prudery often left her quite inadequately prepared for the birth. Most deliveries took place at home; and the poorer the family the less were they able to provide the minimum conditions for a safe birth. Hannah Mitchell was married to a shop assistant earning 25s a week in Bolton in the 1890s. Her account of the birth of her first child is typical:

> I feared the ordeal, but tried to keep my fears to myself, remembering that other women got over it, not once only, but many times . . . At last my own time came. One Friday, having done my weekend cleaning and baked a batch of bread during the day, I hoped for a good night's rest, but I scarcely had retired before my labour began. My baby was not born until the following evening, after twenty-four hours of intense suffering which an ignorant attendant did little to alleviate, assuring me at intervals that I should be much worse yet. At last a kindly neighbour, herself a mother of three children, coming in to see how things were shaping, took matters into her own hands. She sent my husband for the doctor, charging him to insist on immediate attendance, and bustled me into bed. But my strength was gone, and I could do no more to help myself, so my baby was brought into the world with instruments, and without an anaesthetic.
>
> This operation was sheer barbarism and ought to be regarded as 'wilful cruelty' and dealt with accordingly.[14]

The burden of bringing up a family of six or eight children on a wholly inadequate income could only be viewed with apprehension by thousands of working-class women. After the first child or two the dread of unwanted pregnancies grew. In 1914 the Women's Co-operative Guild collected information from members about their experiences of childbirth during the preceding decade.[15] The letters which these women wrote tell a tale of unending struggle with poverty, leading to exhaustion and quiet desperation. Stillbirths, miscarriages and attempts at abortion are chronicled in detail, as also are uncaring doctors and incompetent midwives. In 1900 a quarter of all married women were in childbirth; for thousands of them it could not be anything but a time fraught with anxiety.

At the opposite end of the life cycle there was also fear. It was not fear of death, but of old age. A majority of old people in all classes continued to live together either in their own homes or with relatives who looked after them. But a minority who were less fortunate had to go into the workhouse. The 'Bastilles', as they were still called in the 1890s, had from their inception in 1834 been intended as a deterrent and they had been only too successful in that role. The stigma of the workhouse was so great that working people would accept almost any privation rather than enter it. To avoid a pauper burial and ensure a 'decent' funeral working people were prepared to pay weekly contributions which they could often ill afford into a friendly society or burial club. Almost every middle-class investigator commented on the strength of this tradition among the working classes. It was not necessary to be an inmate to know what workhouse life was like. From an early age children learned to think of it with dread. Stella Davies as a small girl in 1903 lived in a cottage which backed up to the grounds of Crumpsall (Manchester) workhouse, and by climbing on to the midden wall was able to see what went on:

> Our proximity to it [the workhouse] provided us not only with a salutary warning of dreadful possibilities but also with a great deal of interest. Horse ambulances were admitted at the large iron gates and sometimes moans or cries of pain could be heard; pauper lunatics worked in the Workhouse gardens; ragged families trailed up the drive; funerals, the coffin a plain deal box, drove to the workhouse cemetery; children were escorted to the local Board school in a long queue, all wearing the same drab workhouse clothes with the girls in unbleached calico aprons. Now and then an

inmate would come out and be joyfully received by friends or relatives at the gate; sometimes there would be no one and the ex-pauper would wander solitarily away.[16]

The basic unsuitability of the workhouse in old age was that the institution was required to be a deterrent to the able-bodied poor and at the same time a place of refuge for the infirm, the feeble-minded and the sick. Surveys showed that in 1894–5 between 30 and 40 per cent of all persons over 65 were paupers. At this time 20 per cent of all deaths in Bristol occurred in the workhouse, 19 per cent in Manchester and Liverpool, and 36 per cent in Stepney. The poignancy of meeting the 'last enemy' is brought out in Flora Thompson's account of an old soldier, nicknamed 'the Major', who lived alone in the village and who could no longer look after himself:

The day came when the doctor called in the relieving officer. The old man was seriously ill; he had no relatives. There was only one place where he could be properly looked after, and that was the workhouse infirmary. They were right in their decision. He was not able to look after himself; he had no relatives or friends able to undertake the responsibility; the workhouse was the best place for him. But they made one terrible mistake. They were dealing with a man of intelligence and spirit, and they treated him as they might have done one in the extreme of senile decay. They did not consult him or tell him what they had decided; but ordered the carrier's cart to call at his house the next morning and wait at a short distance while they, in the doctor's gig, drove up to his door. When they entered, the Major had just dressed and dragged himself to his chair by the fire. 'It's a nice morning, and we've come to take you for a drive,' announced the doctor cheerfully, and, in spite of his protests, they hustled on his coat and had him out and in the carrier's cart in a very few minutes ... As soon as he realized where he was being taken, the old soldier, the independent old bachelor, the kind family friend, collapsed and cried like a child. He was beaten. But not for long. Before six weeks were over he was back in the parish and all his troubles were over, for he came in his coffin.[17]

These anxieties were not new. Most of them stemmed from the almost complete lack of social security for working people. To middle-class observers at the end of the century this came as something of a shock; but to the people themselves it was simply 'life as we have known it'.[18] From their autobiographies, letters and oral interviews one is left with an impression of long-term fatalism and underlying resentment. But as one poor woman who had to bring up five children on 17s a week replied to the questions she was asked: 'I am afraid I cannot tell you very much, because I worked too hard to think about how we lived.'[19]

IV

Processes of Change

7 .

England Arise!

The picture of late Victorian society presented in the preceding chapters has been more or less static, rather like a still from a running film. Contemporaries however were convinced that they were living in an age of change. This view has been confirmed by social historians, who have usually divided the Victorian period into three parts: first, the twenty years of stress and strain before 1848; then the mid-Victorian age of prosperity and stability; and finally a period of renewed change in the last thirty years or so of the century. We have now to look at the forces making for that change and attempt some assessment of their relative significance.

Among the foremost of the agencies of social change was the labour and socialist movement, whose spectacular rise in the 1880s and 1890s has dazzled several generations of social historians. The heroic age of modern socialism, 1880–1914, was so full of ideals and hopes and controversies, and produced so many outstanding leaders and writers that it is difficult to see the movement in perspective. Throughout Europe mass socialist and working-class parties developed during this period, all demanding fundamental change in society. Great Britain was exceptional in the strength of its trade union movement and the relative weakness of its socialist (Marxist) commitment. Nevertheless, in Britain as elsewhere, the ideology of socialism allied with the organization of trade unionism provided a new form for the articulation of the wants of thousands of ordinary people. The fulfilment of these hopes lay beyond the period of this study, so that what we are looking at is only the spring or seed time. With hindsight we can see the harvest which eventually resulted from the sowing; but to contemporaries of course this was hidden. In the historical process we always ride with our backs to the engine. The danger of anachronism (that is, of ascribing to the late Victorians views and evaluations which could only be held by people who lived later) is here very great. William Morris, like William Blake before him, is probably more widely known and appreciated today than a hundred years ago; Fabian ideas have permeated well beyond the original hopes of Sidney and Beatrice Webb; and the influence of trade unions reached a peak in 1979 which was not foreseen in 1900. The difficulty is that our knowledge of subsequent events, while allowing us to see the long-term significance of the labour movement, may cloud our perception of the 1880s and 1890s, when all was new, exciting, alarming, untried, and often supported by no more than a tiny band of reformers.

By the early 1870s a small minority of workers – mainly skilled craftsmen, textile operatives, coal miners, shipbuilders, engineers and metal workers of various kinds – had succeeded in getting their trade unions accepted and recognised by employers and government. From this base expansion began immediately following an upswing in the trade cycle; but some of the gains, notably among agricultural workers, were not permanent, and with hindsight the growth in the 1870s appears as a false dawn. The truly massive advance in trade unionism began in 1889 and took the U.K. membership from 750,000 (5 per cent of the labour force) in 1888 to over 2 million in 1900 and over 4 million (23 per cent of the labour force) in 1913. The increase was in the membership of existing trade unions and also (more significantly) among unskilled and semi-skilled workers who had hitherto been largely outside the trade union orbit. This 'new unionism' was symbolized by the great dock strike of 1889, which in August successfully closed the London docks and wrested from the employers 'the dockers' tanner' (a day wage of 6d an hour) and abolition of the sub-contracting system. Daily, disciplined marches across London secured favourable publicity for the strike, and its colourful leaders – John Burns, Ben Tillett and Tom Mann – became nationally known figures. Earlier in the year the London gas workers formed a union and won a reduction in working hours; and in the summer of 1888 the match girls' strike at Bryant and May's factory had shown that it might be possible to organize even the poorest and most exploited groups of workers. Across the country a fever of unionism spread rapidly, and the number of trade unionists doubled between 1889 and 1891. The employers fought back, and further union gains were bitterly contested. Ben Turner, who was in the thick of the struggles in the West Riding, recalled that when he joined the Huddersfield Weavers' Union in 1882 it was so weak that it could not even collect regular contributions: 'it was really playing at Trade Unionism, but was as far advanced as the old Radical section felt able to go'.[1] Yet ten years later the whole industrial climate had changed: old unions were revivified and hundreds of unorganized workers – gas workers, tramway workers, blue dyers, plasterers' labourers, tailors and tailoresses – were recruited into new unions in Yorkshire. The great achievement of trade unionism nationally was that by 1914 in most of the major industries a system of collective bargaining had been evolved: the workers, through their representatives, were able to secure improvements in wages and conditions of work.

But there were limits to what trade unions alone could do for their members and it was obvious from the 1870s that legislation favourable to labour could be secured only by political action. After the extension of the suffrage in 1867 and 1884 the two main political parties were prepared to court the working-class vote, which provided organized labour with a certain amount of political power. On this basis was built a Liberal-Labour alliance, by which a few Labour candidates were returned to Parliament on the Liberal ticket. The arrangement worked best in mining constituencies, where the area was socially homogeneous and the union strong.

At the general election of 1885, following the Third Reform Act, the number of Lib-Lab M.P.s increased from two to eleven, and of these six were miners. Since the demise of Chartism such working men as were enfranchised usually voted Liberal, except in Lancashire and parts of London. Indeed, the Liberal Party remained the party of most working men up to 1914. But discontent with Lib-Lab'ism began to be voiced in the 1880s and gathered momentum in the 1890s. It sprang basically from the reluctance of the Liberal Party to appoint more working-class candidates and support the trade unions in their legal struggles with employers. There arose therefore a demand for independent labour representation, free from the constraints of alliance with either Liberals or Conservatives. This movement was reflected within the Trades Union Congress, set up in 1868 to act as a national parliament of labour. Every year from 1887 to 1899 the issue of independent labour representation was raised and hotly debated. On the one side were the new unionists, the socialists, and the advocates of direct sponsorship of working-class candidates, led by the Scottish miners' leader, Keir Hardie, who had himself been refused adoption as a candidate by the Liberals; on the other were the old unionists and the upholders of Lib-Lab'ism as exemplified by Henry Broadhurst, who had left his stonemason's bench, as he said, for the Treasury Bench of a Liberal government. The climax came in 1899–1900, when a carefully worded motion was passed to call a special conference of representatives from 'Co-operative, Socialist, Trade Union, and other working-class organizations' to 'devise ways and means for the securing of an increased number of Labour members in the next Parliament'. Out of this conference emerged the Labour Representation Committee (L.R.C.), which in 1906 became the Labour Party.

The second element in the dynamic of the labour movement was socialism. What precisely the term meant to the many hundreds (later thousands) of earnest working men and women who so described their beliefs is not an entirely straightforward matter. Membership of most socialist organisations signified a commitment to certain principles (of which some version of 'the collective ownership of the means of production, distribution and exchange' was the most important) followed by a list of 'immediate' reforms, such as the eight hour day, state pensions, and free, secular education to sixteen. But it is clear from the reminiscences of old socialists that while they subscribed to these objectives, they often had a variety of other expectations and motivations. For some, the revolt against Victorian society and all that it stood for was paramount; some were appalled by the waste and inefficiency of capitalism and wished to replace it by a more rational system; others found in socialism a new religion; and a

few believed in class struggle and the hope of revolution. Socialism was not only an instrument for the realization of certain
social and political goals. It also had an expressive function in
the lives of many of its more active adherents; they needed
socialism as much as the movement needed them. In the 1880s
and 1890s they had a choice of organizations. The oldest was
the Social Democratic Federation (S.D.F.), founded in 1881 as
the Democratic Federation from various radical clubs in London.
It was basically Marxist, and most of the leading English socialists
were for a short while in its ranks. The Socialist League, under
the leadership of William Morris, split off from the S.D.F. in
1884; and in the same year the Fabian Society was formed by a
group of middle-class intellectuals, whose policy of reformist
socialism was based on a belief in 'the inevitability of gradual-
ness'. In 1893 the Independent Labour Party was founded at a
conference in Bradford, and despite its title was committed to
socialism.

Numerically the socialists were only a small body – probably
no more than 2000 in the 1880s and perhaps 20–30,000 by
1900–but their influence was widespread, especially in London
and the industrial North. Their activities, and above all their
propaganda, set up a ferment of social ideas which captivated a
whole generation of young people in the nineties and carried over
into the first decade of the new century.

> It is curious indeed [reflected the socialist guru, Edward
> Carpenter in 1916] to see how, of all the innumerable
> little societies – of the S.D.F., the League, the Fabians, the
> Christian Socialists, the Anarchists, the Freedom groups, the
> I.L.P., the *Clarion* societies, and local groups of various
> names – all supporting one side or another of the general
> Socialist movement – not one of them has grown to any
> great volume, or to commanding and permanent influence;
> and how yet, and at the same time, the general teaching and
> ideals of the movement have permeated society in the most
> remarkable way, and have deeply infected the views of all
> classes, as well as general literature and even municipal and
> imperial politics.[2]

In the larger towns there was a whole variety of labour clubs, in addition to the trade union branches and the central political organisations. Around the *Clarion* newspaper was developed a series of social activities, especially attractive to youth – cycling clubs, glee clubs, field clubs, and scouting. Parties of young socialist pioneers went out into the villages at the weekends distributing leaflets, holding meetings, consciously spreading the new gospel. In the towns of the West Riding the coffee-houses (the traditional debating grounds for Radicals and others) provided admirable opportunities for the dissemination of socialist ideas.

Hannah Mitchell recaptured the headiness of this springtime of socialism in the 1890s. She and her young husband, both ardent socialists, were then living at Newhall, a colliery village near Burton-on-Trent, when the 'Clarion Van' came into the district. The van was a horse-drawn caravan, fitted with beds, a stove and a few cooking utensils. It provided a mobile platform for socialist propaganda and was in the charge of a capable speaker who relied on local socialists to arrange meeting places and provide hospitality:

> I shall never forget the Sunday meetings when scores of *Clarion* cyclists from Lichfield, Burton and all the surrounding villages descended on Newhall to support the van. Most of these brought their own food, and we were kept busy brewing tea and coffee, while for those whose enthusiasm had sent them out foodless, we emptied our larders . . . Indeed, most of our dinners were rather sketchy for some days.
>
> But our hearts were glad. We were young and full of hope, thinking we had only to broadcast the Socialist message and the workers would flock to our banner. We followed the Van all week, through the surrounding villages, and when it moved on to Lichfield at the weekend, we hired a waggonette and twenty of us drove to Lichfield for the Sunday meetings.[3]

During her courtship in Bolton, Hannah Mitchell attended semi-religious services at the Labour Church run by the local socialists. The Labour Churches were started by John Trevor, a Unitarian minister, and were especially popular as socialist institutions in Yorkshire and Lancashire, where they managed to combine the ethos of religious nonconformity with a broad ethical appeal. The Bradford Labour Institute had formerly been a chapel, and it was there that Margaret McMillan, a pioneer of child welfare and member of the local School Board, gave her first lecture to the Bradford socialists in 1893:

> We reached the platform by climbing up a ladder from the room. One by one we appeared like Jacks from a box – our heads being greeted as we emerged by encouraging cheers. Then the service, for it was a religious service, began. It departed from all the customs of other churches, though we tried more and more to conform and please our various fellow-worshippers. The Swedenborgians repeated the Lord's Prayer with the chairman, but the Social Democratic Federationers did nothing of the kind. The old chapel-goers, or some of them, enjoyed the hymns, but the Secularists did not enjoy them – thought they were mere weakness and held their books anyhow. The lecture was the thing. All waited for that. Some listened intently, critically; these were the Social Democratic Federationers, who were critical, and the Secularists. Mr Isaac Sanctuary, a Swedenborgian, who looked like a mild and handsome reincarnation of Socrates, listened in a kind of dream. Mr Roberts, an old Chartist, heard as it were the trumpet of yesterday. He had a huge head, intelligent blue eyes, young eyes though he was eighty. He tramped in from Clayton every Sunday, dressed in heavy grey cloth – a stuff he sold to navvies – carrying a thick knotted stick. The close song was unanimous – the strong voices rolling out like a sudden wave:
>
> > When wilt thou save Thy people,
> > O God of Mercy, when?[4]

To many of the pioneers socialism had the appeal of a religion; they spoke often of their faith in socialism. Margaret McMillan saw that the new party in Bradford sprang from an impulse that had nothing in common with the older political parties. 'It was called the Independent Labour Party. In reality it was a new religion – a heresy.' Philip Snowden, after addressing his first socialist meeting at Keighley in 1894, experienced the same discovery: 'It was an inspiration. It was like a revival gathering. Socialism to those men and women was a new vision.'[5] There was a tremendous feeling of being part of a movement which would make a reality of this vision, a feeling of taking part in a great crusade. 'England, arise! The long, long night is over', proclaimed Edward Carpenter in a hymn that was sung at labour gatherings for many years. 'Socialism', said Keir Hardie, 'is not a system of economics but life for the dying people.'

The new movement was educational, both in its methods and its broad effects. Socialist Sunday Schools, Adult Schools, and discussion classes were established by the labour clubs, and socialist lectures found their way into existing institutions such as the Secular Sunday Schools wherever possible. Lecturing was one of the ways in which a meagre livelihood could be secured for those who wished to devote themselves whole-time to the cause. Margaret McMillan and Philip Snowden were itinerant I.L.P. lecturers of this order, travelling from place to place and spending the nights in the homes of local comrades. The new socialism was educational also in a broader sense; the flood of pamphlets and journals which it released stimulated intellectual activity and sustained prolonged debate on the fundamentals of democracy and politics which lasted until the First World War. A steady stream of Fabian tracts, Fabian book-boxes, and I.L.P., S.D.F., and Secularist pamphlets provided food for endless discussion and debate. Local journals like the *Yorkshire Factory Times*, the *Bradford Labour Journal*, *Labour Champion*, and the *Huddersfield and Colne Valley Labour News* were read along with the national papers such as *Justice*, *Commonweal*, the *Labour Leader*, and *Clarion*. Robert Blatchford's *Clarion* (begun in 1891) was labour journalism of a new kind, reaching out to the masses, and presenting the socialist case to them in a simple, good-humoured way. Not since Cobbett had any popular political journalist been so effective. In 1894 Blatchford reprinted some of his articles on socialism, as *Merrie England*, and sold 75,000 copies at once and over 2,000,000 during the next fifteen years. The circulation of *Clarion* rose to 80,000. The intelligent young worker who read *Merrie England* was not encouraged to stop there; in the appendix at the end of the book was a reading list which extended far beyond socialist tracts to Emerson, Ruskin and Carlyle.

At this point the socialist movement was able to draw upon an older tradition of working-class self-education, self-improvement, nonconformist moral earnestness and a radical concern for social justice. In 1903 the Workers' Educational Association was founded, and the ideal of 'education for social and industrial emancipation' inspired a new generation of worker-students. Not all members of the W.E.A. were socialists, but many of the activists were. They were also the spiritual and intellectual descendants of the reformers of the 1840s and of that long line of weaver-poets, artisan-naturalists and cobbler-philosophers who flourished in the northern provinces. They were democrats, men and women of the Left, the sort of people who distributed *Clarion* and who bought the Rationalist Press Association's cheap editions of Huxley and Darwin. The original aim of Albert Mansbridge, the founder of the W.E.A. had been to promote among the working classes higher education of the type provided since the 1870s by University Extension but which had reached only the middle classes. From 1907 the W.E.A. entered into a joint arrangement with the universities for the provision of tutorial classes, where Mansbridge's ideal of the partnership of labour and learning found its most complete expression.

There was nothing inevitable in the association of socialism with the bread-and-butter issues of trade unionism, although the most prominent leaders of the new unions were socialists. Theories of socialism, as Lenin pointed out, were not the product of the working class but of intellectuals from the educated classes. Neither revolutionary socialists nor Fabians were over-optimistic about the potentialities of trade unions for bringing about fundamental social change. From their side the old unionists were deeply distrustful of the socialists, whom they suspected of merely wanting to capture the union membership for ulterior ends. Nevertheless, the unique achievement of British labour was the building of a political alliance between these two movements, resulting in the Labour Party. In Europe and America, which also had trade union and socialist movements, no comparable structure developed, although the seeds were there.

The chief architect of what he called the Labour Alliance was Keir Hardie, and the crucial steps in its formation were taken by the generation before the First World War. It had been hoped that the I.L.P. would become a mass socialist party, but its failure to do so in the 1890s was interpreted as showing the need to redouble the efforts to win trade union support. A counter-offensive by the employers, who hoped to emulate the success of their American rivals in union-breaking, convinced some union-ists that they might be unwise to rely on industrial action alone. And in this mood the L.R.C. was established by delegates from the I.L.P., S.D.F., Fabian Society and the unions. The three largest unions – of the miners, cotton workers and engineers – at first held aloof, in contrast to the new unions and the railwaymen. But after the Taff Vale Case in 1900–01, when the House of Lords ruled that a union could be liable for all the damages resulting from a strike (thereby undercutting the very roots of trade union power) the need to exert political pressure to change the law in labour's favour was clear, and there was a rallying of the unions behind the L.R.C. Success came in 1906, when twenty-nine L.R.C. candidates were elected to Parliament, where they assumed the name of Labour Party. The new party did not adopt a socialist programme until 1918, and Lib-Lab'ism, especially among the miners, took some time in dying. The socialism of the Labour Party when it finally emerged was of a peculiarly insular kind: empirical, reformist and welfare-statist.

As an agent of change the labour movement in the 1880s and early twentieth century was more a portent than a force, but a portent nevertheless of great significance. Without subscribing to a Whiggish interpretation of labour history which sees the events of the 1880s as the beginning of a triumphal march towards the present, it remains true that these events signalled a new departure in British social development. The labour movement was the most powerful expression since Chartism of the common people organized for action. It was a truly popular movement in that its inspiration and control were in the hands of individuals and groups drawn from the common people rather than from other classes, though it did not include a majority of the working class. The labour activists and their institutions represented a conscious effort by some working people to control their own destiny, to become the makers instead of the victims of history. This awareness underlay the tremendous enthusiasm and the sense of participation in a great adventure that characterized late Victorian socialists. They believed that society could be changed, and that 'history' was on their side.

One of the strongest motivations towards socialism was the revolt against Victorian civilization in general. John Ruskin had led the way in the 1860s with his attack on orthodox political economy. He criticized the complacent atmosphere in which the comfortable middle classes lived and questioned the whole basis of money making and the values and attitudes associated with it. His writings were widely read and influenced many working men who subsequently joined the socialist movement. William Morris and Edward Carpenter carried the critique a stage further. Carpenter had resigned his fellowship at Trinity Hall, Cambridge, in 1873 and become a University Extension lecturer because he thought it would enable him to 'throw in his lot with the mass-people and the manual workers'. But he was disappointed in this expectation and so in 1881, under the inspiration of Walt Whitman, he turned from lecturing to writing, and established for himself a Thoreau-like existence on a smallholding at Millthorpe near Sheffield. There he joined a local branch of William Morris's Socialist League; and for many years lived as a writer, socialist sage, and advocate of the 'simplification of life'. It is not easy to liberate Carpenter entirely from an Orwellian stereotype of the sandal-wearing, fruit-juice drinking lefty. But Carpenter had little real concern for the squabbles between socialist sects, preferring the politics of personal influence and persuasion among the pilgrims who visited him at his hermitage in Millthorpe. In the 1890s, when the main energies of the labour movement were being channelled into the 'new unionism' of the unskilled workers and the organization of independent labour representation in Parliament, Carpenter began to speak of his 'larger' socialism. By this he meant a catholicity (or opportunism, as his critics alleged) which welcomed all sects and reformers who would in any way support his campaign to overcome (capitalist) 'civiliz- ation'. The following poem is from his *Towards Democracy* (1883):

IN A MANUFACTURING TOWN

AS I walked restless and despondent through the gloomy city,

And saw the eager unresting to and fro – as of ghosts in some sulphurous Hades –

And saw the crowds of tall chimneys going up, and the pall of smoke covering the sun, covering the earth, lying heavy against the very ground –

And saw the huge refuse-heaps writhing with children picking them over,

And the ghastly half-roofless smoke-blackened houses, and the black river flowing below, –

As I saw these, and as I saw again far away the Capitalist quarter, with its villa residences and its high-walled gardens and its well-appointed carriages, and its face turned away from the wriggling poverty which made it rich, –

As I saw and remembered its drawing-room airs and affectations and its wheezy pursy Church-going and its gas-reeking heavy-furnished rooms and its scent-bottles and its other abominations –

I shuddered:

For I felt stifled, like one who lies half-conscious – knowing not clearly the shape of the evil – in the grasp of some heavy nightmare.

For the first half of his life Carpenter was unable to come to terms with his own sexuality; but from about 1881 he seems to have resolved his tensions and frustrations by living with a succession of working men on his smallholding. He regarded his homosexual life as a private affair and for many years his comradely love was not publicly associated with his reputation as a socialist. In later life, however, he wrote openly about homosexuality and also about the liberation of women; though his socialist friends feared that his 'sex bombs' would do their cause no good.

William Morris, one of the most attractive figures in the early socialist movement, had already won fame as an artist, craftsman and poet when he joined the Social Democratic Federation in 1883. However, his dislike of H.M. Hyndman, the leader of the S.D.F., led to Morris's break-away and the foundation of the Socialist League in 1884. He edited and financed *The Commonweal* until 1890, when the anarchists secured control of the League. Like Carpenter, Morris too was led to socialism through his repudiation of capitalist society:

Apart from the desire to produce beautiful things, the leading passion of my life has been and is hatred of modern civilization. What shall I say of it now, when the words are put into my mouth, my hope of its destruction – what shall I say of its supplanting by Socialism?

What shall I say concerning its mastery of, and its waste of mechanical power, its commonwealth so poor, its enemies of the commonwealth so rich, its stupendous organization – for the misery of life! Its contempt of simple pleasures which everyone could enjoy but for its folly? Its eyeless vulgarity which has destroyed art, the one certain solace of labour? All this I felt then as now, but I did not know why it was so. The hope of the past times was gone, the struggles of mankind for many ages had produced nothing but this sordid, aimless, ugly confusion; the immediate future seemed to me likely to intensify all the present evils by sweeping away the last survivals of the days before the dull squalor of civilisation had settled down on the world . . . Think of it! Was it all to end in a counting-house on the top of a cinder-heap, with Podsnap's drawing-room in the offing, and a Whig committee dealing out champagne to the rich and margarine to the poor in such convenient proportions as would make all men contented together, though the pleasure of the eyes was gone from the world, and the place of Homer was to be taken by Huxley?[6]

Morris set out his vision of life in a socialist utopia in *News from Nowhere* (1890). As much as possible of nineteenth century civilization having been destroyed, work was now pleasant and desirable. Handicraft dominated production and the machine had been relegated to its 'proper' or subordinate place. A simplification of life and taste had come about. Dress, for instance, was loose-fitting, practical but elegant. Pottery and furnishings were in simple, cottage style; and an emphasis on life, not books, had effectively resulted in de-schooling. Industrial towns had been broken up and country life revitalized. The churches were no longer used as religious institutions but simply as communal buildings. People in the new society were physically different from their ancestors in the nineteenth century, and were much more beautiful. The emphasis was on banishing all ugliness, in environment as well as in person. Women were emancipated; no longer was there need for divorce courts, since property had been abolished. Morris's ideals, despite certain elements of fantasy and archaism, provided an inspiration for the activists in the socialist movement – and, more widely, in the Arts and Crafts movement and in the planning of garden cities.

The problem for late Victorian socialists was how to move forward from their socialist visions to effective political power. Not until much later were the socialists, through the Labour Party, able to gain the support of any sizeable part of the working class. In the late nineteenth and early twentieth centuries the impact of socialism on the people as a whole was marginal. Traditional attitudes of fatalism and political scepticism were hard to overcome. A sympathetic observer claimed in 1884 that:

The mass of persons in England take a languid interest in political action, and a capricious line on social questions. They have had reason to believe that politics are the mere game of two hereditary and privileged parties, in which it signifies little which gets a temporary ascendancy. They are convinced of the hollowness of political cries, and are under the impression that the public service is a phrase by which politicians mean private advantage.[7]

Because of such disenchantment the typical attitude of large numbers of the common people was not political but populist. Their social philosophy was no more than a simple feeling that they were somehow the victims of the system and its ruling elites. A deep-seated conviction that the world was divided into 'them' and 'us', a kind of secular Manichaeism or dualism, provided a basis of support for causes (rather than movements) which seemed to demonstrate a clash between the people (right) and the Establishment (wrong). Throughout the nineteenth century there was no lack of opportunity for the display of such sentiment, much of it of the flag-wagging, jingoistic, xenophobic, no-popery kind. A typical rallying point of populist sentiment in the 1870s was the Tichborne cause, when the fraudulent claimant to a baronetcy and estates in Hampshire became the hero of thousands in his attempt to prove his case. The legal proceedings lasted from 1867 to 1874, a Magna Charter Association was founded, and its periodical, the *Englishman*, had a weekly circulation of 70,000. By support of the claimant the Tichbornites were expressing their opposition to the Establishment and their approval of a champion who appeared to challenge its codes and practices. Thoughtful working men and their middle-class sympathizers could regret this 'flood of human idiotism', as John Ruskin called it. But elements of populism remained strongly entrenched. From this part of working-class culture – centred on the pub, the race course and the music hall – the socialists could expect little support. Their strength lay elsewhere.

This is not to devalue the labour and socialist movement as an agent of change but simply to set it in perspective. Radical and reform movements by their very nature tend to attract certain types of personality and activists are always in a minority. It is noteworthy that many of the pioneers of socialism were, or had been, involved in other reform movements. The early Fabians, for example, came from various backgrounds, including spiritualism, 'New Life' and transcendentalism. In the last thirty years of the nineteenth century there was no shortage of reform causes, each seeking change in its own particular direction: secularism, land nationalization, Henry Georgeism (single taxers), Marxism, anarchism, republicanism, theosophy, anti-war (peace societies), vegetarianism, Malthusianism, feminism, co-operation, temperance, university settlements, neighbourhood guilds, allotments and small-holdings, eugenicism, – even (as one disgusted food reformer put it) anti-everythingarianism. From this angle the late Victorians appear as anything but complacent and self-satisfied. On the contrary, they saw clearly the limitations of many aspects of their society and tried hard to change them. They frequently met with little immediate success. But they could take heart from the assurance of William Morris:

> Men fight and lose the battle, and the thing they fought for comes about in spite of their defeat, and when it comes turns out not to be what they meant, and other men have to fight for what they meant under another name.[8]

8

The Woman Question

Labour was not the only section of society pressing for social and political emancipation in the last quarter of the nineteenth century. It was frequently noticed that another majority group, women, were increasingly demanding changes of far-reaching import. In newspapers, journals and novels the 'woman question' was widely debated. All aspects of women's life – economic, political, social, educational, sexual – came under scrutiny, revealing deep-seated discontents and resentments on the one hand and male fears and prejudices on the other. Publicity strengthened the self-confidence of women in seeking unprecedented social transformation. Their revolt was against their inferior position in a man's world. Middle and working-class women experienced this inferiority in different ways, and it was not easy for the women's movement to develop a common consciousness. Moreover the sexual divisions in society were so strong that they were regarded as 'natural' and eternal by many women and most men, so that to challenge them was to strike at the certainties of the age. Indeed, it was almost impossible for women to define themselves except in terms set by a male-dominated society, and it was long before feminists were able to break out of this mould. Nevertheless, change there was, partly through economic and social developments in society at large, and partly through movements for women's emancipation.

The Victorian ideal of womanhood centred on marriage and the home. Woman's mission in life was to be the guardian of moral, spiritual and domestic values. She was, in the words of Coventry Patmore's apotheosis of married love, 'The Angel in the House'. Before marriage, girls were to be kept sexually ignorant and quite innocent or 'pure-minded'. Tennyson, Ruskin and other Victorian writers habitually likened maidens to flowers.

Feminine human nature was held to be characterized by frailty, passivity, submissiveness, silence, and desexualized affection. All women, it was theorized, had retained 'a remnant of the innocence of Paradise' and this innate innocence was designed as a protection of female chastity. Angelic women would not be troubled by the temptations of sexual pleasure. Woman's sexual fulfilment was to be found only in her role as wife and mother; and a woman who indulged in sexual gratification for its own sake rather than for procreation degraded her womanhood. The ideal woman did not have to work outside the home but was supported by her husband. Her role was to manage the household economy in an efficient way and sanctify the home by her loving tenderness and chaste discipline. Home was to be a haven, a sanctuary, a place of peace and emotional security. In all of this she was subordinate to her husband's wishes. If the marriage turned out to be a disaster she was enjoined by the popular manuals of the day to remember that her 'highest duty is so often to suffer and be still'.[1]

Female inferiority and the stereotype of the womanly woman were reinforced by Victorian biological, anthropological and medical theories. In an age which, as we have seen earlier, worshipped science, the whole weight of scientific orthodoxy was brought in to support traditional views of male superiority. From a combination of biological and social-Darwinian assumptions it was argued that women were 'naturally' more emotional, intuitive, dependent and timid, and more like children than men. Even Havelock Ellis, a pioneer sexologist and radical supporter of women's emancipation, could make the remarkable statement that 'Nature has made women more like children in order that they may better understand and care for children.'[2] Although women did as well as men in examinations it was argued that this was merely because they had a facility for reproducing facts which they had stored away; they were less original than men and all the great geniuses in human history had been male. Herbert Spencer, still widely read in the late nineteenth century, used the concepts of evolution to show that sexual difference was the result of adaptation to the conditions necessary for social survival. Woman's position in society was the natural result of processes designed to strengthen her central function – reproduction. The medical doctors and eugenicists likewise agreed that woman's reproductive role dominated female character. Nearly all female illness was ascribed to disorder of the womb in some shape or form; and medical advice was usually directed to emphasising the duty of maternalism.

That these pseudo-scientific arguments were little more than rationalizations of male prejudice is now obvious. Ernest Newman, the music critic, perceived this in 1895:

> [M]en have started out with the theory of the natural inferiority of women, have assumed – like Rousseau, because it suited them to do so – that her 'true' sphere was the home and her 'true' function maternity, and then persuaded themselves that they had biological reasons for keeping her out of the universities and for denying her a vote.[3]

But the view that the inferiority of women stemmed from biologically-determined sexual difference was hard to refute in a male-dominated world. Not only most men but also many women accepted as natural the idea of separate spheres, public and private, male and female. The strength of the maternal role ascription appears in the diary of Beatrice Webb in 1894 when she had already decided to forego motherhood on her marriage to Sidney. She confided that if she had the training of a young woman she would

> From the first . . . impress on her the holiness of motherhood – its infinite superiority over any other occupation that a woman may take to. But for the sake of that very motherhood I would teach her that she must be an intellectual being . . . It pains me to see an intelligent girl, directly she marries, putting aside intellectual things as no longer pertinent to her daily life. And yet the alternative – so often chosen nowadays by intellectual woman of deliberately foregoing motherhood seems to me to thwart all the purposes of their nature. I myself – or rather we – chose this course in our marriage – but then I had passed the age when it is easy or natural for a woman to become a childbearer – my

physical nature was to some extent dried up at 35 after ten years stress and strain of purely brainworking and sexless life. If I were again a young woman and had the choice between a brain-working profession or motherhood, I would not hesitate which life to choose (as it is I sometimes wonder whether I had better not have risked it and taken my chance).[4]

The ideal woman was essentially a middle-class stereotype. Although arguments based on biological sexual differences applied to all women, the middle-class scientists and sociologists assumed female behaviour appropriate in their own class. Nevertheless the ideal was also acceptable to many members of the working class, even though their straightened economic and living conditions precluded some of the ignorance and innocence which afflicted middle-class girls. The pursuit of respectability placed a high premium on moral purity and family values. Below the respectable working classes the gap between ideal and reality was so great that middle-class norms were irrelevant, as the plight of the women in George Hewins's family, quoted in Chapter Four, makes plain.

The family, even for the comfortable middle classes, was not always a haven of love and emotional security. Memoirs and novels of late Victorian family life reveal patriarchal dominance, maternal worries and sibling jealousies which could make the family an ordeal of tyranny for women. This is not to deny the many experiences of female happiness and fulfilment within the family, nor to suggest that most women wished to question the institutional role of the family as such. But there is evidence – as in the testimony of working-class women in *Life as We have Known it*, *Maternity* and *Round about a Pound a Week* – to suggest that feelings of frustration, anger, desperation and resentment of their inferior status were more common among women than has often been recognised. For some middle-class women equally, the material comforts of their home life failed to reconcile them to the enormities of a male-dominated existence. Two very different but equally sensitive observers, Virginia Woolf and Beatrice Webb, recorded their experiences of a system

160

in which male tyranny and arrogance left them feeling resentful and rebellious.

Virginia Woolf's father, Leslie Stephen, was in many ways very liberal-minded for a Victorian paterfamilias, and his daughters enjoyed many freedoms denied in more conventional households. But it never occurred to him to treat them equally with their brothers. The resentment that this and various petty tyrannies nurtured in Virginia Woolf exploded in her portrait of her father as Mr Ramsay in *To the Lighthouse* (1927), her great novel of late Victorian domestic life and of the power of fathers to make 'people do what they did not want to do, cutting off their right to speak'.[5] In his old age, twice widowed, and pathetically self-centred, Leslie Stephen relied upon his daughters to look after him but subjected them to a battery of constant bullying and complaints which he would never have deployed with men. Every Wednesday afternoon Vanessa would bring him the weekly household accounts for inspection and settlement. Virginia was appalled by the way he treated her sister:

The books were presented directly after lunch. He put on his glasses. Then he read the figures. Then down came his fist on the account book. His veins filled; his face flushed. Then there was an inarticulate roar. Then he shouted . . . 'I am ruined.' Then he beat his breast. Then he went through an extraordinary dramatisation of self pity, horror, anger. Vanessa stood by his side silent. He belaboured her with reproaches, abuses. 'Have you no pity for me? There you stand like a block of stone . . . ' and so on. She stood absolutely silent. He flung at her all the phrases about shooting Niagara, about his misery, her extravagance, that came handy. She still remained static. Then another attitude was adopted. With a deep groan he picked up his pen and with ostentatiously trembling hands he wrote out the cheque. Slowly with many groans the pen and the account book were put away. Then he sank into his chair; and sat spectacularly with his head on his breast. And then, tired of this, he would take up a book; read for a time; and then say half plaintively, appealingly (for he did not like me to witness

these outbursts): 'What are you doing this afternoon, Jinny?'
I was speechless. Never have I felt such rage and such
frustration.[6]

Beatrice Webb's education was similar to Virginia Woolf's. Her
rich father allowed his daughters complete freedom to read
whatever they liked and after the death of her mother Beatrice
was in charge of the household and assisted her father closely.
But she came up sharply against the rock of absolute male
dominance when she fell in love with Joseph Chamberlain, the
Radical imperialist. On one occasion, after a discussion about
the views of Herbert Spencer who was an old family friend,
Chamberlain said 'It is a question of authority with women, if
you believe in Herbert Spencer you won't believe in me.' Beatrice
Webb confided in her diary:

> This opens the battle. By a silent agreement we find ourselves
> in the garden. 'It pains me to hear any of my views contra-
> verted' and with this preface he begins with stern exactitude
> to lay down the articles of his political creed. I remain
> modestly silent; but noticing my silence he remarks that he
> requires 'intelligent sympathy' from women. 'Servility', Mr
> Chamberlain, think I, not sympathy but intelligent servility:
> what many women give men, but the difficulty lies in chang-
> ing one's master, in jumping from one *tone* of thought to
> another – with intelligence. And then I advance as boldly as
> I dare my feeble objections to his general proposition feeling
> that in this case, I owe it to the man to show myself and be
> absolutely sincere.[7]

When she reflected a little later Beatrice saw that marriage to
Chamberlain would mean the destruction of her own personality
and the impossibility of an independent career:

> If the fates should unite us (against my will) all joy and light
> heartedness will go from me. I will be absorbed into the life
> of a man whose aims are not my aims; who will refuse me
> all freedom of thought in my intercourse with him; to whose
> career I shall have to subordinate all my life, mental and
> physical, without believing in the usefulness of his career,

whether it be inspired by earnest conviction or ambition . . .
If I married him I should become a cynic as regards my own
mental life.

Male dominance in the family had a darker side for some women.
Not only was the family system exploitive of their unpaid labour
and psychic dependence, it also exacted a sexual price. The
Victorians were well aware of the need to contain male sexuality;
'the fire glowing' within each male had to be covered with 'the
asbestos coating of moral decency'.[8] Within marriage the wife
was expected to submit always to the sexual demands of her
husband, and with unreliable – if any – methods of contraception,
the dread of unwanted pregnancy was ever present. It was high
praise for a working-class woman to say of a husband that 'he
doesn't bother me too often'.[9] But the coating of moral decency
was not always present; children and young women were sometimes sexually abused within the family. Beatrice Webb, when
investigating East End sweatshops in 1888, discovered that incest
was common:

> The fact that some of my workmates – young girls, who were
> in no way mentally defective, who were, on the contrary, just
> as keen-witted and generous-hearted as my own circle of
> friends – could chaff each other about having babies by their
> fathers and brothers, was a gruesome example of the effect
> of debased social environment on personal character and
> family life . . . The violation of little children was another
> not infrequent result.[10]

She, like other middle-class investigators, attributed this to gross
overcrowding and inadequate bedroom privacy. But incest was
not confined to the poor. Virginia Woolf was sexually abused by
her half-brother; and Eric Gill had incestuous relations with his
sisters and daughters. The Victorians, despite all their passion
for surveys and statistics, did not collect figures for incest. Overcrowding, prostitution, illegitimacy, drunkenness, gambling
could be investigated and made the bases for social crusades. But
the taboo on incest was complete. Beatrice Webb had to omit all
reference to it when she published the results of her investigations

into the East End sweatshops as an article in the *Nineteenth Century*. Incest was unmentionable because it desecrated the sacred institutions of home and family. There could be no outside protection for young women from the lust of fathers and brothers. There is a problem of how to reconcile this with the many accounts in fiction and memoirs of deep and loving relationships between brothers and sisters and fathers and daughters. In the absence of relevant data however a balanced historical perspective is impossible. The erotic tensions within the Victorian family are suggested by such issues as the long-debated legislation on marriage with a deceased wife's sister. Without necessarily subscribing to Freudian interpretations of incest, it is possible to hypothesize a situation in which male dominance made the women of a family, especially the single ones, vulnerable to fears and anxieties if not to actual sexual molestation.

Outside the home women encountered other forms of sexual discrimination, for example in employment opportunities. At the end of the nineteenth century about 35 per cent of all women aged fifteen and above were in paid employment, but only 10 per cent of married women. This had not always been so. Earlier in the century, before the separation of home and workplace effected by the industrial revolution, wives had been a more important part of the labour force, and in 1851 nearly a quarter of them were still classified as at work. By 1900 most women who worked were single, and their employment outside the home was effectively limited to domestic service, textiles, dressmaking, school teaching and office work. Conventionally certain jobs were always thought of as women's work and others as exclusively male. The distinction was based largely on local custom together with more general beliefs that women were suited to jobs requiring nimble fingers or no great physical strength. Women's inferior status in the world of work was emphasized by inequality of remuneration. Most women's jobs were in low-paid occupations, and even when the work was equivalent to men's – as in printing, nailmaking or post office clerking – it was paid at a lower rate.

In manufacturing industry women usually earned about half the average weekly earnings of men. Only in textiles was this exceeded. In Lancashire female cotton weavers were paid the same piece-rates as men; though their actual earnings were usually somewhat less on account of men's superior physical strength and mechanical skills. A higher proportion of the women in mill towns worked outside the home than elsewhere. In 1901 three-quarters of the single women in the main weaving towns of Blackburn, Burnley and Preston were at work and about one third of the married women. In all, over a quarter of a million women were employed in the Lancashire cotton mills. For those who were married this frequently meant working a 'double shift' – the day in the mill and the evening and Sunday looking after the family. Opportunities for middle-class women in professional or non-manual occupations were severely limited, and here too it was expected that women would be paid less than men.

Women's earnings were also depressed by the concept of the family wage. Ideally the husband should earn enough to support his family and the wife should stay at home to manage the household. The idea was strongly supported by trade unionists who argued that the employment of women tended to lower men's wages. Speaking at the Trades Union Congress in 1877 Henry Broadhurst, secretary of the T.U.C. Parliamentary Committee, declared:

> They [the men] had the future of their country and their children to consider, and it was their duty as men and husbands to use their utmost efforts to bring about a condition of things, where their wives would be in their proper sphere at home, instead of being dragged into competition for livelihood against the great and strong men of the world.[11]

But this precept could not be followed by the lowest-paid workers, who were unable to subsist on a single wage. The notion that a woman's earnings were only auxiliary persisted, and made it virtually impossible to secure equality with male wages. This was the more unjust in view of the number of 'surplus' women. At the end of the nineteenth century there were in England and Wales over a million more women than men, which meant that large numbers of women were denied the opportunity of marriage. They were thus doubly penalized: first, by exclusion from what they had been taught to regard as their prime role of wife and mother; and second, by limitation to low-paid jobs when they tried to support themselves.

Throughout late Victorian Britain the inferiority of women was thus ubiquitous. Male and female roles were strictly defined and the whole weight of social orthodoxy was brought to bear on transgressors of this division. The popular stereotype did not distinguish between sexual differences which were biological, and differences of gender which were culturally determined. With control of all forms of power, both within the family and without, men were able to ascribe their dominance to sexual, not gender differences. And like all successful hegemonic groups they persuaded those whom they dominated that this was perfectly natural and inevitable. Women were in fact socialized into believing that they were inferior and therefore subordinate to males.

But not all women (nor all men) accepted this majority view. At first a few, and then an increasing number of women began to question their lot. As the movement gathered momentum in the last quarter of the nineteenth century the 'woman question' came to the fore. Any fundamental change in the position of women was bound to affect society as a whole and was likely to be met with resistance. Processes of social change in Britain have usually been cumulative, uneven, and, as William Morris noted, not always in line with the expectations of reformers. Probably the two developments which in the long run did most to change the lives of a majority of women were the advent of safe and reliable contraception and opportunities for employment outside the home. In the 1890s this could hardly have been foreseen, though the beginnings of change were already apparent.

The decline in fertility rates after 1870 implies some form of family limitation. Artificial methods of contraception, chiefly the vaginal sponge and the sheath, had been available for many years but were unreliable or clumsy, and for poorer people quite expensive. They were therefore not widely used. Family limitation depended on the exercise of that essentially Victorian virtue 'restraint', meaning abstinence or withdrawal. The unsatisfactoriness of such methods is amply documented by the number of unwanted pregnancies and the flourishing trade in abortion and abortifacients. Women's power to control their own fertility had still a long way to go. Nevertheless, attitudes were slowly changing. Hannah Mitchell's socialist husband agreed to her request to use birth control after the birth of their one-and-only child. The long silence on abortion and unwanted pregnancy was beginning to be broken: Lady Bell commented on abortion in Middlesbrough; and Somerset Maugham's first novel, *Liza of Lambeth* (1897), based on his experiences while a medical student, is a tale of illicit love and miscarriage among working-class women. In 1898 the case of the Chrimes brothers, who tried to blackmail women who purchased their abortifacient pills by mail, exposed the plight of thousands of women seeking to terminate their pregnancies.

More promising from the viewpoint of late Victorian women looking for some degree of emancipation was the widening of employment opportunities. These were a direct consequence of the development of technological innovations such as the telephone and typewriter, and also to the general expansion of the tertiary sector of the economy with its consequent demand for more white-collar and white-blouse employees. The main beneficiaries of this expansion after 1880 were middle-class women together with some working-class females who were able to move into lower middle-class occupations. Jobs as typists, telephone operators, post office employees, school teachers and civil servants became increasingly available to women. A favoured few, following in the footsteps of Elizabeth Garrett Anderson who had pioneered women's right to become medical practitioners in the 1860s, were able to become physicians; though in 1901 there were only 212 women out of 22,000 doctors in England and Wales. Very few women were admitted to the higher grades of the civil service or the professions. If to modern readers the amount of change seems modest enough, to contemporaries who lived through the last thirty years of the century the position of women had altered considerably. In an article in the *English-woman's Review* for 1904 an Englishman who had lived abroad continuously between 1874 and 1904 with only one short visit in 1888, was astonished at what he found on his return:

So far as I remember in days gone by the only lines of employment open to girls or women were: teaching, assisting in a shop, dress-making, or bar-keeping. In these days there is hardly an occupation, or even a profession, into which a girl may not aspire to enter. Type-writing provides a living for many thousands, perhaps hundreds of thousands. There are women newspaper reporters almost as numerous as men. Accountants and book-keepers crowd the trains morning and evening, going to and from their work, while many branches of postal, telegraph and telephone work are entirely managed by women, as also are photographic studios. Sixteen years ago the A.B.C. refreshment rooms were in their infancy. Now they are counted by the hundred, each with a staff of from ten to fifteen girls. Hardly a district but has its lady doctor, and some of these have risen to great eminence. Girls of every rank think no more of riding a bicycle through the busy thoroughfares of London, than they do of going into an A.B.C. shop for a cup of tea. Go back to 1875, and try to think, if you can, what would have been said of a woman riding a bicycle down Piccadilly on a June afternoon.[12]

This last observation is another interesting example of the manner in which new technology could affect the lives of women in a positive way. Bicycles in the form of velocipedes (boneshakers) and penny-farthings had become popular in some middle-class masculine circles in the seventies and eighties, but the machines were heavy and cumbersome. The invention of the safety bicycle with equal-sized wheels, chain drive and pneumatic tyres in the late 1880s and 1890s completely transformed the nature of cycling. The bicycle suddenly became enormously popular and the craze for cycling reached a peak in 1895–7. There were cycling clubs, cycling journals, novels about cycling, and parades of fashionable cyclists in London parks. It was estimated that the number of cyclists was over a million and a half by 1896, and the annual cycle production at the height of the boom was 750,000. For women, especially young middle-class women, cycling opened up a new dimension of freedom. It offered a healthy form of recreation and the means to go wherever one pleased. It was a means of escape from chaperonage (despite the establishment of a Chaperon Cyclists' Association in 1896) and an opportunity for equality between the sexes. Lastly, it speeded up the reform of women's dress as long skirts were both inconvenient and dangerous when cycling. A movement for 'rational' dress in the form of knickerbockers or the divided skirt revived memories of Amelia Bloomer and her followers earlier in the century. However women who dared to wear 'rationals' were often subjected to ridicule and hostility. The bicycle became a symbol of freedom, closely associated with the emancipated 'new woman' of the nineties. The feelings of liberation and independence released by the bicycle are recalled in many women's memories of the period such as those of Flora Thompson, Gwen Raverat and Hannah Mitchell. Popular enthusiasm for the bicycle is recaptured for all time in the music-hall song, Daisy Bell:

> Daisy, Daisy, give me your answer, do!
> I'm half crazy, all for the love of you!
> It won't be a stylish marriage,
> I can't afford a carriage,
> But you'll look sweet upon the seat
> Of a bicycle made for two!

The bicycle was in general a socially-levelling agent. At first bicycles were expensive (£30 or more for the best quality) but after 1897 prices dropped rapidly and second-hand machines were cheap enough to be within the range of working-class girls. Moreover the manufacture of bicycles provided jobs for women: by 1914 a quarter of all workers in bicycle factories were female. Although cycling and the increased demand for women's labour contributed to the emancipation of women, this was an indirect effect of the change. From the 1860s, however, more direct pressure in the form of the women's movement had been gathering strength. A series of campaigns to extend women's rights and opportunities, led by a notable group of middle-class feminists, produced debates and legislation on prostitution and venereal disease, women's education, divorce, property rights, and the suffrage. The Married Women's Property Act of 1882 removed most of the common law disabilities which denied a married woman the right to own property and earnings. In 1883 the Contagious Diseases Acts of the 1860s, under which prostitutes could be compelled to undergo medical examination for venereal disease and be detained if infected, were suspended and then repealed, as a result of Josephine Butler's national crusade. The campaign united evangelical, anti-statist feeling with feminist protest against the double moral standard – double that is as between men and women and also as between working-class and middle-class women. Conditions for divorce had been eased for the well-to-do in 1857; and the Matrimonial Clauses Act of 1878 facilitated legal separation and maintenance for badly-used wives. The opening up of secondary and higher education to women was particularly dear to intelligent middle-class feminists. In 1872 the Girls' Public Day School Company was founded and from then on girls' secondary day (or 'high') schools developed steadily. At the ancient universities, women's colleges were established, two at Cambridge, 1869–72, and four at Oxford, 1879–93. Women students were not admitted as members of the universities of Oxford and Cambridge and could not therefore take degrees, but were allowed to attend lectures and take degree examinations. In 1887 Agnata Ramsay of Girton College, Cambridge, was placed first in the classics examination; and three years later Philippa Fawcett of Newnham was placed above the senior wrangler in mathematics. There were also women's colleges in London and the university there granted women full admission in 1880. In universities and university colleges elsewhere women were admitted to most faculties by the 1890s. Acts of Parliament in 1869, 1870, 1880 and 1894 gave certain women the franchise at local government level and made women eligible, for example, to sit on school boards.

These changes made only a small dent in male domination of society as a whole. But for the women affected by them they were momentous. Margaret Cole (née Postgate) found the social activities and intellectual freedom of Girton exhilarating when she went up in 1911:

> My first impression of College was one of freedom – freedom
> to work when you liked; to stop when you liked; to cut,
> even, lectures which turned out unhelpful or uninteresting;
> to be *where* you liked *when* you liked, with *whom* you liked
> (subject to not making too anti-social a racket); to get up
> and go to bed when you pleased and if desirable to go on
> reading, writing, or talking till dawn . . . This freedom . . .
> was enjoyed within a framework of regulation which modern
> Cambridge might well think only a slight improvement on
> a concentration camp; but to creatures fresh from school it
> was next door to Utopia.[13]

For middle-class girls the opportunity to have a room of one's
own, to be able to organize one's life free from patriarchal
dominance, to have cocoa, tea or coffee parties unsupervised, to
discuss whatever one liked with friends, to play games of hockey,
and cycle round the town – all this was immensely liberating,
despite many restrictions and controls imposed by the college
authorities. For older women new freedom could be found in the
exercise of their rights in local government. Despite the confused
and illogical state of the franchise laws some women were able
to vote and hold office at the local government level. The 1870
Education Act had set up school boards to manage the new
elementary schools and feminists did their best to get women
elected to them. At the end of the century there were perhaps
two hundred or more women members of school boards. Women
were relatively well represented on the London School Board. In
Bradford, Margaret McMillan was elected to the school board
in 1894 and began her pioneering work to establish nursery
schools, school clinics, and school meals. Women were also
elected as poor law guardians. Concern for the poor, the sick
and the aged was traditionally part of women's philanthropic
work and women's participation in poor law administration was
therefore the more acceptable. Although women ratepayers had
been able to vote for members of the boards of guardians since
1834, their eligibility to stand for election as guardians was only
established in 1875. At the end of the century it was calculated
that there were about 975 women guardians, some of whom

were working-class, in England and Wales. They had to be prepared to face male prejudice. Louisa Twining, after forty years of workhouse visiting and management, warned prospective women guardians that 'they must expect to find at least one opponent, not to say enemy, on every Board'.[14] This is well borne out in the following account by a member of the Women's Co-operative Guild in Lincolnshire:

I was first asked to become a candidate for the Board of Guardians previous to the property qualification being done away with, but declined. When the Act of 1894 was passed I consented to stand, and won a contested election. Twice since then, at the termination of three years' office, I have been returned without opposition.

The Vicar of the Parish opposed my nomination the first time, but on the last occasion of election, the Churchwarden sent me my nomination paper filled up, without any solicitation, showing some prejudice overcome.

The Chairman of the Board, January 1895, told the women members privately that he was much against women coming there (we were then elected but had not taken our seats), he kindly inviting us to an interview in the Board Room to make our acquaintance and explain some of our duties. He would be like the boy with the physic, he said, make the best of it. He thought we should be useful to see that the children's heads were kept clean, etc. Then he was anxious to know if we should wish to sit when speaking at the Board, as if we did, some men would too, and it was difficult enough to keep order now.

It was a great relief (so he said) when I assured him we three were accustomed to public speaking, and would not dream of addressing the Chair unless standing . . . I am the first woman Vice-Chairman of the House Committee, and Chairman of the Nursing Committee the last three years.

Then when it was first proposed to send women to Poor Law Conferences, a cry was raised at the Board, 'Let the women stay at home and cook their husbands' dinners'. Since then for three years in succession, I have been elected as one of two representatives to the Central Poor Law Conference.[15]

Participation in local government and higher education were important as assertions of women's rights, and as experiences valuable in themselves. They provided opportunities for some women to develop interests outside the home and family, and to demonstrate a practical equality or superiority with men in certain areas of the national life. They challenged the rigid doctrine of separate spheres for men and women and showed that women could play a part in public and professional life. But the degree of emancipation was fairly modest. In the first place it was largely limited to middle-class women. Second, married women were barred in many areas by relics of the legal doctrine of couverture, which held that husband and wife were one person and that the wife had no independent legal existence. Rights dependent on property, such as a ratepayers' franchise, discriminated against married women. Third, the changes were well within the bounds set by male dominance. For instance, women students at the university were required to behave with all the decorum of young ladies while at the same time being expected to measure up to the standards of a male system of higher learning. Middle-class parents were often a little fearful of sending their daughters to university lest the experience should unfit them for their expected role of wife and mother. Certainly some of the pioneers of women's education remained unmarried, like Frances Buss, Dorothea Beale, Emily Davies and Margaret and Rachel McMillan. The campaign for education was regarded by some women as a higher calling, and celibacy was embraced as a form of sexual liberation. But others like Barbara Bodichon (née Leigh Smith) and Barbara Hammond (née Bradby) found a role as intellectual partners to academic or professional husbands.

These economic, social and legal changes brought a measure of emancipation for middle-class women. To feminists, however, the central issue increasingly became the vote. Denial of the suffrage was taken as the badge of women's inferior status; and the feeling of injustice was exacerbated by the Reform Acts of 1867 and 1884 which extended the franchise to some working men but not to working-class or middle-class women. The case for women's suffrage had been powerfully presented by John Stuart Mill in the 1860s, and the debates over the next thirty years added little to his classic text, *The Subjection of Women*, published in 1869. If women were not given the vote it was not for lack of forceful intellectual argument. Mill regarded equality for women as an integral part of a modern, liberal society, in which

> human beings are no longer born to their place in life, and chained down by an inexorable bond to the place they are born to, but are free to employ their faculties, and such favourable chances as offer, to achieve the lot which may appear to them most desirable.

Only women were denied this basic right:

> In no instance except this, which comprehends half the human race, are the higher social functions closed against any one by a fatality of birth which no exertions, and no change of circumstances, can overcome; for even religious disabilities (besides that in England and in Europe they have practically almost ceased to exist) do not close any career to the disqualified person in case of conversion.
>
> The social subordination of women thus stands out an isolated fact in modern social institutions; a solitary breach of what has become their fundamental law; a single relic of an old world of thought and practice exploded in everything else.

Mill swept aside arguments based on sexual differences:

> What is now called the nature of women is an eminently artificial thing – the result of forced repression in some directions, unnatural stimulation in others. It may be asserted without scruple, that no other class of dependents have had their character so entirely distorted from its natural proportions by their relation with their masters.

And he roundly declared:

> I believe that their disabilities . . . are only clung to in order

174

to maintain their subordination in domestic life; because the generality of the male sex cannot yet tolerate the idea of living with an equal. Were it not for that, I think that almost every one, in the existing state of opinion in politics and political economy, would admit the injustice of excluding half the human race from the greater number of lucrative occupations, and from almost all high social functions; ordaining from their birth either that they are not, and cannot by any possibility become, fit for employments which are legally open to the stupidest and basest of the other sex, or else that however fit they may be, those employments shall be interdicted to them, in order to be preserved for the exclusive benefit of males ... Under whatever conditions, and within whatever limits, men are admitted to the suffrage, there is not a shadow of justification for not admitting women under the same. The majority of the women of any class are not likely to differ in political opinion from the majority of the men of the same class, unless the question be one in which the interests of women, as such, are in some way involved; and if they are so, women require the suffrage, as their guarantee of just and equal consideration.[16]

The female suffrage movement began in the wake of the agitation for the second Reform Bill. A federation called the National Society for Women's Suffrage (1867) was formed by Lydia Becker, a Manchester liberal, and succeeded in getting a succession of bills for women's suffrage presented in the House of Commons throughout the 1870s and later. The movement was respectable, well-to-do, and dominated by a handful of middle-class leaders. Ideologically it shared the beliefs of liberal individualism and most of its support came from liberals and radicals. But the moderate, rational, constitutional approach achieved little. Thirty years after the presentation of the first women's petition to Parliament in 1866 the franchise for women seemed as far off as ever, despite innumerable petitions and private member's bills. Like the Chartists seventy years earlier, the suffragists therefore turned to the consideration of more militant measures. For the Women's Social and Political Union, founded by Mrs Emmeline

Pankhurst

militant measures

Pankhurst in 1903, militancy at first meant heightened publicity through street marches, demonstrations, banners, and colourful episodes, together with non-violent tactics such as refusal to pay taxes, heckling of politicians, and shouting protests at meetings. From 1909 the campaign was intensified by a minority of suffragettes to include the use of physical force, arson and destruction of property. The final stages of this agitation, with its dramatic story of imprisonment, forced-feeding, and attacks on politicians, belongs to the epilogue to late Victorian Britain and will be taken up later. But the vote for women was not won before the First World War engulfed the nation and put an end for the time being to social and political reform. Women aged 30 were enfranchised in 1918; and in 1928 they were finally on equal terms with men.

The long delay in answering the Appeal of One Half the Human Race, Women, against the Pretensions of the Other Half, Men,[17] which today seems inexcusable, can be explained in many different ways, apart from male prejudice. Three factors in particular illustrate the complexity of effecting change. First was the importance of class; second, the limitations imposed by the party political system; and third, the strength of opposition and indifference. Each of these was in itself a formidable obstacle, but together they proved insuperable.

The local suffrage societies were composed mainly of middle-class women, many of whom would have been happy to settle for a restricted, property-based franchise. The leaders of the national movement were the wives and daughters of middle-class men in business and the professions. Lydia Becker, Millicent Garrett Fawcett, the Pankhursts, the Pethick-Lawrences, Isabella Ford, Charlotte Despard, Esther Roper, Teresa Billington-Grieg, were all of this social background; though Eva Gore-Booth and her sister Constance (later Countess Markievicz) and Lady Constance Lytton came from the landed gentry and aristocracy. Annie Kenney, a Lancashire cotton worker and disciple of the Pankhursts, provided a token working-class presence among the national suffragette leadership. The limited social base of the movement restricted its appeal. Only in Lancashire and Yorkshire was there any significant progress in enlisting working-class women from the ranks of textile workers and the Women's

Co-operative Guilds. Links between the women's suffrage and labour movements were mainly at the personal level. Mrs Pankhurst and her husband Richard were active supporters of the I.L.P. in the 1890s, as also was Isabella Ford in Leeds; and Keir Hardie was a staunch ally of the suffragists. The W.S.P.U. in its early days in Manchester worked closely with the I.L.P. and trade union movement; but after 1905 Mrs Pankhurst and her elder daughter Christabel moved away from the working-class and labour movement, and the W.S.P.U. lost the support of working-class women.

The difficulties of working with the political labour movement were similar to the problems encountered earlier with the Liberals. In both cases considerations of party politics frustrated support from the women's 'natural' allies. Probably a majority of liberals looked favourably on women's suffrage, which was in accordance with liberal principles, and the friends of the movement in the House of Commons were usually from the Liberal party, particularly its radical wing. But some Liberals were lukewarm in their support and the party leadership, notably Gladstone and Asquith, opposed women's suffrage when they were in office. The reasons for this are not far to seek. Most proposals to enfranchise women were not calls for universal adult suffrage but an extension based on property (household) qualifications, which would have given the vote only to a small group of better-off, elderly and single women, who might be expected to support conservatism rather than liberalism. 'Girls and widows are Tories, and channels of clerical influence,' wrote the historian Acton in a letter to Gladstone's daughter.[18] Labour too was suspicious that a limited franchise would merely strengthen middle-class and propertied interests. Socialists and trade unionists were pressing for complete adult suffrage (which had not been granted under the 1867 and 1884 Acts) and feared that the enfranchisement of some women on a property basis would weaken the struggle and not greatly benefit the working class. Despite the later tactics of militancy and working-class women's radical suffragism in the Northwest, the overall image of the women's political movement was too conservatively middle class to win the enthusiastic support of many Labourites. Experience had taught working-class leaders to be wary of middle-class reformers; and working-class ideals of respectability and male authoritarianism in the home were not favourable to feminist aspirations. At Westminster the shifting coalitions of supporters and opponents frustrated attempts to pilot a bill for women's enfranchisement. Many who were prepared to support such a bill in principle fell away when they saw the price which their party might have to pay.

For the Conservative Party, which was continuously in office for twenty years after 1885 (apart from short breaks in 1886 and 1892–95), there was little temptation to support women's suffrage. Conservatives generally disliked the idea of extension of democracy and feared that the enfranchisement of women would lead to universal adult suffrage. Since the Liberal leadership was also opposed to enfranchisement there was no need to follow Disraeli's tactic in 1867 of enfranchising working men in order to 'dish the Whigs'. The Conservatives could afford to ignore the issue and concentrate on other things.

Opposition to women's suffrage was not all mindless and bigoted misogyny. The doctrine of separate spheres was deeply ingrained in many women as well as men. In June 1889 the *Nineteenth Century* published an 'Appeal against Female Suffrage' signed by 104 well-known women, including Mrs Humphry Ward, Beatrice Webb, Eliza Lynn Linton, Mrs Leslie Stephen and Mrs Matthew Arnold; and two months later added a supplementary list of nearly two thousand names. The Appeal claimed that women's direct participation in politics 'is made impossible either by the disabilities of sex, or by strong formations of custom and habit resting ultimately upon physical difference, against which it is useless to contend'.[19] Women already had their own spheres of work in local government, school boards, and workhouses; and their personal influence and family role would be weakened, it was said, by party political involvement. The Queen had earlier abhorred 'this mad, wicked folly of "Woman's Rights" with all its attendant horrors'; and opined that Lady Amberley, who supported the cause, 'ought to get a good whipping'.[20] Beatrice Webb later retracted her opposition to women's suffrage, which she referred to as a 'false step'. But the very fact that she could earlier have lent support to the 'antis' is indicative of the complex nature of the issues involved. Resentful as she was of male dominance, Beatrice Webb was not prepared to acknowledge the importance of the suffrage question as an instrument of women's emancipation. Her anti-feminism in the late 1880s and 1890s sprang from a failure to reconcile what she felt were the domestic, family and personal needs of women with the tactics of the women's movement.

Moreover the movement itself was divided. The National Society for Women's Suffrage (from 1897 the National Union of Women's Suffrage Societies) was federal in structure and constitutional in tactics. These suffragists were led until 1890 by Lydia Becker and thereafter by Millicent Garrett Fawcett. But in 1903 a militant section of suffragettes, the Women's Social and Political Union, was formed by Mrs Pankhurst and turned to increasingly violent measures. A third organisation, the Women's Freedom League, split off from the W.S.P.U. in 1907 in protest at the authoritarian leadership of Mrs Pankhurst and her daughter Christabel. The 1889 Appeal revealed the divisions between women on the suffrage issue, the W.S.P.U. the divisions among the suffragists themselves. As the militancy of the W.S.P.U. increased the divisions grew deeper, and in 1908 the Women's National Anti-Suffrage League was formed.

The limited success of the women's suffrage movement in late Victorian Britain should not blind us to the very real contribution that the campaign made to the eventual changing of the position of women. In the 1890s it kept the woman question in the public eye; and the militant tactics of the 1900s brilliantly achieved the publicity that was their aim. In this respect the movement for women's political advancement linked up with or reinforced wider expressions of women's emancipation. Radical social change is ultimately dependent on a redrawing of the boundaries of the permissible and thinking the unthinkable. This takes time, especially in matters which closely affect the individual like sexual morality. People have to become accustomed to notions that they previously considered utterly unacceptable. New ways of thinking about women had to be familiarized before women's position in society could be altered fundamentally. This involved more than finding new opportunities for paid employment or new occupations for women of the leisured classes. It posed an entirely new dimension of femininity and promised wholly new lives for women. The appearance of the New Woman in the later nineteenth century was disturbing because she upset deeply-held assumptions and threatened the conventional bases of society. Changes in the lives of half the human race could not but change the lives of everyone.

The New Woman in real life was probably a relatively rare phenomenon (although a godsend to the humorists in *Punch* and elsewhere). But in the literature of the 1890s she became a symbol of female emancipation. Novels in themselves can seldom be considered agents of social change; but as evidence of what interested contemporaries and how they looked at the problems of their time, novels are invaluable. They alert us to the sensibilities of an age. In a preface written to *Tess of the D'Urbervilles* in 1892, Thomas Hardy agreed that his novel 'embodies the views of life prevalent at the end of the nineteenth century', but cautioned that 'a novel is an impression, not an argument'.[21] In Hardy's two great novels, *Tess of the D'Urbervilles* (1891) and *Jude the Obscure* (1895), social and sexual relations between men and women are very different from the idealized Victorian stereotype. Tess gives birth to an illegitimate child, then marries another man but is abandoned by him. She murders her earlier seducer and is finally hanged. Challengingly, Hardy subtitled *Tess* 'A Pure Woman', and made it clear that he regarded Tess as a victim of an unjust system, a sport of the Immortals (in the Aeschylean phrase). Sue Bridehead in *Jude* is an intelligent and vivacious young schoolteacher whose sexual inhibitions lead to an unsuitable marriage, divorce, children out of wedlock, and the miserable death of Jude. Hardy had reservations about the institution of marriage:

> the general question [is] whether marriage, as we at present understand it, is such a desirable goal for all women as it is assumed to be; or whether civilisation can escape the humiliating indictment that, while it has been able to cover itself with glory in the arts, in literatures, in religions, and

in the sciences, it has never succeeded in creating that homely thing, a satisfactory scheme for the conjunction of the sexes.[22]

William Hale White (Mark Rutherford) in his novel, *Clara Hopgood* (1896), followed Hardy's *Tess* in flouting Victorian sexual proprieties. Madge Hopgood falls in love with a respectable young man and while sheltering in a barn during a thunderstorm surrenders to sexual passion and becomes pregnant. She realises that she does not really love the man, and despite his offer to marry her prefers to have the child outside marriage. Her sister Clara is attracted to a widower, but in spite of her love for him she arranges that he should marry Madge. Clara then goes to Italy and dies in the fight for freedom in the Risorgimento. Other late Victorian writers similarly expressed doubts about marriage and sexual relationships. H.G. Wells' *Love and Mr Lewisham* (1900) is a light-hearted account of the conflict between sexual desire and pursuit of a career. In *The New Machiavelli* (1911) Wells returned to the unsatisfactory nature of marriage: 'modern conditions and modern ideas, and in particular the intenser and subtler perceptions of modern life, press more and more heavily upon a marriage tie whose fashion comes from an earlier and less discriminating time', when the wife was subservient to her husband. But now 'woman insists upon her presence. She is no longer a mere physical need, an aesthetic byeplay, a sentimental background; she is a moral and intellectual necessity in a man's life'.[23]

The New Woman was presented more starkly in Grant Allen's novel, *The Woman Who Did* (1895). It is the story of Herminia, a feminist who deliberately has a child by her lover whom she refuses to marry on the grounds that marriage is degrading and a denial of her freedom. Her lover dies during the honeymoon and she henceforth has to live a life of poverty and social and family ostracism while bringing up her daughter, whom she dreams will carry on her ideals of the Higher Woman and Perfect Freedom. But despite great hardship her (Herminia's) martyrdom is in vain, because her daughter repudiates her ideals completely and blames her for her illegitimacy. In order not to stand in the way of her daughter's marriage to a young squire, Herminia finally commits suicide. The novel is uncompromising in its feminism. Herminia found the higher education offered at Girton a mockery of real emancipation and she left without taking the degree examinations. For her the women's suffrage agitation was not as important as social and moral emancipation, though 'of course I'm a member of all the women's franchise leagues and everything of that sort – they can't afford to do without a single friend's name on their lists at present'. She completely repudiated 'the monopoly of the human heart, which is known as marriage', which was simply a form of slavery. She saw herself as a moral pioneer and therefore doomed to martyrdom: 'every great and good life can but end in a Calvary'.[24]

Equally tragic, and in some ways more dangerous to orthodoxy because it combined feminism with agnosticism, was Olive Schreiner's *The Story of an African Farm* (1883). Again the heroine, Lyndall, is the archetypal, independent feminist, fiercely resenting the subordination of women, who have been moulded 'to fit [their] sphere as a Chinese woman's foot fits their shoe'. She looks forward to the future 'when love is no more bought or sold', and each woman's life 'is filled with earnest, independent labour'. Marriage she regards as a form of serfdom:

> With good looks and youth marriage is easy to attain. There are men enough; but a woman who has sold herself, even for a ring and a new name, need hold her skirt aside for no creature in the street. They both earn their bread in one way.

Lyndall therefore rejects an offer of marriage, but consents to living with a man to whom she is attracted:

> I cannot marry you, she said . . . because I cannot be tied; but, if you wish, you may take me away with you, and take care of me; then when we do not love any more we can say good-bye.[25]

In due course she gave birth, alone and among strangers, but the baby lived for only two hours; and shortly afterwards Lyndall died too.

Olive Schreiner was a young woman in her twenties who in

the lonely surroundings of the South African Karoo asked the same questions about religion and sex and women that were being asked by socialists and feminists in London – which suggests the need to set British feminism in context. The woman question was raised in other European countries as well as in America and Australasia, and everywhere followed a similar pattern of development. Beginning with demands for access to the professions, secondary and higher education, and the right of women to their own property, the movements went on to demand the vote. Along the way they also undertook moral crusades against drink, sexual licence and prostitution. Ideologically part of individualist liberation, in practice the women's movement proved something of an embarrassment to Liberal parties. Similarly although socialists usually supported equality for women, socialism and feminism were at best uneasy allies. The immediate gains from women's emancipation mainly benefited middle-class women; and as long as the class divisions of society remained as rigid as they were an improvement in the status of middle-class women did not necessarily benefit women of the working class. The woman question was entangled with questions of class and status as well as sex. From this perspective the attack on the masculine world appears as part of wider changes in advanced western societies, involving increased social and political democratization and rising standards of living for all.

9

The Condition of the People

I

In 1839 Thomas Carlyle had warned about the 'Condition of England Question' and voiced the widespread concern about the plight of the labouring classes. A flurry of investigations into living and working conditions produced a spate of reports by select committees, royal commissions, statistical societies and local bodies in the 1830s and 1840s, which led to a certain amount of legislation. After 1848 and with the onset of mid-Victorian prosperity public interest in these questions died down, although social reformers continued to campaign against specific social abuses such as prostitution and drunkenness. Then in the 1880s this general social complacency was rudely shaken and a second age of inquiry began. Issues of overcrowding, poverty, sexuality and immorality suddenly reappeared on the political and social agenda in response to pressure from articulate sections of the population. A sense of shock and a demand that 'something should be done' constituted an important element in the process of social change in late Victorian Britain.

In 1883 a small penny pamphlet with the arresting title, *The Bitter Cry of Outcast London*, appeared. It was written by Andrew Mearns, a Congregationalist minister, and described in vivid detail the living conditions in some of London's worst slums. Despite all the efforts of the Christian churches, declared Mearns,

> only the merest edge of the great dark region of poverty, misery, squalor and immorality has been touched . . . Whilst we have been building our churches and solacing ourselves with our religion and dreaming that the millennium was coming, the poor have been growing poorer, the wretched

more miserable, and the immoral more corrupt; the gulf has been daily widening which separates the lowest classes of the community from our churches and chapels, and from all decency and cililization . . . We are simply living in a fool's paradise if we suppose that . . . [we] are doing a thousandth part of what needs to be done, a hundredth part of what *could* be done by the Church of Christ. We must face the facts; and these compel the conviction that THIS TERRIBLE FLOOD OF SIN AND MISERY IS GAINING UPON US. It is rising every day.[1]

The pamphlet spoke of 'rotten and reeking tenements', drunken parents and neglected children, families of seven persons living in one room, and women and children working in sweated occupations like trouser-finishing and matchbox-making. 'Incest is common' alleged Mearns – though under cross-examination before the Royal Commission on the Housing of the Working Classes later he modified this to the assertion that 'you do meet with it [incest] and frequently meet with it, but not very frequently'. The *Bitter Cry* was greeted with horror and surprise. It was taken up by the *Pall Mall Gazette*, whose editor, W.T. Stead, had a keen nose for the publicity which such causes could arouse. Stead's crusading zeal both increased the circulation of his paper and made housing reform and slum conditions an immediate issue, while playing down the evangelical origins and purposes of Mearns' pamphlet.

The sensation created by the *Bitter Cry* was due more to its timing than to the novelty of its subject matter. The mid-Victorians had been made familiar with the conditions of working-class life in London through the work of Henry Mayhew, George Godwin, George Augustus Sala, James Greenwood and others. Richard Rowe's *Life in the London Streets or Struggles for Daily Bread* appeared in 1881; and Walter Besant's popular *All Sorts and Conditions of Men* in 1883. Some of the evidence in the *Bitter Cry* was in fact taken from G.R. Sims' *How the Poor Live* (1883), reprinted from the *Pictorial World*; and working-class housing was already being discussed by Joseph Chamberlain and Lord Salisbury before Mearns' pamphlet was published. Nevertheless the *Bitter Cry* sparked off a whole series of investigations, surveys, and exposés of the condition of the poor which continued for the next twenty-five years. The problems of housing raised questions about poverty, crime, morality and the economy, and, in fact, led to a general inquest into the social state of late Victorian Britain as perceived by the middle and upper classes. The frame of mind in which these enquiries were carried out was that of explorers into unknown territory. General Booth of the Salvation Army entitled his book (urging social reform as a way to salvation) *In Darkest England and the Way Out* (1890), in direct imitation of H.M. Stanley's journeys into Darkest Africa. Even more sensational was W.T. Stead's investigation, aided by the Salvation Army, of child prostitution in London, with its lurid details of the 'Maiden Tribute of Modern Babylon'. In the case of Eliza Armstrong (1885) Stead arranged to purchase a child for £5 for purposes of prostitution. He successfully exposed the nature of the evil, boosted the sales of his paper, and suffered a three-month gaol sentence.

The weakness, of course, of all these accounts of poverty was that they were entirely subjective, anecdotal and impressionistic. As a basis for action they failed to satisfy the more rigorous demands of a positivistic generation of social thinkers full of ideas about social science, scientific socialism, and scientific investigation. Charles Booth, a well-to-do shipowner and philanthropist, was sceptical about statements concerning the proportion of the population of London who were living in extreme poverty. In 1886 he began a survey of poverty in London, beginning with the East End and ultimately covering the whole of the metropolis. His findings were published at intervals from 1889 onwards, culminating in the massive seventeen-volume *Life and Labour of the People in London* (1903). Booth's main sources of data were the 1881 and 1891 censuses and the reports of the school board visitors, supplemented by information from school divisional committees, teachers, relieving officers, district visitors, the Charity Organisation Society, police and clergy. He and his staff of seven assistants also engaged in a certain amount of participant observation in order to familiarize themselves with the streets and lives of people referred to in the visitors' accounts. In all, four million people were covered by the investigation which took seventeen years to complete. Beatrice Webb, as Booth's cousin and enthusiastic young helper, was not entirely unbiased in her assessment of his achievement; but she was not the only contemporary to hail 'the grand inquest into the conditions of life and labour of . . . the richest city in the world' as 'a landmark alike in social politics and in economic science'. Later critics have objected to some of Booth's methods which were perhaps not as value-free as he imagined. Nevertheless the impact of *Life and Labour* on the thinking of all concerned with social problems at the end of the nineteenth century would be hard to exaggerate. For the first time an attempt had been made to measure poverty systematically, to define its nature and analyse its causes.

Booth discovered that 35.2 per cent of East Londoners and 30.7 per cent of all Londoners were living below the poverty line, defined as an income of 18–21s per week for a 'moderate family'. He classified the population according to 'social condition', and his primary purpose was to distinguish between those living in 'poverty' and those in 'comfort'. He established eight classes, lettered A to H. The lowest class, A, consisted of occasional labourers, loafers and semi-criminals. Then came class B, the very poor, who were 'in want'; they depended on casual labour and led a 'hand to mouth' existence. Classes C and D were the poor who 'lacked comfort' but were not 'in want'. Above them were the true working classes, E and F, who lived 'in comfort'; and the middle classes, G and H, who enjoyed 'plenty' and 'luxury' respectively. Booth summarized his findings as in the table on p. 188.[2]

Like all figures these statistics were open to various interpretations, and Booth himself was reluctant to draw simplistic conclusions from them. But for liberals and reformers the shocking 'fact' was that over thirty per cent of the population of the largest and richest city in the kingdom was living at or beneath the level of bare subsistence. Moreover, it could not be argued that the metropolis was exceptional; for in 1899 a similar survey in York produced results closely parallel to Booth's. Seebohm Rowntree, in his *Poverty: A Study of Town Life* (1901), found that 27.84 per cent of the total population of York were living in poverty.

Classes	Nos	%	
(a) East London			
A (lowest)	10,979	1.2	
B (very poor)	100,062	11.2	In poverty or in want 35.2%
C (intermittent earnings)	74,247	8.3	In poverty or in want 35.2%
D (small regular earnings)	128,887	14.5	
E (regular standard earnings)	376,953	42.3	
F (higher class labour)	121,240	13.6	In comfort or in affluence 64.8%
G (lower middle class)	34,392	3.9	In comfort or in affluence 64.8%
H (Upper middle class)	44,779	5.0	
(b) London as a whole			
A (lowest)	37,610	0.9	
B (very poor)	316,834	7.5	In poverty or in want 30.7%
C D (poor)	938,293	22.3	
E F (working class, comfortable)	2,166,503	51.5	
G H (middle class and above)	749,930	17.8	In comfort or in affluence 69.3%

Rowntree drew a distinction between 'primary' and 'secondary' poverty.

Families regarded as living in poverty were grouped under two heads:

(a) Families whose total earnings were insufficient to obtain the minimum necessaries for the maintenance of merely physical efficiency. Poverty falling under this head was described as 'primary' poverty.

(b) Families whose total earnings would have been sufficient for the maintenance of merely physical efficiency were it not that some portion of it was absorbed by other expenditure, either useful or wasteful. Poverty falling under this head was described as 'secondary' poverty.

The number found to be in a state of primary poverty was 7230, or about ten per cent of the total population of the city; and those in secondary poverty numbered 13,072 or about eighteen per cent. Rowntree's poverty line was calculated at 21s 8d per week for a family of two adults and three children. It was the minimum required to maintain physical efficiency, included only the barest essentials and allowed nothing for such things as bus fares, newspapers, drink, tobacco, or subscriptions to church, chapel, sick club or trade union. The estimate

> was based upon the assumptions that the diet is selected with a careful regard to the nutritive values of various food stuffs, and that these are all purchased at the lowest current prices. It only allows for a diet less generous as regards variety than that supplied to able-bodied paupers in work-houses. It further assumes that no clothing is purchased which is not absolutely necessary for health, and assumes too that it is of the plainest and most economical description.
>
> No expenditure of any kind is allowed for beyond that which is absolutely necessary for the maintenance of *merely physical efficiency*.

Rowntree noted that working people could expect to experience a cycle of alternate periods of want and comparative plenty. During childhood, unless the father was a skilled worker, the family would be in poverty. Then, when the older children began to earn and still lived at home, a more comfortable period would follow. The children would in their turn marry, leave home, and enjoy relative prosperity, until the number of their children forced them back into poverty. Finally, in old age, when they could no longer work, the labourer and his wife would again be in want. The proportion of the working class who at one period or another of their lives suffered from poverty to the point of being physically deprived was thus greater than the numbers below the poverty line at any given moment.

Rowntree's findings were the more impressive in that they were based on a house-to-house survey of all 11,560 working-class families in the town. Detailed comparison with Booth's figures is not possible because of different methods of classification and definitions of poverty. But the overall results of the two enquiries were so similar that Rowntree felt justified in claiming: 'I feel no hesitation in regarding my estimate of the total poverty in York as comparable with Mr Booth's estimate of the total poverty in London, and in this Mr Booth agrees.' Later surveys in 1912–13 in Bolton, Stanley (Co. Durham), Northampton, Warrington and Reading showed considerable variations in the incidence of working-class poverty; but it seems likely that Rowntree's figures for York are fairly representative of the state of urban poverty at the end of the century. His response to the poverty was also representative of socially-minded people:

> That in this land of abounding wealth, during a time of perhaps unexampled prosperity, probably more than one-fourth of the population are living in poverty, is a fact which may well cause great searchings of heart. There is surely need for a greater concentration of thought by the nation upon the well-being of its own people, for no civilization can be sound or stable which has at its base this mass of stunted human life. The suffering may be all but voiceless, and we may long remain ignorant of its extent and severity, but once we realise it we see that social questions of profound importance await solution. What, for instance, are the primary causes of this poverty? How far is it the result of false social and economic conditions? If it be due in part to faults in the national character, what influences can be exerted to impart to that character greater strength and thoughtfulness?

The voicing of such questions was symptomatic of the later years of the nineteenth century. Historians nowadays are reluctant to talk about the 'spirit of the age'; but people living in the 1880s were conscious of changes in social perceptions which they described in this way. Beatrice Webb ascribed the changed outlook to 'a new consciousness of sin among men of intellect and men of property', and explained that by this she did not mean a personal, but a collective or class consciousness: 'a growing uneasiness, amounting to conviction, that the industrial organisation, which had yielded rent, interest and profits on a stupendous scale, had failed to provide a decent livelihood and tolerable conditions for a majority of the inhabitants of Great Britain'.[4] Middle-class feelings of guilt were one type of response to the revelations of 'poverty in the midst of plenty', as the popular

slogan put it, and soon found practical expression in the settlement movement and 'social work' in slum areas. But over the
twenty-five years from 1883 the concern which had begun as an
inquiry into the housing question and then extended into an
investigation of poverty, broadened into an inquest into social
policy as a whole. The assumptions and certainties of mid-
Victorian individualist, *laissez-faire* society were challenged and
new possibilities of collectivist and state action were aired. Such
solutions have been seen as foreshadowing later developments
towards a welfare state, though we have here to be careful not
to impute motives and aims which would be anachronistic.

The rediscovery of poverty demolished a number of shibbol-
eths. Booth and Rowntree showed that the condition of those
living in poverty was not due primarily to drink, improvidence,
idleness and general fecklessness. These last were to be seen as
symptoms rather than causes. The root of the poverty of Booth's
Class B (the very poor), whom he considered to be the nub
of the problem, was the casual and irregular nature of their
employment. Rowntree too found that the immediate cause of
primary poverty in over half the cases was low wages, which
were simply insufficient to maintain a 'moderate' family. Other
causes of primary poverty in York were death of the chief wage
earner (15.63 per cent), illness or old age (5.11 per cent), and
'largeness of family', i.e. the presence of more than four children
(22.16 per cent). If the causes of poverty were largely insufficient
earnings and factors beyond the control of the individual it
followed that the poor could not be blamed for their poverty.
They were the victims of circumstance, not moral delinquents. A
combination of inadequate wages, irregular work and low-grade
housing locked the very poor into a culture of poverty from
which they could not escape. The social explorers had gone out
to bring back tales of the poor; but their lurid and shocking
revelations were shown to be but manifestations of a disease
called poverty. When this was recognised attention turned from
relief to prevention. Booth himself, who had been a liberal
individualist in the 1880s, became convinced of the need for
reform of the Poor Law, the establishment of state-funded old-age
pensions, and a certain amount of 'limited socialism'.

The traditional means of relieving the suffering of the poor were private charity and the Poor Law. Both of these methods were now called into question. In the 1860s it was widely held that 'indiscriminate' alms-giving was responsible for the 'demoralization' of the poor. To remedy this, measures were taken to administer the Poor Law more strictly and discourage outdoor relief by an efficient application of the workhouse test. In 1869 the Charity Organisation Society was established to co-ordinate charitable activity. By its casework approach of carefully investigating each individual applicant the C.O.S. pioneered modern methods of social service; but its strongly individualist philosophy, paternalism, and investigative methods were resented by working people. When Beatrice Webb first encountered the C.O.S. in 1883 she regarded it as 'an honest though short-circuited attempt to apply the scientific method of observation and experiment, reasoning and verification, to the task of delivering the poor from their miseries by the personal service and pecuniary assistance tendered by their leisured and wealthy fellow-citizens'. But she soon became deeply opposed to its philosophy and methods and referred to it as 'my friend the enemy'. She later interpreted the struggle over poverty and the Poor Law as the triumph of collectivist over individualist principles. As the nature and extent of poverty became better known the demand for state intervention to bring about remedies increased. Such demands however came from Conservatives and Liberals as well as Socialists, and did not necessarily reflect a neat division between individualists and collectivists. After 1906 these categories became even more blurred as, under the leadership of the new Liberals, the state moved into areas of social welfare previously reserved for voluntary agencies.

One by one the cherished ideals of mid-Victorian Britain came under scrutiny and were either modified or quietly abandoned. General William Booth and his wife Catherine, after experiences as Methodists, had in the 1860s founded an East End mission which became the Salvation Army. Its doctrines and teachings were those of revivalist evangelicalism: the need for salvation, sudden conversion, hell-fire, a puritan life-style. The Army aimed to reach the 'poor and lost' and was not afraid to use methods which were considered vulgar by respectable religionists. Even so, in the 1880s Booth was aware that the Army was not as successful in the slums as he hoped: pure evangelism was not enough. The exposure of poverty and its relation to social evils convinced Booth that a new strategy for salvation was necessary. To be effective spiritually the Army would have first to remedy social ills. 'We can't go and talk to people about their souls while their bodies are starving,' said one Salvation lass working in the slums. Night Shelters, Slum posts, and a Social Reform Wing were set up to attend to the temporal welfare of the poor. *In Darkest England* outlined a plan for the establishment of colonies for the unemployed, as well as rescue agencies for 'the submerged tenth' which Booth estimated at three million. Booth insisted that

> in providing for the relief of temporal misery I reckon that I am only making it easy where it is now difficult, and possible where it is now all but impossible, for men and women to find their way to the Cross of our Lord Jesus Christ.[5]

Nevertheless the shift in emphasis to a social programme was a marked departure from earlier attitudes and implied recognition of the need to change the poor's environment.

A similar reordering of priorities occurred in the case of Samuel Barnett, the Vicar of St Jude's, Whitechapel in East London. Work in the slums of the East End in the 1870s convinced Barnett and his wife, Henrietta, that missions, philanthropy and the C.O.S., which they had strongly supported, were inadequate to deal with the problems of poverty. 'They had discovered for themselves', wrote Beatrice Webb, who knew them well,

> that there was a deeper and more continuous evil than unrestricted and unregulated charity, namely, unrestricted and unregulated capitalism and landlordism. They had be-come aware of the employment of labour at starvation rates; of the rack-renting of insanitary tenements; of the absence of opportunities for education, for refined leisure and for the enjoyment of nature, literature and art among the denizens of the mean streets; they had come to realise that the principles

of personal service and personal responsibility for ulterior consequences, together with the application of the scientific method, ought to be extended, from the comparatively trivial activity of almsgiving to the behaviour of the employer, the landlord and the consumer of wealth without work. Their eyes had been opened, in fact, to all the sins of commission and omission, whether voluntary or involuntary, committed by the relatively small minority of the nation who, by means of their status or possessions, exercised economic power over the masses of their fellow-countrymen. Thus without becoming Socialists, in either the academic or the revolutionary meaning of the term, they initiated or furthered a long series of socialistic measures, all involving increased public expenditure and public administration, of which Samuel Barnett's advocacy in 1883 of universal state-provided old-age pensions may be taken as a type – an advocacy which, be it added, eventually converted Charles Booth, and led to his remarkable demonstration of the expediency and practicability of pensions to the aged poor.

This Fabian version of the Barnetts' achievements is not the whole story, though it accounts for a considerable part. Toynbee Hall, of which Samuel Barnett was the founder, was the product of the social thinking of the late 1860s and 1870s maturing in the context of 1883–4. A sense of social responsibility had led a number of clergymen and middle-class social reformers to take up residence among the working classes in the belief that only thus could the gap between rich and poor be bridged. What the East End lacked was, in the words of Edward Denison, a 'resident gentry'. Barnett's proposal was for a settlement, sponsored by Oxford University, where graduates and undergraduates could live, some permanently, others during vacations, while they engaged in social, charitable, educational and local government activities in the surrounding area. He secured support from a number of socially-minded dons in Oxford, where the influence of T.H. Green had created a small following of men imbued with humanist and liberal-Christian sympathies and a commitment to social action. Toynbee Hall, named after a young Oxford tutor

at Balliol, was started in 1884 and was followed by more settlements in London and other towns. By 1913 there were 27
settlements in London, 12 in other English towns, 5 in Scotland
and one in Belfast. The number of university-educated young
men who could satisfy their social consciences by work in settlements was obviously limited. But the number of people who
could vicariously identify with this ethos by reading *Robert
Elsmere* was legion. Like its author, Mrs Ward, they did not deny
the existence of moral evil but they were aware of its connection
with physical and social conditions. These were removable, and
the task ahead was how to remove them.

Dissatisfaction with the inadequacy of private philanthropy
inevitably led to a questioning of the Poor Law, for the C.O.S.
had been designed to work closely with the guardians. With each
successive enquiry into social conditions the scale of the problem
was seen to grow inexorably. Massive details of hours of work,
wages, and all aspects of industrial relations were gathered in
the forty-nine volumes produced by the Royal Commission on
Labour (1892–4). The limitations of the Poor Law in providing
for the needs of old age were documented in the Royal Commission on the Aged Poor (1893–5); and the Select Committee
of the House of Commons on Distress from Want of Employment
(1896) recognised that unemployment was a problem requiring
special treatment. The demands of the 1890s for unemployment
relief and old age pensions were met later by state intervention
outside the Poor Law. But the changing attitudes to poverty and
the increasing cost of institutional provision for the poor led to
the setting up of a Royal Commission on the Poor Law and the
Relief of Distress to investigate the working of the Poor Law
since 1834. In 1909 it produced its famous Majority and Minority
Reports. Both reports recommended changes such as the abolition
of the guardians and the transference of the administration of the
Poor Law to Public Assistance Committees, and more specialized
provision for children, old people and the able-bodied unemployed. But the Majority Report, which was supported by the
C.O.S., retained the Poor Law in fact though not in name;
whereas the Minority Report (closely associated with the Webbs)
wanted the 'break-up' of the Poor Law entirely. The Royal

Commission had been set up by the Conservatives shortly before leaving office, but their Liberal successors found the proposals politically unacceptable and virtually ignored them. The early and mid-Victorians had been only too successful in associating relief through the Poor Law with shame and fear. As a result the Liberal legislation of 1906–14 to deal with 'the condition of the people' – school meals and medical service, old age pensions, labour exchanges, unemployment insurance and national health insurance – had to be free of all taint of the Poor Law if it were to be acceptable to working people. Social reform measures, like all legislation, have a political context – in this case the need to take account of the delayed effects of the franchise extension of 1884 and the Local Government Acts of 1888 and 1894.

The popular presence was also expressed in other ways. So far we have presented the changes in late Victorian Britain as due in part to a sense of guilt or heightened social responsibility on the part of some of the educated classes. But there was also an element of fear. The Victorians had always been aware of the existence of some members of the lower orders who were completely outside the pale of respectability because they either would not or could not accept its values of morality, improvement and self-help. They were 'the residuum', 'the dangerous classes', 'the submerged tenth'. Booth's survey showed the extent of this group and distinguished it from 'the true working classes'. He identified the problem as essentially the casual and irregular nature of the labour of Class B. Like others of his generation he subscribed to the theory that the conditions of urban existence had led to a degeneration of the race. The brutal and savage aspects of life among the casual poor exposed by the social explorers were not to be ascribed to the moral failings of the individual but to the influence of a slum environment. A Darwinian twist was given to the theory of urban degeneration by the suggestion that improved sanitation and the amelioration of the worst social evils through humanitarian efforts had frustrated the laws of nature and allowed a greater proportion of the 'unfit' to survive. Whatever the explanation of the residuum, the image it conjured up was frightening to the middle classes. With memories of the Paris Commune of 1871 in the background it seemed that the bitter

cry of the outcasts might easily turn to violence and revolution.
In 1886 these fears were partially realised.

The combination of economic depression and severe weather
caused great distress in the winter of 1885–6, especially among
dock and building workers. A demonstration of London's unemployed in Trafalgar Square on 8 February 1886 turned into a
riot when the crowd of about twenty thousand set off to march
to Hyde Park. In Pall Mall, under provocation from some young
clubmen, stones were thrown and windows were broken. The
rioters then went on to smash windows, loot shops, rob the
occupants of carriages, and terrorize the West End. During the
next two days, which were foggy, gangs of 'roughs' gathered
in Trafalgar Square, and London was full of rumours of
crowds of men marching from the south and east to pillage
the west. London was in a state of panic. Shopkeepers
boarded up their windows, banks closed, and troops stood by.
Threatening meetings and riots were reported from Norwich,
Birmingham, Northampton, Sheffield, Great Yarmouth, and
Manchester. Throughout the summer of 1886 and the whole
of 1887 tension remained high in the metropolis as groups of
unemployed camped out in the parks and squares and gathered
in large demonstrations and marches. In the autumn of 1887
meetings in Trafalgar Square were forbidden and a free speech
demonstration was called for 13 November. The resulting
battle of 'Bloody Sunday' was marked by violence and brutality
as the police broke up the crowd. The next Sunday a young
man was killed in a protest demonstration. His funeral was
made the occasion of a great socialist and radical mobilization,
with a speech by William Morris and the singing of his 'Death
Song for Alfred Linnell':

> Not one, not one, nor thousands must they slay,
> But one and all if they would dusk the day.

Middle-class fears that the violence of the poor might be the
prelude to revolution were fed by the rhetoric of some socialist
leaders. *The Times* reported the meeting in Trafalgar Square on
8 February 1886 thus:

The whole of the square where the fountains are was densely packed with people . . . There was a great roar of voices as *the man with the red flag* mounted the stonework overlooking the square, and all faces which had previously been turned south now looked north. Mr Burns had a stentorian voice . . . He . . . [denounced] the House of Commons as composed of capitalists who had fattened on the labour of the working men, and in this category he included landlords, railway directors, and employers . . . To hang these, he said, would be a waste of good rope, and as no good to the people was to be expected from these 'representatives' there must be a revolution to alter the present state of things. The people who were out of work did not want relief, but justice. From whom should they get justice? From such as the Duke of Westminster? . . . The next time they met it would be to go and sack the bakers' shops in the West of London. They had better die fighting than die starving, and he again asked how many would join the leaders of the Socialists – a question in reply to which a great many hands were held up . . . Those whom he was addressing, he said, pledged themselves to revolutionary doctrines, which elicited cries of 'No, No.' He concluded by asking the question, When we give a word for a rising, will you join us? to which a large number of the audience replied they would, and almost as large a number declared they would not.[6]

As this ambivalent response suggests, the crowds who demonstrated in 1886–7 were not revolutionary. George Bernard Shaw, writing in the *Pall Mall Gazette* (11 February 1886) observed: 'Angry as they are, they do not want revolution, they want a job.'

The significance of the events of February 1886 lay not so much in the events themselves as in the middle-class response to them. For a brief moment the residuum had appeared as a visible and terrifying force instead of a 'social problem' kept out of sight except to those who wished to investigate it. The Two Nations of Disraeli's *Sybil* (1845) had plainly not disappeared as some had fondly supposed, but remained to haunt the 1890s. The image of the abyss, from which the nation had pulled back just in time, continued into the twentieth century, reflected in titles such as Charles Masterman's *From the Abyss* (1902) and Jack London's *People of the Abyss* (1903). The fifth chapter of *In Darkest England* was headed 'On the Verge of the Abyss' and the same metaphor is found in the work of H.G. Wells and E.M. Forster (*Howards End*, 1910). The need to do something about 'the condition of the people' was clearly recognised: the problem was what?

II

The 'condition of the people' was essentially a middle-class construct, a way of looking at social reality and identifying certain 'problems'. Many ways of solving these problems were suggested, but the most acceptable was that most typical of middle-class reformer's solutions: education. It was attractive because it seemed to offer a way to effect real social change that was non-revolutionary, immediately practical, and in harmony with the ideals of rationality, improvement and progress. For the more conservative-minded, the schoolmaster as policeman was no new idea, and was given a fresh urgency by the publicity about the residuum. The educational changes in the last quarter of the century were not due in the first instance to the rediscovery of poverty, though once that rediscovery had been made it added to the pressure for change. Education as a rule does not initiate social change but rather reflects or reinforces a process that has already begun. However, once radical changes in the educational system have been made, the working out of the logic of such changes does produce important modifications in society at large. So it was in the 1880s and 1890s. Decisions taken in the late 1860s bore fruit twenty years later.

The crucial turning point was the Education Act of 1870. By that date a system of public elementary education had been established by voluntary religious societies, the two main providing bodies being the British and Foreign Schools Society (Nonconformist) and the National Society (Church of England). Thanks to their rivalry (free trade in education) provision for some 1.7 million of the 2.5 million children of school age was provided, though the average actual attendance was only about 1.1 million. The 1870 Act was intended to fill the gaps; and thus began a process of supplementing and, ultimately, replacing the voluntary schools with state schools. Nevertheless the dual system continued for many years, and voluntary schools remained strong in rural areas where the Church of England was dominant. Further Education Acts in 1876, 1880 and 1891 made education virtually compulsory and free. Despite its name, the 1870 Education Act was not intended to provide liberal education but something more akin to instruction. The schools were not popular schools initiated by demand from below but working-class schools provided from above. As H.G. Wells observed, 'The Education Act of 1870 was not an Act for a common universal education, it was an Act to educate the lower classes for employment on lower-class lines, and with specially trained, inferior teachers who had no university quality.'[7] Elementary education meant not a stage in the educational process but a minimal education for those who could not afford to pay for something better. The nature of the changes effected during the years 1870–95 becomes clear when the working of the system is examined.

At the centre of the educational structure were school boards, elected by the ratepayers and empowered to spend funds raised by local rates. This was the most democratic franchise of the time and members did not require a property or residential qualification. Many of the schools they built in the 1880s and 1890s are with us still: huge two or three-storeyed red brick edifices, with a central hall and surrounding classrooms, railed-in playground, and separate entrances for boys and girls. Rivalling only the churches in size and number, the board schools were greeted as symbols of social change, to be either welcomed or viewed with apprehension. For the middle classes the message was clear:

SHERLOCK HOLMES: Look at those big, isolated clumps of buildings rising up above the slates, like brick islands in a lead-coloured sea.
DR WATSON: The Board Schools.
SHERLOCK HOLMES: Lighthouses, my boy! Beacons

of the future! Capsules, with hundreds of bright little seeds in each, out of which will spring the wiser, better England of the future.[8]

But for some of the London poor the response was more equivocal. The board school represented the loss of their children's earnings, and in some cases the destruction of their homes which were pulled down to make way for school buildings. When they discovered what went on in the schools they were even more ambivalent.

The emphasis from the start was on discipline. Since the 1870 Act conscripted a large army of children of the poor who had not previously been in school, the problem was how to control them while teaching simple mastery of the Three Rs. Faced with a class of seventy or more children for five and a half hours daily the teachers demanded instant obedience and uniform responses. A vast amount of punishment was inflicted: every sum wrong and every spelling mistake was liable to be visited by a stroke of the cane (for boys) or a ruler on the knuckles (for girls). Serious infractions of the rules – truancy, insubordination, disrespect, bad language – received more severe caning in front of the class or the whole school. Punishment books were kept to record the nature and amount of each punishment and by whom inflicted. A London headmaster who was a pupil teacher in 1889–93 recalled:

> I never remember seeing my headmaster in school when he had not a cane hanging by the crook over his left wrist. Every assistant master had a cane and so had the pupil teachers, but we were not allowed to have a crook so that if any question arose they were only pointers. There were no backs to the desks and backs of boys were straightened by means of a stroke of the cane.[9]

There was of course nothing novel in this use of corporal punishment, which was widely accepted throughout society. Working-class, no less than middle-class, autobiographies are full of memories of mothers smacking the bare bottoms of young children, of fathers taking off a heavy leather belt and administering a beating, of ritualized birchings in workhouses, reformatories and public schools. Nevertheless the daily canings on the hand in board schools left an indelible impression on a whole generation of children who remembered their schooling – and hence their views of education – with mixed feelings. Happiness at school was remembered when a teacher was kind and fired the child's imagination in some way.

The system under which the board schools operated was 'payment by results'. Children were classified, roughly by age, into 'standards', and the appropriate work and level of attainment for each standard was defined by the central Education Department. Grants to schools were dependent on the number of children who passed an examination in each subject at each standard, together with the number of attendances throughout the year. The children were examined orally by H.M.I.s (Her Majesty's Inspectors of Schools) each year. The teachers were thus under pressure to get as many children as possible through the examination and this they could do most easily by rote learning. As the day of the examination approached, the drilling of the children to answer the expected questions intensified; no spontaneity or originality could be allowed to risk an upset. Such a system did little to develop a child's individuality or self-reliance; but, as R.H. Tawney wrote later, 'the elementary schools of 1870 were intended in the main to produce an orderly, civil, obedient population, with sufficient education to understand a command.'[10]

By 1895 the institutions for free, compulsory elementary education were in place. Thereafter the system of payment by results was modified. The minimum school-leaving age was advanced from 10 to 11 and later to 13, although exemptions for part-time work and certificates of proficiency to excuse attendance were continued. It had been the intention in 1870 that the state should concern itself only with elementary education, but pressure from within the system forced an advance to secondary and technical education. By various subterfuges such as the use of 'Whiskey Money' (funds made available to local government from customs and excise legislation of 1890) provision was made for evening continuation classes in subjects beyond the elementary level.

From the mid–1880s the Department of Science and Art, which had been originally intended to provide classes in applied science and scientific principles for industrial workers, was directing its efforts towards secondary education for the lower-middle and upper-working classes. Finally in 1902 a new Education Act made provision for secondary schools. It also abolished the school boards and transferred their powers to Local Education Authorities. Thus, by the end of the Victorian period, the first phase of what has been called 'the silent social revolution' had been accomplished. These changes can be interpreted in several different ways.

As an exercise in socialization of the residuum and the working classes the system of state schooling developed between 1870 and 1902 was generally considered by middle-class observers to have been a success. There was much talk of the 'civilizing' mission of education and a consensus of opinion that the schools had ameliorated to some extent the problems of juvenile crime, street violence and drunkenness through the diffusion of middle-class values. Sidney Webb, usually critical of the London School Board, wrote in 1904 of 'the wonderful discipline of the public elementary school' and credited the Board with effecting a transformation in 'the manners and morals of the London manual working class'; and Charles Booth was similarly enthusiastic. Outside the board school system – in the town and village voluntary schools – the achievement was less impressive. Everywhere, the social function of the school was paramount, and the close association between education and social class was emphasized. Middle-class children did not go to public elementary schools but to fee-paying public schools or private, proprietary establishments. By 1900 there were about a hundred public schools with perhaps thirty thousand pupils, providing education for the elite. For less affluent members of the middle class and some of the upper working class the ancient grammar schools offered secondary schooling beyond the Three Rs. In the suburbs a variety of independent schools, often in large private houses, were the mainstay of lower middle-class education. H.G. Wells in his autobiography recaptured the atmosphere of one such school, Bromley Academy, where the bald, portly Mr

Thomas Morley (Licentiate of the College of Preceptors) laboured intensively but irregularly to turn 25–35 unwilling boys into respectable young clerks and shop assistants. Between Mr Morley's pupils and the schoolboys from the local elementary school there was only hostile class feeling.

To working-class parents and children the educational changes so enthusiastically welcomed by H.M.I.s and middle-class social reformers appeared somewhat different. The authoritarian and disciplinary ethos of the schools was reminiscent of other contacts with the state and middle-class agencies. To enforce the 1870 Act, school attendance officers (in London termed visitors) were appointed. The 'school board man' or 'truant officer' became a symbol of interfering officialdom. In London the visitors collected detailed information about the lives of the poor which Booth and other investigators used in their surveys. By the time they were abolished the school boards in many areas had become much disliked by working-class parents. The classroom disobedience, truancy and 'larking about' which were condemned by teachers and H.M.I.s as evidence of indiscipline or moral delinquency were to some extent a resistance to norms which the schools were attempting to inculcate.

The new legislation also destroyed an older tradition of independent working-class schools. Historians of education have followed the lead of Victorian educationalists who were anxious to professionalize teaching, and who took every opportunity to denigrate working-class private schools, and ultimately drove them into extinction. These schools (sometimes called dame schools because they were often run by women) had between ten and thirty pupils as a rule, and were frequently held in the home of the teacher, who was without any formal educational training. There was no segregation of pupils by sex, age or ability; and the teaching and learning was individual and informal. Fees of 3*d*–9*d* a week were paid to the teacher by the parents. Government inspectors and middle-class reformers condemned such schools as mere baby-minding establishments. They noted with strong disapproval the absence of settled or regular attendance. The pupils came and went at all times during the day. School hours were nominal and adjusted to family needs – hence the number of two and three year olds who were sent to be 'out of the way' or 'kept safe'. The accommodation was overcrowded and sometimes stuffy, dirty, and insanitary. The pupils were not divided into separate classes, and the teacher was a working man or woman who continued to work while teaching.

To the middle classes such efforts appeared woefully inadequate: the schools were simply not real schools at all. Yet throughout the first three-quarters of the nineteenth century their numbers remained large. Official nineteenth century enquiries gave a ratio of attendance at working-class private schools to public elementary (working-class) schools of about one to three. In Bristol in 1875 (five years after the 1870 Act), 4280 pupils still attended private venture schools, which was 24 per cent of the number attending public elementary schools. Only after 1875, when the state made a determined effort to eliminate them, did the working-class private schools disappear, and even then a few lingered on into the twentieth century.

Working people clung tenaciously to an institution for which they had to pay fees and which was in many ways inferior to the alternative state-sponsored elementary school because the private school offered the kind of education which many of them wanted, rather than the education which the middle class thought they should have. The grounds on which Her Majesty's Inspectors objected to working-class private schools were the very ones that endeared them to many of the common people. Because they paid fees to the teachers (not always punctually) the working classes controlled the schools completely. The teachers were working people like the parents, not socially-superior, 'educated' persons, and they were prepared to take the children at the times and on the conditions acceptable to a working-class family. The schools were efficient in teaching basic literacy, as even the H.M.I.s had reluctantly to admit. To many labouring people the atmosphere of a small, warm, stuffy dame's cottage may have seemed preferable to the cold, draughty and impersonal nature of large school buildings. They felt at home there, and among their own kind. The working-class private school was in this sense a part of the culture of the common people, and its role raised fundamental class issues. Like the trade union, it was an agency of working-class self-help which the middle classes did not welcome. Schools for the people were one thing: the people's own schools were quite another. They had therefore to be killed off, and this was done by the Education Act of 1876 which laid down that only attendance at a 'certified efficient school' qualified a child to leave school for employment. So effective was the destruction of the working-class private school that after the 1880s the memory of it was forgotten. Thereafter the concept of private schooling was annexed exclusively by the middle classes. 'The triumph of [state-] provided elementary schooling and the ideological capture of "private schooling" was complete.'[11]

V

Epilogue

10

The End of Equipoise

The Victorian age did not come to a sudden end with the death of the queen in 1901. Some aspects of Victorianism had already faded in the last quarter of the nineteenth century, others only came to full fruition later. Historians have usually seen 1914 as a more significant date than 1901, with the outbreak of the First World War marking the end of an epoch. The Edwardian epilogue provides contrast and similarity, change and continuity with what had gone before. By the end of the century the changes outlined in Part Four had effectively undermined the confidence and cohesion of mid-Victorian society. The balances betwen various conflicting elements which had been precariously maintained in the third quarter of the century were no more: the age of equipoise was ended.[1] In its place came the unsettlement of the late 1880s and 1890s, continuing until 1914. The jubilees of 1887 and 1897 presented a façade of national unity; but underneath, the nation was divided on the nature of the eternal social, religious and political certainties.

As the year 1900 approached there was much fashionable talk of '*fin de siècle*'. *The Yellow Book* and the drawings of Aubrey Beardsley (much reproduced in recent years) expressed most representatively the daring and challenging rejection of Victorianism. The explicit sexuality of Beardsley's drawings, the flamboyant homosexuality of Oscar Wilde, the celebration of decadence, paganism, perversity and the bizarre fascinated the young and shocked their elders. In preparation for the new century appeared the 'new woman', the 'new humour' (Jerome K. Jerome, W.W. Jacobs, Israel Zangwill), the 'new hedonism' (Grant Allen), the 'new unionism' (John Burns, the Webbs), and of course '*l'art nouveau*'. Max Beerbohm caught the mood of aestheticism which had begun in the 1880s and set the tone for the avant-garde:

Fired by [Oscar Wilde's] fervid words, men and women hurled their mahogany into the streets and ransacked the curio-shops for the furniture of Annish days. Dados arose upon every wall, sunflowers and the feathers of peacocks curved in every corner, tea grew quite cold while the guests were praising the Willow Pattern of its cup. A few fashionable women even dressed themselves in sinuous draperies and unheard-of greens. Into whatsoever ballroom you went, you would surely find, among the women in tiaras and the fops and the distinguished foreigners, half a score of comely ragamuffins in velveteen, murmuring sonnets, posturing, waving their hands. Beauty was sought in the most unlikely places. Young painters found her robed in the fogs, and bank clerks, versed in the writings of Mr Hamerton, were heard to declare, as they sped home from the City, that the underground railway was beautiful from London Bridge to Westminster, but not from Sloane Square to Notting Hill Gate.[2]

To mock middle-class values and habits – '*épater le bourgeois*' as Flaubert put it – was a favourite occupation of many a young *fin de siècle* writer. Some were little more than poseurs, but others, notably George Bernard Shaw, used the tactic of shocking to challenge orthodoxies and present an alternative, socialist point of view. As a movement of art and letters *fin de siècle* was of only restricted appeal. As an effervescence it betokened deeper currents of cultural and social change, all directed to removing Victorian restraints and upsetting the Victorian equilibrium.

In contrast to this sharp and often witty critique, but also essentially new, was the concept of imperialism. The period 1880–1914 has been labelled the Age of Empire as a means of emphasizing one of its main characteristics and differentiating it from the mid-Victorian heyday. It was the period in which the Western European states, the U.S.A. and Japan divided up a large part of the rest of the world between themselves as colonies. In this process Britain took a lion's share, annexing large parts of Africa and consolidating its hold on India.

When I left the Foreign Office in 1880, [Lord Salisbury told a Glasgow audience in May 1891] nobody thought about Africa. When I returned to it in 1885, the nations of Europe were almost quarrelling with each other as to the various portions of Africa which they could obtain. I do not exactly know the cause of this sudden revolution. But there it is. It is a great force – a great civilizing, Christianizing force.[3]

This civilizing, Christianizing mission was the generally accepted view of British imperialism. Economic gains such as new markets, new sources of raw materials and their exploitation by British capital made imperialism attractive to financiers and business-men. Strategic considerations dictated the need to acquire bases to protect the routes to India, 'the brightest jewel in the imperial crown'. For the middle classes India and the colonies provided new career opportunities 'for tens of thousands of young men born to decent station'.[4] For the working classes, few of whom had any direct contact with the empire apart from a handful who enlisted as soldiers, imperialism was mainly a matter of vicarious glory and patriotic feeling.

The popularity of empire reached a crescendo in the 1897 jubilee celebrations and during the Boer War (1899–1902), when the two Boer republics of Transvaal and the Orange Free State fought to prevent the extension of British influence in South Africa. At first the war went badly for the British, whose forces were soon besieged in several towns, including Mafeking in Bechuanaland, commanded by Colonel Robert Baden-Powell. After a siege lasting 217 days Mafeking was relieved on 17 May 1900 and the news was celebrated with such wild carnival in the streets of London and other towns that it could only be described as 'mafficking'. The hysterical, flag-wagging jingoism of the crowds confirmed the worst fears of liberals and socialists that imperialism would serve to cement the masses behind the existing order by encouraging a sense of national unity and identity and playing upon popular xenophobia. Demands for social reform at home might be deflected by glories from abroad. The 'natural' imperialists were the aristocracy and the Conservative party, but, by the end of the century, there were also Liberal Imperialists

Late Victorian Britain

(Limps) who included Lord Rosebery, H.H. Asquith, R.B. Haldane and Edward Grey. They were opposed by more radical elements in the Liberal party (like the young David Lloyd George) who remained true to the old Gladstonian tradition of 'little Englandism', and who were now called 'pro-Boers'. Among socialists and trade union leaders imperialism aroused little enthusiasm and usually strong opposition; though some Fabians were anti-Boer on grounds of the superior efficiency and civilizing (i.e. modernizing) effects of Great Power states.

Imperialism had many different faces and related to many of the social and intellectual strands mentioned in earlier chapters. But the most popular and comprehensive contemporary presentation of Britain's imperial role was in the works of Rudyard Kipling. Few writers have caught the imagination of their generation more vividly than the author of *Barrack-Room Ballads*, which was reprinted three times in 1892 and some fifty times during the next thirty years. Hailed as the new Dickens on his arrival in London in 1889, Kipling produced a steady succession of novels, short stories and verses dealing with India, army life, seafaring, the jungle and many other things.[5] Eminently quotable, his words were recited, sung and parodied for years afterwards. If, as seems likely, the popularity of a writer rests on a basis of assumptions which are shared by the readers, it would seem that what Kipling had to say about empire (and much else) was a faithful reflection of the position of imperialism in contemporary British culture.

As the unofficial poet laureate of the Empire Kipling's first aim was to make his countrymen and women aware of the reality of the overseas territories and their relevance to life in Britain. 'What do they know of England who only England know?', he asked. The diamond jubilee in 1897 had reminded the nation that the queen reigned over an empire upon which the sun never set. Patriotism was no longer insular but implied a wider loyalty. Kipling believed in the superior qualities of the English race which had enabled it to overcome barbarism and bring the blessings of 'civilization' and efficient organization to 'backward' peoples. His touchstone was 'the Law', an almost tribal concept interpreted as a philosophy of self-reliance:

Keep ye the Law – be swift in all obedience –
Clear the land of evil, drive the road and bridge the ford.
Make ye sure to each his own
That he reap where he hath sown;
By the peace among Our peoples let men know we serve the
    Lord!

For the white races empire was a duty. In 'The White Man's
Burden', a poem addressed to the Americans on their responsi-
bilities in the Philippines in 1898, Kipling urged them:

> Take up the White man's burden –
> Send forth the best ye breed –
> God bind your sons to exile
> To serve your captives' need.

Such language sprang from attitudes which today we recognise
as racist. Kipling and his followers would not have understood
this. Theories of race and eugenicist arguments were widely
favoured in Fabian socialist and other intellectual circles. For
Kipling a white man was superior not so much because of the
colour of his skin but because he acknowledged a 'higher' code
of conduct than 'lesser breeds without the Law'. In the best-
known of all Kipling's ballads, 'Gunga Din', a cockney soldier's
comment on the dark-skinned Indian servant who sacrificed his
life for him was that 'for all 'is dirty 'ide, 'E was white, clear
white, inside.' Kipling legitimized imperialism through an appeal
to moral values and an almost puritan sense of duty. He was,
however, sailing close to the wind: and what had begun as
patriotism easily degenerated into jingoism during the Boer War.

The careful wording of Kipling's poems was sometimes over-
looked and his meaning quite distorted. For instance, the first
couplet of 'The Ballad of East and West' was often quoted alone:

Oh, East is East, and West is West, and never the twain
    shall meet,
Till Earth and Sky stand presently at God's great Judgement
    Seat;

Whereas the next two lines completely alter the sense of the
poem:

But there is neither East nor West, Border, nor Breed, nor
Birth,
When two strong men stand face to face, though they come
from the ends of the earth!

Again, 'Recessional', which was written on the occasion of the
1897 jubilee, quickly became a hymn in celebration of empire:

> God of our fathers, known of old,
> Lord of our far-flung battle-line,
> Beneath whose awful Hand we hold
> Dominion over palm and pine –
> Lord God of Hosts, be with us yet,
> Lest we forget – lest we forget!

In fact it was a warning against the sin of hubris and a call to
humility in face of the ephemeral nature of all empire:

> Far-called, our navies melt away;
> On dune and headland sinks the fire:
> Lo, all our pomp of yesterday
> Is one with Nineveh and Tyre!
> Judge of the Nations, spare us yet,
> Lest we forget – lest we forget!

That the common view of what Kipling was saying was not
always accurate, is, however, of much less importance than his
general role as a popular propagandist or apologist for imperialism. He helped to make empire a household word, familiarized
on biscuit tins and cigarette cards, in music-halls and boys'
stories.

Kipling's view of empire was very much from below. He
did not write about generals and viceroys but about engineers,
journalists, rank-and-file soldiers and native peoples. And he
wrote in a style close to the popular idiom of the ballad and the
hymn. His championing of the common soldier, hitherto despised
or ignored by respectable society, was entirely original and presented imperial themes in a personal, easily-understood way. The
cockney dialect and song rhythms of his verse were not far
removed from the music-hall ditties of the time.

The cause of empire was actively promoted in many other

ways. The Boy Scout movement, founded in 1907–8 by Baden-Powell, the hero of Mafeking, was the fruit of his Boer War experiences and his concern for the future of the British race and its Empire. Scouting drew upon the Victorian public school traditions of 'playing the game', 'good form', 'character' and so on, and extended them to the elementary schoolboy in the form of the Scout law of honour, loyalty and duty. Baden-Powell took seriously the idea of the deterioration of the race, and feared that in the Darwinian struggle for national survival Britain might lose her imperial superiority unless she deliberately strengthened the patriotism of youth. His aim in forming the Boy Scouts, he said, was 'to counteract if possible the deterioration moral and physical which shortened our rising generation, and to train the boys to be more efficient and characterful citizens'.[6] He talked of the need to build up 'self-reliant, energetic manhood'; and feared lest the empire should succumb like Rome through national decadence. The response to Baden-Powell's *Scouting for Boys* was immediate and the Scouts rapidly became the largest youth movement in the country.

The attempt to promote imperial loyalty in the young was not left to voluntary organizations alone, but was institutionalized in the schools. 'Empire Day' was the 24th May, the birthday of Queen Victoria, and was celebrated accordingly. Robert Roberts described the fervour of the occasion in the Salford elementary school which he attended:

We drew union jacks, hung classrooms with flags of the dominions and gazed with pride as they pointed out those massed areas of red on the world map. 'This, and this, and this', they said, 'belong to us!' When next King George with his queen came on a state visit we were ready, together with 30,000 other children, to ask in song, and then (in case he didn't know) tell him precisely the 'Meaning of Empire Day'.

'The children were first presented with a bun', says the log book, 'and a piece of chocolate kindly provided by Alderman F. and after forming fours on the croft proceeded to a stand erected on the road. Each boy wore a rosette of red, white and blue ribbon and each girl wore a blue sash over a white dress'. (Those without white dresses were allowed to stand at the rear.) In happy unison we sang, 'Here's a health unto His Majesty', 'Three cheers for the red white and blue', and

> What is the meaning of Empire Day?
> Why do the cannons roar?
> Why does the cry, 'God save the King!'
> Echo from shore to shore?
> Why does the flag of Britannia float,
> Proudly o'er fort and bay?
> Why do our kinsmen gladly hail,
> Our glorious Empire Day?
> *Response*
> On our nation's scroll of glory,
> With its deeds of daring told,
> There is written a story,
> Of the heroes bold,
> In the days of old,
> So keep the deeds before us,
> Every year we homage pay,
> To our banner proud,
> That has never bowed,
> And that's the meaning of Empire Day![7]

Later Roberts was doubtful whether the working classes had gained much materially from the empire: 'They didn't know, it was said, whether trade was good for the Empire, or the Empire was good for trade, but they knew the Empire was theirs and they were going to support it.'

One aspect of imperialism, and that a legacy from the colonial past, did not inspire feelings of pride and glory: Ireland. Throughout the nineteenth century the 'Irish question' plagued successive English governments and none was able to satisfy Irish grievances, which stemmed from policies designed to maintain Irish economic, religious and political inferiority. When reforms were grudgingly conceded they were usually too little and too late. By the 1880s the central question was whether Ireland should be granted 'home rule' and this became a dominant political issue between the Liberal 'home rulers' and the Conservative 'unionists'. In Parliament the balance between the two parties was held by the Irish members who voted together as a bloc. Gladstone in 1886 introduced his first Home Rule bill, which provided for an Irish parliament in Dublin while reserving matters of defence and foreign policy for the Westminster parliament. But the bill was defeated by a split in the Liberals, 93 of whom voted against it. In 1893 Gladstone tried again. This time his (second) Home Rule bill narrowly passed through the Commons but was then defeated in the Lords. The Liberals were not in a position to pursue the matter again until they returned to power in 1906. Much preoccupied with social reform legislation, they were reluctant to make trouble for themselves, the more so as they were no longer dependent on the Irish nationalist vote. Moreover it was certain that the House of Lords, with its built-in Conservative majority, would defeat any new attempt to pass a Home Rule bill.

However events in 1909–11 changed this situation. The Chancellor of the Exchequer, Lloyd George, needing more money for naval rearmament to meet the challenge of Germany's military build-up and also for his Old Age Pensions scheme, proposed among other measures a modest land tax. The Conservatives opposed the budget uncompromisingly and were goaded to extremes by Lloyd George's speeches delivered up and down the country. His 'People's Budget' was passed by the Commons but then rejected by the House of Lords. It was held to be unconstitutional for the Lords to thwart the will of the Commons, for this would undermine the basis of democratic government. Since the Conservatives had a permanent majority in the Lords the Liberals had little alternative but to seek to amend the powers of the upper chamber. As Lloyd George said, 'the House of Lords is not the watchdog of the Constitution; it is Mr Balfour's poodle'. The sequence of events which followed the rejection of the budget led to a constitutional crisis, including two general elections in January and December 1910 and the passing of the Parliament Act in 1911 under circumstances reminiscent of the 1832 Reform

Bill crisis. Henceforth the Lords were able only to delay for two years the implementation of a bill which had passed the House of Commons. This removed the last obstacle to Home Rule, and as the Liberals' majority had been greatly reduced in the 1910 elections so that they were once again dependent on the support of the Irish nationalists, a third Home Rule bill was introduced in 1912. Unlike its predecessors this bill was federalist in conception, and provided for an Irish parliament in Dublin and 42 Irish members in the Westminster parliament. Under the new Parliament Act it was due to come into effect in 1914, over the Lords' veto. But the mood in Ireland was now very different from 1886 and the bill failed to take account of the special problem of the Protestant minority in Ulster. Their whole way of life – economic, social and religious – was different from the rest of Ireland, and the prosperity and growth of Belfast challenged the primacy of Dublin. The Conservative party, frustrated at Westminster, decided to exploit the Ulster problem in order to defeat the bill. They were convinced that the break-up of the United Kingdom would be the prelude to the break-up of the British Empire. The lengths to which they were prepared to go to prevent this took the country to the verge of civil war.

Violent and lawless measures were nothing new in the history of Ireland since the 1798 rising, but the use of revolutionary tactics by Conservatives was a new phenomenon. Under the leadership of Sir Edward Carson, and openly supported by Bonar Law, the leader of the Conservatives, the unionists in Ulster prepared to resist Home Rule by force of arms. There was much alarming talk: Bonar Law, speaking at a great party rally at Blenheim in July 1912 declared, 'I can imagine no length of resistance to which Ulster will go, which I shall not be ready to support, and in which they will not be supported by the overwhelming majority of the British people.' In Ulster, processions, Orange marches, demonstrations and pledges were followed by military parades and the formation of an army of Ulster Volunteers. By the end of 1913, 100,000 men had enlisted. They regarded themselves not as rebels but as loyalists, and were so regarded by some army officers, who could not therefore be relied on to 'coerce' them. In March 1914 the Commander-in-Chief in

Ireland, General Paget, told his officers of the possibility of civil war in Ireland and said that those who wished might resign; whereupon 57 out of 70 officers of the 3rd Cavalry Brigade together with other officers in the infantry said they would do so 'if ordered north'. This 'mutiny at the Curragh' was intensely unpopular in the country. But a month later the Larne gun-running landed thirty thousand rifles and bayonets and three million rounds of ammunition for the Ulster Volunteers from Germany. Not to be outdone, the National Volunteers (recruited from the nationalists in opposition to the Ulster Volunteers) organized a similar gun-running at Howth, near Dublin, in broad daylight on 26 July 1914. British troops tried unsuccessfully to stop them marching to Dublin, and in the clash three people were killed and thirty-eight injured. Two rival private armies were now prepared to fight for union or independence. Ireland was drifting towards civil war. Rebellion in Ireland had always been associated in the English mind with disaffected Catholics and the discontented poor. Now came the Conservative defiance of law and the spectacle of eminent imperialists like Lord Milner urging resistance to Home Rule by force if compromise failed. What now of the complacent Victorian confidence that the British, unlike some other nations, acknowledged the rule of law to be the supreme principle of government?

A similar readiness to turn to tactics of physical force appeared elsewhere. The women's suffrage movement, disillusioned by the slow progress it had made, in 1905 took to militancy. A pattern of illegal acts was planned; these would lead to imprisonment, martyrdom, publicity in the newspapers, and increased funds and support for the W.S.P.U. Such was the rationale of the new policy. Assaults on policemen, interruption of Liberal party meetings, mass lobbying of Parliament, padlocking of suffragettes to the railings outside No. 10 Downing Street, breaking of windows in government offices, physical attacks on ministers (Asquith, Lloyd George, Churchill) – all contributed to a mood of desperate defiance. Once arrested, sentenced and imprisoned, the suffragettes carried on their protest within the gaols. As middle-class ladies they were appalled by the degrading conditions of imprisonment: coarse clothes, unappetizing food, primitive sanitary arrangements, the dehumanizing regime. Lady Constance Lytton, daughter of the second Earl of Lytton, was so disgusted by the treatment of working-class, as distinct from aristocratic and middle-class, women which she witnessed during her first imprisonment that she disguised herself as 'Jane Warton', a seamstress, and deliberately got herself arrested in Liverpool and imprisoned in Walton gaol. Despite a heart disease, which she refused to mention and which was undetected in a cursory medical examination, she went on hunger strike. She was forcibly fed eight times and released in a state of collapse.

The tactic of hunger striking was at first successful in gaining early release. But in September 1909 the government ordered forcible feeding. This was done by pouring a nourishing liquid through a tube inserted through the mouth or nostrils. The prisoner had to be held down if she fought against the process. Sylvia Pankhurst described her experiences:

I struggled, but was overcome. There were six of them, all much bigger and stronger than I. They flung me on my back on the bed, and held me down firmly by shoulders and wrists, hips, knees and ankles. Then the doctors came stealing in. Someone seized me by the head and thrust a sheet under my chin. My eyes were shut. I set my teeth and tightened my lips over them with all my strength. A man's hands were trying to force open my mouth; my breath was coming so fast that I felt as though I should suffocate. His fingers were striving to pull my lips apart – getting inside. I felt them and a steel instrument pressing round my gums, feeling for gaps in my teeth. I was trying to jerk my head away, trying to wrench it free. Two of them were holding it, two of them dragging at my mouth. I was panting and heaving, my breath quicker and quicker, coming now with a low scream which was growing louder. 'Here is a gap', one of them said. 'No, here is a better one. This long gap here!' A steel instrument pressed my gums, cutting into the flesh. I braced myself to resist that terrible pain. 'No, that won't do' – that voice again. 'Give me the pointed one!' A stab of sharp, intolerable agony. I wrenched my head free. Again they grasped me.

Again the struggle. Again the steel cutting its way in, though I strained my force against it. Then something gradually forced my jaws apart as a screw was turned; the pain was like having the teeth drawn. They were trying to get the tube down my throat, I was struggling madly to stiffen my muscles and close my throat. They got it down, I suppose, though I was unconscious of anything then save a mad revolt of struggling, for they said at last: 'That's all!' and I vomited as the tube came up. They left me on the bed exhausted, gasping for breath and sobbing convulsively.

The same thing happened in the evening, but I was too tired to fight so long.

Day after day, morning and evening, the same struggle. Sometimes they used one steel gag on my jaw, sometimes two. 'Don't hurt more than you can help,' the senior sometimes said when his junior prodded with the sharp point of steel. My gums, where they prised them open, were always sore and bleeding, with bits of loose, jagged flesh; and other parts of the mouth got bruised or pinched in the struggle.[8]

Attempts at conciliation were made by the government during 1910–11 but the refusal of Asquith and Lloyd George to introduce a bill unequivocally granting female suffrage led to renewed outbursts of violence. More windows were broken, the contents of public letter boxes were set alight, and a campaign of arson and property damage was begun. Golf greens were mutilated, the orchid house at Kew Gardens was burned, and a bomb wrecked Lloyd George's new house in Surrey. Churches, railway stations, cricket pavilions, art galleries, clubhouses, and the residences of known anti-suffragists were burned and vandalized. Hunger striking continued; and the government passed the famous 'Cat and Mouse' Act which permitted the re-arrest of prisoners who had been released because their health was suffering. Throughout 1913 militancy increased, and with it a new emphasis on martyrdom when Emily Wilding Davison threw herself in front of the king's horse on Derby Day at Epsom and died from her injuries. Two flags in the purple, white and green colours of the W.S.P.U. were found pinned inside her coat. Her

funeral in London was the occasion of a mass demonstration.
Two thousand suffragettes formed a guard of honour who es-
corted the coffin through the streets lined with spectators from
Victoria Station to St George's Church in Bloomsbury. Mrs
Pankhurst, dressed in deep mourning, was arrested at the church,
but pledged that she would 'carry on our Holy War for the
emancipation of our sex'.

Martyrdom and arson however did not have the effect that
Mrs Pankhurst and her daughter Christabel hoped for. Support
for the W.S.P.U. declined; and the autocratic methods of the
Pankhursts alienated even their closest allies, the Pethick-
Lawrences. Christabel became increasingly millenarian in her
pronouncements; and Mrs Pankhurst urged unceasing militancy:

> Those of you who can express your militancy by facing Party
> mobs at Cabinet Ministers' meetings when you remind them
> of their falseness to principle – do so. Those of you who can
> express your militancy by joining us in our anti-Government
> bye-election policy – do so. Those of you who can break
> windows – break them. Those of you who can still further
> attack the secret idol of property so as to make the Govern-
> ment realise that property is as greatly endangered by
> Women Suffrage as it was by the Chartists of old – do so.
> And my last word to the Government: I incite this meeting
> to rebellion. I say to the Government: You have not dared
> to take the leaders of Ulster for their incitement to rebellion,
> take me if you dare.[9]

But the W.S.P.U. (though not without its quota of Irish patriots
among the leadership) was no Irish volunteer force. Arson did
not attract the support of the masses and the self-imposed martyrdom of hunger striking was perceived as the protest of a tiny
minority. These tactics won publicity but not support. The movement was an annoyance and embarrassment rather than a threat
to the government. The most significant thing about the W.S.P.U.
in relation to the weakening of the Victorian consensus was that
respectable middle-class women were prepared to go to such
lengths in their militancy and violence. Nothing could be further

from the hallowed Victorian stereotype of the home-centred, submissive female.

A movement with greater political muscle was labour. It too turned towards the tactics of extreme militancy in the years before the First World War. The period 1896–1914 was one in which real wages overall did not increase as they had done in previous decades. In some industries such as coal mining, building and the railways real wages fell as prices outdistanced earnings. During the same period trade union membership grew massively, from 1.5 million in the early 1890s to over 4 million in 1913. Unions generally reacted more quickly to reductions in money wages than to falls in real wages caused by rising prices. Thus the full effects of the years of stationary or falling real wages were not felt immediately but were delayed until workers' awareness that their position had worsened motivated them to militancy. Economic fluctuations alone seldom account for strike action. Rising prices, pressure for increased output, employers' refusal or reluctance to recognise traditional bargaining procedures, and an increased class-consciousness that emphasized relative inequalities in wealth, all fuelled an explosive mixture that only needed a spark, such as an employer's proposed wage cut, to set it off. The 'labour unrest', as it was euphemistically called, was a series of disputes involving many different industries and localities, but dominated by coal mining and the railways. Some of the strikes were short and local, others were national stoppages of several months' duration. Their tone was often bitter and unyielding, and they were sometimes accompanied by riot and physical repression. Contemporary observers complained of a mood of 'strike fever'.

The rising tension was observable from 1908 when the number of days lost through stoppages was over ten million – four or five times the figure for the immediately preceding years. Faced with a sharp recession, the North East's employers in shipbuilding and engineering announced wage cuts in 1908 , which were promptly followed by strikes and lockouts lasting up to six months. The cotton workers were treated similarly and held out for seven weeks on strike. There was less unrest in 1909 except among coal miners, who resented new working arrangements and resorted to strike action which lasted until the following year. Later in 1910 the miners at Tonypandy in the Rhondda rejected the price list for a new seam and after much haggling were locked out. The South Wales Miners' Federation then called out the whole of the 12,000 men employed by the coalowners, the Cambrian Combine. Strikes also began in neighbouring pits and soon 30,000 men were locked out or on strike. Attempts to introduce blackleg labour were fiercely resisted and windows were smashed. Police reinforcements and troops were brought in, and a general was appointed to take charge of both civil and military forces should it be necessary to use the latter to 'quell disorder'. Keir Hardie protested at unnecessary police violence; and Tonypandy became a byword in Welsh mining lore. The strike dragged on until August 1911, when the men went back on the employers' terms. Before then – during the long hot summer of 1911–seamen, dockers, tramwaymen and railwaymen came out on strike. Incidents of arson and rioting occurred in Liverpool and South Wales, and troops opened fire, killing four people in the two clashes. But the strike wave had not yet reached its peak. That came in 1912, when more than forty million working days were lost by stoppages. A national miners' strike brought out a million men from the end of February to April. The London dockers struck from May until August, but had to go back defeated. Industrial unrest continued throughout 1913 and into 1914, though not on the same scale as in 1912. Strikes in the Midlands metal trades occurred in 1913; but the main conflict was in Dublin, where James Larkin's Irish Transport Workers' Union held out for eight months.

Larkin was an advocate of revolutionary syndicalism, a movement which attracted a number of militant trade union leaders and socialists in the years before the First World War. It was influenced partly by the Anarcho-Syndicalists of France and more directly by American developments. The Industrial Workers of the World was an organization founded in Chicago in 1905, proclaiming that 'the working class and the employing class have nothing in common', and looking to the day when the capitalists would be defeated by the combined strength of the workers organized in revolutionary unions. Tom Mann, the dockers'

leader, had absorbed syndicalist ideas during his travels in Australasia and the United States and returned to spread them among
transport workers and the trade union movement generally.
Marxism and the ideas of the American Marxian-syndicalist
Daniel De Leon were also enthusiastically received by some
working-class intellectuals, as at Ruskin College, Oxford, where
they split off in 1908 to found their own Labour College and
the Plebs League. Syndicalism made most headway among the
members of the Amalgamated Society of Railway Servants and
among the South Wales miners, who published an influential
pamphlet in 1912 under the title *The Miners' Next Step*. It set
out a programme of immediate trade union demands and added
the full syndicalist gospel of unceasing hostility towards employers and the ultimate take-over of the mining industry 'in
the interests of the workers'. Syndicalism was not as effective
organizationally as it was intellectually. It widened the horizons
of many militants in such areas as the notion of workers' control,
and forged a link between trade union action and left-wing
politics. Industrial unionism, as syndicalism was sometimes
called, scared conservatives and liberals alike and gave credence
to the newspaper talk of revolutionary conspiracies and anarchy.
Its emphasis on class, especially the open advocacy of class
struggle, indicated a mood in which fundamental social and
political realignments were being looked for. In place of the
image of the respectable, moderate working man was posed the
revolutionary proletarian. That syndicalism was not sufficiently
strong to overturn mainstream trade unionism and labour was
not so obvious in 1910–14 as it is today. In context it served to
heighten a general feeling of unrest, insecurity and, for some,
desperation.

The great French historian, Elie Halévy, remarked on the
simultaneous revolt of the syndicalists, the feminists and the Irish;
and the same theme was developed more dramatically by George
Dangerfield in *The Strange Death of Liberal England*.[10] The
three movements were in no sense allies and they had little in
common beyond a certain shared psychology of revolt. Yet each
in its different way repudiated some aspect of the values of the
Victorian compromise. Industrial conflict, violence and riot were

not in themselves anything new; but the context in which they were experienced after 1906 made them seem somehow less acceptable than formerly. Belief that progress had been made towards a rational basis for a stable, balanced society was jolted. Contemporaries, as always, found it hard to put their finger on exactly what was happening though they sensed that they were living in the midst of important changes. Lloyd George in 1910 foresaw the nature of the years ahead:

> Humanity is like the sea. It is never quite free from movement, but there are periods of comparative calm and others of turbulence and violent disturbance. Everything points to the fact that the storm cone has been hoisted and that we are in for a period of tempests.[11]

The social strife which he had in mind was abruptly ended by the outbreak of war in August 1914. But by then the great Victorian era was well and truly past.

Notes and References
Tables
Further Reading
Index

Notes and References

1 PROGRESS AND POVERTY

(1) Martin J. Wiener, *English Culture and the Decline of the Industrial Spirit, 1850–1980* (Harmondsworth, 1985).

(2) G.M. Young, *Victorian England: Portrait of an Age* (1936), p. 85.

(3) Gilbert and Sullivan opera, *Iolanthe* (1882).

(4) Neal Blewett, 'The Franchise in the United Kingdom, 1885–1918', *Past and Present*, no. 32 (December 1965), p. 31.

(5) Patrick Joyce, *Work, Society and Politics: the Culture of the Factory in Later Victorian England* (1982).

2 THE ELITE

(1) George C. Brodrick, *English Land and English Landlords* (1881), p. 153.

(2) Anthony Trollope, *The Last Chronicle of Barset*, (2 vols., 1867), vol. II, p. 151.

(3) T.H.S. Escott, *England: Its People, Polity and Pursuits* (new edn., 1891), p. 314.

(4) W.L. Guttsman, *The British Political Elite* (1965), p. 78.

(5) Lady Gwendolen Cecil, *Life of Robert, Marquis of Salisbury,* (4 vols. 1921–32), vol. III, pp. 212–13.

(6) Speech at Exeter, 2 February 1892, in *Ibid*, vol. IV, p. 401.

(7) Lady Tweedsmuir, *The Lilac and the Rose* (1952) and quoted in Leonore Davidoff, *The Best Circles* (1973), p. 26.

(8) Frances Evelyn Greville, Countess of Warwick, *Life's Ebb and Flow* (1929), pp. 48–9.

(9) *Ibid*, pp. 190–91.

(10) Siegfried Sassoon, *Memoirs of a Fox-Hunting Man* (1928), in *Complete Memoirs of George Sherston* (1940 edn.), pp. 132, 155.

(11) L.E. Jones, *A Victorian Boyhood* (1955), p. 77.

(12) *Ibid*, pp. 70–71.

(13) Davidoff, *op. cit.*, p. 15.

(14) *Ibid*, p. 43; and p. 32 for the *Punch* illustration.

(15) Greville, *op. cit.*, pp. 37–8.

(16) Vita Sackville-West, *The*

Edwardians (1930),
pp. 87–8.

(17) Ouida, *Under Two Flags*
(1901 edn.), pp. 2, 12.

3 COMFORTABLE
ENGLAND

(1) *see* David Daiches, *Some Late
Victorian Attitudes* (1969),
p. 55.

(2) W.D. Rubinstein (ed), *Wealth
and the Wealthy in the
Modern World* (1980), p. 55.

(3) Beatrice Webb, *My
Apprenticeship* (1926), p. 47;
see also p. 52.

(4) Gwen Raverat, *Period Piece:
A Cambridge Childhood*
(1954), p. 54. The other
quotations are from pp. 55–9,
226–8.

(5) F.M. Mayor, *The Rector's
Daughter* (1924.
Harmondsworth, Penguin
edn., 1978), pp. 16, 38–9.

(6) M. Vivian Hughes, *A London
Family, 1870–1900* (1946),
p. 538.

(7) H.G. Wells, *Experiment in
Autobiography*, (2 vols.,
1934), vol. I, pp. 69–70,
73.

(8) See J.A. Banks, *Prosperity
and Parenthood* (1954),
chapter VI.

(9) Shan F. Bullock, *Robert
Thorne, The Story of a
London Clerk* (1909), p. 22;
and quoted by Richard N.
Price in Geoffrey Crossick
(ed.), *The Lower Middle Class
in Britain, 1870–1914*
(1977), p. 97.

(10) George and Weedon
Grossmith, *The Diary of a
Nobody* (1892. 1947 edn.),
pp. 15–16, 18, 41.

(11) See Hugh McLeod, in
Crossick, *op. cit.*,
p. 61.

(12) C.F.G. Masterman, *The
Condition of England* (1911
edn.), p. 67.

(13) Wells, *op. cit.*, pp. 150–51.

(14) Jerome K. Jerome, *The Idle
Thoughts of an Idle Fellow*
(1886), p. 5.

4 LABOURING LIFE

(1) The title of an investigation
of working-class families in
Lambeth carried out by the
Fabian Women's Group,
1909–13, and published in
Maud Pember Reeves,
*Round About a Pound a
Week* (1913; new edn., ed.
Sally Alexander, 1979).

(2) This and the following four
quotations are from B.
Seebohm Rowntree, *Poverty:
A Study of Town Life* (1901;
new edn., 1903), pp. 150–52,
231–2, 285–6.

(3) S. and B. Webb, *The Minority
Report of the Poor Law
Commission, Part II, The
Unemployed* (1909),
p. 188.

(4) Lady Florence Bell, *At the
Works: a Study of a
Manufacturing Town* (1907;
1911 edn.), p. 118.

(5) See John Burnett, David
Vincent and David Mayall
(eds.), *The Autobiography of*

the Working Class: an
Annotated, Critical
Bibliography, vol.I,
1790–1900 (Brighton,
1984).

(6) Alfred Williams, *Life in a
Railway Factory* (1915; 2nd
edn., 1920). The quotations
are from pp. 86, 136, 217,
251–4.

(7) Allen Clarke, *The Effects
of the Factory System*
(1899; 3rd. edn., 1913),
pp. 41–3.

(8) Joyce, *op. cit.*

(9) Clarke, *op. cit.*, pp. 27–8.

(10) Elizabeth Roberts, *A
Woman's Place: an Oral
History of Working-Class
Women, 1890–1940* (Oxford,
1984), p. 57. The next three
quotations are from pp. 57,
58, 65–6.

(11) Robert Roberts, *The Classic
Slum: Salford Life in the First
Quarter of the Century*
(Manchester, 1971; Penguin
edn., Harmondsworth,
1977), p. 37.

(12) Mrs Murray, a Derbyshire
housewife, at the turn of the
century, quoted in Carol
Adams, *Ordinary Lives: A
Hundred Years Ago* (1982),
pp. 149–151.

(13) C. Henry Warren, *Happy
Countryman* (1939), p. 119,
quoted in Raphael Samuel
(ed.), *Village Life and Labour*
(1975), pp. 45–6.

(14) Thomas Hardy, *Tess of the
D'Urbervilles* (1891), chapter
XLIII.

(15) George Hewins, *The Dillen:
Memories of a Man of*

Stratford-upon-Avon, ed.
Angela Hewins (Oxford,
1981), pp. 65, 80, 84,
96.

5   CERTAINTIES

(1) T.E. Hulme, *Speculations*
(1924), pp. 50–51.

(2) Beatrice Webb, *op. cit.*,
p. 15.

(3) Quoted in Helen Merrell
Lynd, *England in the
Eighteen-Eighties* (New
York, 1945), pp. 69–70.

(4) Webb, pp. 130–31.

(5) Winwood Reade, *The
Martyrdom of Man* (1877
edn.), pp. 513, 515.

(6) Walter Bagehot, *Economic
Studies* (1880), p. 5.

(7) Alfred Marshall, *Principles of
Economics* (8th edn., 1959),
p. 12.

(8) Harold Perkin, *The Origins
of Modern English Society,
1780–1880* (1969).

(9) Robert Giffen, *The Progress
of the Working Classes in the
Last Half Century* (1884),
p. 29.

(10) Charles Booth, *Life and
Labour of the People in
London*, Third Series:
Religious Influences (1902),
vol. II, p. 222.

(11) Booth Collection, London
School of Economics, quoted
in Hugh McLeod, *Class and
Religion in the Late Victorian
City* (1974), p. 141.

(12) Flora Thompson, *Lark Rise
to Candleford* (1945),
pp. 206–7, 215.

(13) *Primitive Methodist Magazine*, 1896, pp. 830–1, quoted in John Briggs and Ian Sellars (eds.), *Victorian Nonconformity* (1973), pp. 35–6.

(14) Eric Gill, *Autobiography* (1940), pp. 60–1, 71.

(15) Jones, *A Victorian Boyhood*, pp. 5–6.

(16) Hughes, *A London Family*, pp. 67, 71–3.

(17) William Kent, *The Testament of a Victorian Youth: An Autobiography* (1938), pp. 289–91.

(18) Booth, *op. cit.*, p. 237.

(19) Robert Tressell, *The Ragged Trousered Philanthropists* (1965 edn.; first published 1914), p. 142.

(20) Thompson, *op. cit.*, p. 215.

6 DOUBTS AND ANXIETIES

(1) Letter to Sir William Hunter, 1873, in Noel Annan, *Leslie Stephen: The Godless Victorian* (New York, 1984 edn.), p. 159.

(2) F.W.H. Myers, *Essays: Modern* (1883), pp. 268–9.

(3) Letter from Benjamin Jowett to Margot Asquith, 11 March 1889, in Margot Asquith, *Autobiography*, (2 vols., 1920–2), pp. 122–3.

(4) Mrs Humphry Ward, *Robert Elsmere* (1912 edn.), p. 558.

(5) E. Lynn Linton, *The True History of Joshua Davidson, Christian and Communist* (1874), pp. 276–9.

(6) James Thomson, *The City of Dreadful Night and other Poems* (1932), p. 30.

(7) I am indebted to Professor F.B. Smith for this reference. *see* his article, 'Three Neglected Masterpieces: Joshua Davidson, The Martyrdom of Man, London – A Pilgrimage', in *Meanjin Quarterly*, March 1973, pp. 114–26.

(8) Reade, *Martyrdom*, pp. 543–44.

(9) Gill, *Autobiography*, pp. 110–11.

(10) Masterman, *Condition of England*, p. 221.

(11) Bell, *op. cit.*, p. 81.

(12) George Bourne [Sturt], *Change in the Village* (1912; repr. 1959), p. 17.

(13) Bell, *op. cit.*, pp. 154–55.

(14) Hannah Mitchell, *The Hard Way Up: the Autobiography of Hannah Mitchell, Suffragette and Rebel* (1968), pp. 101–102.

(15) Margaret Llewelyn Davies (ed.), *Maternity: Letters from Working-Women collected by the Women's Co-operative Guild* (1915; repr. 1978).

(16) C. Stella Davies, *North Country Bred: A Working-Class Family Chronicle* (1963), p. 73.

(17) Thompson, *op. cit.*, p. 79.

(18) Margaret Llewelyn Davies (ed.), *Life as We Have Known It: By Co-operative Working*

Women (1931: repr. 1977).

(19) *Maternity*, p. 110.

7 ENGLAND ARISE!

(1) Ben Turner, *About Myself, 1863–1930* (1930), p. 90.
(2) Edward Carpenter, *My Days and Dreams* (1916), p. 126.
(3) Mitchell, *op. cit.*, pp. 107–8.
(4) Margaret McMillan, *Life of Rachel McMillan* (1927), p. 77.
(5) Philip Snowden, *An Autobiography*, (2 vols., 1934), vol. I, p. 67.
(6) William Morris, *How I became a Socialist* (1896), reprinted from articles in *Justice*, June, 1894.
(7) James E. Thorold Rogers, *Six Centuries of Work and Wages*, (2 vols., 1884), vol. I, p. 14.
(8) William Morris, *A Dream of John Ball* (1888).

8 THE WOMAN QUESTION

(1) Mrs Ellis, *The Daughters of England* (1845), p. 73, and quoted in Martha Vicinus (ed.), *Suffer and Be Still: Women in the Victorian Age* (Bloomington, Indiana, 1972), p. x.
(2) Quoted in David Rubinstein, *Before the Suffragettes* (Brighton, 1986), p. 5.
(3) Ernest Newman, 'Women

and Music', *Free Review*, no. 4 (1895), quoted in *ibid*, p. 7.

(4) Beatrice Webb, Ms. diaries, 28 July 1894, quoted in Barbara Caine, 'Beatrice Webb and the "Woman Question"', *History Workshop Journal*, no. 14 (1982), pp. 37–8.
(5) Quoted in Annan, *Stephen*, p. 130.
(6) Virginia Woolf, *Moments of Being* (1985 edn.), p. 144.
(7) Webb, Ms. diaries, 12 January, 16 March, 1884, quoted in Caine, *op. cit.*, pp. 26–7.
(8) P. Gaskell, *The Manufacturing Population of England* (1833), p. 80.
(9) Jill Liddington and Jill Norris, *One Hand Tied Behind Us* (1978), p. 31.
(10) Webb, *Apprenticeship*, p. 321.
(11) Minutes, T.U.C., 1877, quoted in Marian Ramelson, *The Petticoat Rebellion* (1967), p. 103.
(12) 'The Woman at Work', *Englishwoman's Review*, vol. 35 (1904), quoted in Rubinstein, *op. cit.*, pp. 72–3.
(13) Margaret Cole, *Growing Up Into Revolution* (1949), pp. 37–8.
(14) Louisa Twining, *Workhouses and Pauperism* (1898), p. 125.
(15) Davies (ed.), *Life as We Have Known It*, pp. 129–31.
(16) John Stuart Mill, *The Subjection of Women* (1983 edn.), pp. 29–30, 35–6, 38–9, 91–2, 96–7.

(17) Title of the early feminist classic (1825) written by William Thompson.

(18) Roger Fulford, *Votes for Women* (1958), p. 79.

(19) Quoted in Brian Harrison, *Separate Spheres* (1978), p. 116.

(20) Quoted in Fulford, *op. cit.*, p. 65.

(21) Thomas Hardy, *Tess of the D'Urbervilles* (5th and later edns.), preface, p. viii.

(22) *New Review* (1894), p. 681, in Michael Millgate, *Thomas Hardy: A Biography* (Oxford, 1982), p. 357.

(23) H.G. Wells, *The New Machiavelli* (1911), pp. 258, 400.

(24) Grant Allen, *The Women Who Did* (1906 edn.), pp. 7, 39, 171.

(25) Olive Schreiner, *The Story of an African Farm* (1892 edn.), pp. 173–4, 180, 228.

9 THE CONDITION OF THE PEOPLE

(1) Andrew Mearns, *The Bitter Cry of Outcast London*, 1883, ed. Anthony S. Wohl (Leicester, 1970), pp. 55–6.

(2) Booth, *Life and Labour*, vol. I, pp. 35, 62; vol. II, p. 21, in E.P. Hennock, 'Poverty and social theory in England: the experience of the eighteen-eighties', *Social History*, I (1976), p. 73.

(3) Rowntree, *Poverty*, pp. 295–6. The following quotations are from pp. 297, 299, 304.

(4) Webb, *Apprenticeship*. This and the following quotations are from Chapter IV, pp. 180, 195, 207–8.

(5) General [William] Booth, *In Darkest England and the Way Out* (1890), p. 4.

(6) *Times Weekly Edition*, 12 February 1886, quoted in E.J. Hobsbawm (ed.), *Labour's Turning Point* (1948), p. 138.

(7) Wells, *op. cit.*, p. 93.

(8) Arthur Conan Doyle, 'The Naval Treaty', *Memoirs of Sherlock Holmes* (1926 edn.), p. 208, quoted in John Hurt, *Education in Evolution* (1971), p. 223.

(9) G.A.N. Lowndes, *The Silent Social Revolution* (1937), p. 17.

(10) R.H. Tawney, *Education, the Socialist Policy* (1924), p. 22, quoted in Brian Simon, *Education and the Labour Movement, 1870–1920* (1965), p. 119.

(11) Phil Gardner, *The Lost Elementary Schools of Victorian England* (1984), p. 188, to which I am much indebted.

10 THE END OF EQUIPOISE

(1) *see* W.L. Burn, *The Age of Equipoise* (1964), pp. 330–1.

(2) Holbrook Jackson, *The Eighteen Nineties* (1913. Paperback edn., 1939), p. 22.

(3) Keith Hutchison, *The Decline*

and Fall of British
Capitalism (1951), p. 28.

(4) Escott, *op. cit.*, p. 5.

(5) The Kipling quotations in the
following paragraphs are
from *Barrack-Room Ballads*
(1892) and *The Five Nations*
(1903).

(6) John Springhall, *Youth,
Empire and Society* (1977),
p. 57.

(7) Robert Roberts, *The Classic
Slum* (1971. Paperback edn.,
1977), pp. 142–3.

(8) E. Sylvia Pankhurst, *The
Suffragette Movement*
(1935), pp. 443–4.

(9) Andrew Rosen, *Rise
Up, Women!* (1974),
pp. 176–7.

(10) See Elie Halévy, *A History of
the English People in the
Nineteenth Century*, vol VI,
Part III (1961 edn.); and
George Dangerfield, *The
Strange Death of Liberal
England* (1935, and later
edns.).

(11) E.H. Phelps Brown, *The
Growth of British Industrial
Relations* (1959),
p. xxxv.

Tables

1   Population (Great Britain), 1871–1911

	Population (Millions)	Percentage increase in previous decade
1871	26.07	
1881	29.71	14.0
1891	33.03	11.2
1901	37.00	12.0
1911	40.83	10.4

From: B. R. Mitchell and P. Deane, *Abstract of British Historical Statistics* (1962)

2   Birth and Death Rates (England and Wales), 1871–1915

	Average annual birth-rate (per 1000 population)	Average annual death-rate (per 1000 population)
1871–75	35.7	22.0
1876–80	35.4	20.8
1881–85	33.5	19.4
1886–90	31.4	18.9
1891–95	30.5	18.7
1896–1900	29.3	17.7
1901–05	28.2	16.1
1906–10	26.3	14.7
1911–15	23.6	14.3

From: *Census of England and Wales, 1921, Preliminary Report*

Tables

3 Size of Family in Relation to Date of First Marriage Great Britain, Marriages under 45 Years of Age, of 1870–1915

Live births per woman	Date of first marriage		
	1870–9	1900–9	1915
	Number of women per 1,000 with specified numbers of live births		
0	83	113	150
1	53	148	212
2	72	187	235
3, 4	181	277	254
5, 6	189	147	94
7, 8, 9	245	99	45
10 or more	177	29	10
Total	1000	1000	1000

From: A. M. Carr-Saunders, D. Caradog Jones and C. A. Moser *A Survey of Social Conditions in England and Wales* (1965), reproduced by kind permission of Oxford University Press

4 Average Ages at Marriage, Childbearing and Death, England and Wales, 1850–1950

	Year of birth					
	1850	1870	1890	1910	1930	1950
1. First marriage						
Men	27	27	28	27	26	24
Women	26	26	26	25	24	22
2. Birth of first child						
Men	29	29	30	29	28	26
Women	28	28	28	27	26	24
3. Birth of last child						
Men	37	36	35	32	30	28
Women	36	35	33	30	28	26
4. Spouse's death						
Men	56	60	62	64	66	68
Women	55	58	61	63	65	67
5. Own death as widow or widower						
Men	75	77	79	80	81	82
Women	75	79	81	81	82	83

From: Michael Young and Peter Willmott, *The Symmetrical Family* (1973), reprinted by kind permission of the publishers, Routledge and Kegan Paul

5 Changes in the life cycle of women (England and Wales), 1850–1950

	Date of birth					
	1850	1870	1890	1910	1930	1950
Average age at (first) marriage	26	26	26	25	24	22
Average age at birth of first child	28	28	28	27	26	24
Average age when last child aged 11	47	46	44	41	39	37

From: Young and Willmott, op. cit.

6 Average number of children in 1911 according to social class

Upper and Middle Class	2.77
Textile Workers	3.19
Skilled Workers	3.53
Semi-Skilled Workers	3.59
Unskilled Workers	3.92
Agricultural Workers	3.99
Miners	4.33

From: E. H. Hunt, *British Labour History, 1815–1914* (1981)

7 Urban Population, 1871–1901

	Numbers of towns in England and Wales with population over 50,000 in 1871 and 1901	
	1871	1901
Number of towns with population over 50,000	37	75
Population of 1 million and under 5 million	1(London)	1 (London)
700,000 and under 1 million	–	–
500,000 and under 700,000	–	3 (Liverpool) (Manchester) (Birmingham)
300,000 and under 500,000	3	3 (Leeds) (Sheffield) (Bristol)
200,000 and under 300,000	2	7
100,000 and under 200,000	8	19
50,000 and under 100,000	23	42
Total population in these towns (000's omitted)	8,293	14,507
Population of England and Wales (000's omitted)	22,712	32,528
Percentage of total population living in towns of 50,000 and over	36.5%	44.6%

From: David C. Marsh, *The Changing Social Structure of England and Wales* (1965), reprinted by kind permission of the publishers, Routledge and Kegan Paul

Tables

8 National Income

Year	Net national income at current prices		Net national income at 1900 prices	
	Total (£m.)	Per head (£)	Total (£m.)	Per head (£)
1870	936	29.9	774	24.8
1875	1,113	33.9	912	27.8
1880	1,076	31.1	932	26.9
1885	1,115	31.0	1,115	31.0
1890	1,385	36.9	1,416	37.8
1895	1,447	36.9	1,587	40.5
1900	1,750	42.5	1,750	42.5
1905	1,776	41.3	1,757	40.9
1910	1,984	44.2	1,881	41.9
1915	2,591	56.3	1,916	41.7

From: B. R. Mitchell and P. Deane, *Abstract of British Historical Statistics* (1962)

9 Occupations of males and females aged 10 years and over in England and Wales at the Census of 1881 and 1901

	Numbers in 000's			
Occupations	*Males*		*Females*	
	1881	1901	1881	1901
1. General and local government	97	172	7	26
2. Defence	107	168	–	–
3. Professional	231	312	188	295
4. Domestic, etc	88	141	1,519	1,691
5. Commercial	308	531	8	60
6. Conveyance of men, goods, etc	782	1,248	11	19
7. Agriculture	1,288	1,159	64	58
8. Fishing	29	24	(0.294)	(0.166)
9. In mines, etc	521	800	8	5
10. Metals, machines, etc	775	1,167	38	61
11. Precious metals, jewels, etc	68	134	10	19
12. Building, etc	763	1,126	2	2
13. Wood, etc	162	233	18	25
14. Brick, etc	104	142	24	33
15. Chemicals, etc	62	102	8	27
16. Skins, etc	66	80	15	25
17. Paper, etc	116	188	42	91
18. Textiles	482	492	613	663
19. Dress	346	415	606	712
20. Food, etc	550	774	161	299
21. Gas, water, etc	25	68	(0.182)	(0.114)
22. Other, etc	788	681	60	61
23. Without, etc	1,555	1,977	6,590	9,018
Total	9,313	12,134	9,992	13,190

From: David C. Marsh, op. cit.

Tables

10 Agricultural Change, 1870–1914

England and Wales: Acreage under various types of crops and grass, and numbers of livestock, 1870–1914

	1870	1880	1890	1900	1910	1914
Total cultivated area (acres)	25,957,035	27,363,782	27,872,335	27,538,130	27,292,588	27,114,004
Permanent Pasture (acres)	11,107,860	13,267,606	14,792,439	15,320,922	15,972,144	16,115,750
Total Arable Land (acres)	14,849,175	14,096,176	13,079,896	12,217,208	11,320,444	10,998,254
Total Green Crops (acres)	2,890,029	2,779,207	2,647,754	2,554,867	2,390,920	2,403,496
Total Corn Crops (acres)	8,123,780	7,471,815	6,715,920	6,076,759	5,826,063	5,758,651
Wheat (acres)	3,374,901	2,835,462	2,324,363	1,796,210	1,756,057	1,807,498
Barley (acres)	2,127,597	2,203,321	1,895,386	1,750,070	1,537,061	1,504,771
Oats (acres)	1,743,704	1,759,651	1,889,352	2,076,960	2,062,824	1,929,626
Horses	1,093,838	1,227,167	1,242,893	1,305,605	1,341,809	1,399,547
Cattle	4,361,883	4,812,760	5,322,756	5,607,084	5,866,568	5,877,944
Sheep	21,646,735	19,546,962	19,910,998	19,277,229	19,958,299	17,259,694
Pigs	2,012,448	1,879,917	2,613,935	2,249,519	2,216,599	2,481,481

From: W. Ashworth, *An Economic History of England, 1870–1939* (1960)

Further Reading

These suggestions for further reading are limited to books which are fairly easily available in libraries and bookshops, including second-hand bookshops which should be haunted regularly by all would-be Victorianists. Many of the books contain full bibliographies. The place of publication is London unless shown otherwise.

GENERAL

It is essential to set the period covered by this study in the wider context of nineteenth century history, not least because many of the themes pre-dated 1875–1901. For this purpose the following can be recommended: Edward Royle, *Modern Britain: A Social History, 1750–1985* (1987); F.M.L. Thompson, *The Rise of Respectable Society: A Social History of Victorian Britain, 1830–1900* (1988); Donald Read, *England 1868–1914: the Age of Urban Democracy* (1985); Henry Pelling, *Modern Britain, 1885–1955* (1960). All these contain many themes not included in this book. For the political history R.C.K. Ensor, *England, 1870–1914* (first published in the Oxford History of England series in 1936) is the best starting point; and the later part of G.M. Young's *Victorian England: Portrait of an Age* (1936; 2nd edn., 1953) has many thoughtful insights. The wider European dimension is provided in E.J. Hobsbawm, *The Age of Empire, 1875–1914* (1987). The results of recent research are often first published as articles in such journals as *Past and Present, History Workshop, International Review of Social History, Social History, English Historical Review, Victorian Studies*.

THE VICTORIAN ACHIEVEMENT

Since most of us have a hankering after the illusory certainty of statistics, reassurance may be found most conveniently in B.R. Mitchell and Phyllis Deane, *Abstract of British Historical Statistics* (Cambridge, 1962); David C. Marsh, *The Changing Social Structure of England and Wales, 1871–1961* (1965); and A.M. Carr-Saunders, D. Caradog Jones and C.A. Moser, *A Survey of Social Conditions in England and Wales* (Oxford, 1965). E.H. Hunt, *British Labour History, 1815–1914* (1981) is broader than its title might suggest and is a most valuable source for many aspects of working-class life. The relevant chapters of any good economic history of the nineteenth century will be found useful, e.g. Peter Mathias, *The First Industrial Nation: an Economic History of Britain, 1700–1914* (1969); E.J. Hobsbawm, *Industry and Empire: An Economic History of Britain since 1750* (1969); François Crouzet, *The Victorian Economy* (1982); and, for more detail, Sidney Pollard, *Britain's Prime and Britain's Decline: The British Economy, 1870–1914* (1989). On the Great Depression one should consult S.B. Saul, *The Myth of the Great Depression, 1873–1896* (1969) in the Studies in Economic History series, which has a good bibliography. For urbanism the two superb volumes of H.J. Dyos and Michael Wolff (eds.), *The Victorian City: Images and Realities* (1973) are compulsory reading, as also are the two companion volumes for the rural world, G.E. Mingay (ed.), *The Victorian Countryside* (1981). A challenging book which sparked off a lively controversy on a most perplexing topic is Martin J. Wiener, *English Culture and the Decline of the Industrial Spirit, 1850–1980* (1985). For the social implications of demographic change the work of J.A. Banks and Olive Banks is central. See in particular the seminal study by J.A. Banks, *Prosperity and Parenthood: A Study of Family Planning among the Victorian Middle Classes* (1954); and his later *Victorian Values* (1981); also J.A. and Olive Banks, *Feminism and Family Planning in Victorian England* (Liverpool, 1964). Other important works in this field are Angus McLaren, *Birth Control in Nineteenth-Century England* (1978); and Richard Allen Soloway, *Birth Control and the Population Question in England, 1877–1930* (Chapel Hill, North Carolina, 1982). This study does not deal with politics in any detail but the social implications of the 1867 and 1884 Reform Acts are brought out in the two introductory pamphlets, H.J. Hanham, *The Reformed Electoral System in Great Britain, 1832–1914*, (Historical Association, 1968); and F.B. Smith, *British Parliamentary Reform since 1867* (1971). An important study of the social roots of politics is Patrick Joyce, *Work, Society and Politics: The Culture of the Factory in Later Victorian England* (1982).

SOCIAL STRUCTURE

It is a revealing comment on modern social historians that they have shown far less interest in the Victorian aristocracy than in the middle and working classes. The later chapters of F.M.L. Thompson, *English Landed Society in the Nineteenth Century* (1963), although written more than twenty-five years ago, are still the best starting point for a study of the landed classes; but they can now be supplemented with J.V.

Further Reading

Beckett, *The Aristocracy in England, 1660–1914* (Oxford, 1986). An excellent sociological approach to the late Victorian aristocratic elite is Leonore Davidoff, *The Best Circles: Society, Etiquette and the Season* (1973; new edn., 1986). Keith Middlemas, *Pursuit of Pleasure: High Society in the 1900s* (1977), although primarily concerned with the 1900s has much to say that is relevant to the 1880s and 1890s. First-hand sources are the memoirs of members of the aristocracy and gentry such as those quoted in the footnotes to Chapter Two; and others are listed in Davidoff and Middlemas. Vita Sackville-West's novel, *The Edwardians* (1930) is a wonderful encapsulation of the gentlemanly pattern of life in the late Victorian and Edwardian era.

The middle classes have been better served. W.D. Rubinstein's essay in W.D. Rubinstein (ed.), *Wealth and the Wealthy in the Modern World* (1980) is important as showing the power of finance and the City in British life. A most useful collection of essays on the lower middle class is Geoffrey Crossick (ed.), *The Lower Middle Class in Britain, 1870–1914* (1977). A case-study of a middle-class Victorian suburb is H.J. Dyos, *Victorian Suburb: A Study of the Growth of Camberwell* (Leicester, 1961). But it is from the wealth of primary sources that one can best appreciate middle-class life. The middle classes were nothing if not articulate and their memoirs are goldmines of eminently readable material. One of the best of these is Beatrice Webb, *My Apprenticeship* (1926) which is wonderfully informative on many different aspects of social life. In greater detail we also have *The Diary of Beatrice Webb*, eds. Norman and Jeanne MacKenzie, (vol. I 1873–92; vol. II 1892–1905, 1986). Another delightful series of reminiscences is Gwen Raverat, *Period Piece: A Cambridge Childhood* (1954); and the well-known trilogy, by Flora Thompson, *Lark Rise to Candleford* (1945) has many vivid flashes of social insight. M. Vivian Hughes, *A London Family, 1870–1900* (1946) is especially useful for middle-class girls' education; and H.G. Wells, *Experiment in Autobiography*, (2 vols. 1934) reinforces the picture of lower middle-class life so brilliantly portrayed in his novels. Middle-class hopes and fears are well brought out in C.F.G. Masterman's *The Condition of England* (1909). And of course we must not forget that bible of Victorian domesticity, Mrs Isabella Beeton's *Book of Household Management* (1861) which was continuously and fully in print throughout the period (before degenerating into a mere collection of recipes later). Perhaps the most painless way of learning about the late Victorians is through their novels. H.G. Wells and Arnold Bennett are at their best when describing life among the lower middle classes, as also are George Gissing and George Moore. There are also many forgotten late-nineteenth-century novels and stories, like W. Pett Ridge's *Outside the Radius: Stories of a London Suburb* (1899), whose discovery is one of the delights of book hunting. Late Victorian humour is perhaps something of an acquired taste; but if one can put up with a certain archness and some dreadful puns, then Jerome K. Jerome's *Three Men in a Boat* (1889) and *The Idle Thoughts of an Idle Fellow* (1886) are to be recommended. And there is one minor classic, George and Weedon Grossmith's *The Diary of a Nobody* (1892) which never fails to amuse.

The economic and social framework of working-class life is set out in several of the general histories mentioned above, e.g. Hunt, Hobsbawm, Dyos and Wolf, Mingay. To these should be added two books by John Burnett, *Plenty and Want: A Social History of Diet in England from 1815 to the Present Day* (1968); and *A History of the Cost of Living* (1969). For urban working-class life Standish Meacham, *A Life Apart: The English Working Class, 1890–1914* (1977) is excellent and has a useful short bibliography. Raphael Samuel (ed.), *Miners, Quarrymen and Saltworkers* (1977) deals with the work experience of three non-factory groups of workers. Books by sympathetic middle-class investigators which are much quoted by historians are B. Seebohm Rowntree, *Poverty: A Study of Town Life* (1901); and Lady Florence Bell, *At the Works: A Study of a Manufacturing Town* (1907). An unusually fine account of heavy manual labour is the book by a self-educated Wiltshire hammerman, Alfred Williams, *Life in a Railway Factory* (1915; new edn., 1986). On rural conditions see Raphael Samuel (ed.), *Village Life and Labour* (1975); Pamela Horn, *Labouring Life in the Victorian Countryside* (Dublin, 1976); and Alun Howkins, *Poor Labouring Men: Rural Radicalism in Norfolk, 1870–1923* (1985). Rural skills are recaptured in the works of George Ewart Evans, based on oral evidence: *Ask the Fellows Who Cut the Hay* (1965); *The Farm and the Village* (1969); *Tools of their Trades: An Oral History of Men at Work, c.1900* (1970). Change in the countryside is sensitively chronicled by George Sturt [Bourne] in *The Bettesworth Book* (1901; new edn. 1978); *Memoirs of a Surrey Labourer* (1907; repr. 1930); *Change in the Village* (1912; new edn. 1969); *The Wheelwright's Shop* (Cambridge, 1923; new edn. 1963). Thomas Hardy's novels offer a unique experience of rural life in southern England. A generation ago it was widely held that few working people left any records; but recent research has uncovered a rich haul of their autobiographies, now recorded and annotated in John Burnett, David Vincent and David Mayall (eds.), *The Autobiography of the Working Class*, 3 vols. (vol.1: 1790–1900; vol.2: 1900–45; vol.3: Supplement) (Brighton, 1984–9). Two very useful selections are John Burnett (ed.), *Useful Toil: Autobiographies of Working People from the 1820s to the 1920s* (1976); and *Destiny Obscure: Autobiographies of Childhood, Education and Family from the 1820s to the 1920s* (1982).

Further Reading

Of the many autobiographies which might be mentioned, the following are each in their way representative of different working-class traditions: C. Stella Davies, *North Country Bred: A Working-Class Family Chronicle* (1963); and George Hewins, *The Dillen: Memories of a Man of Stratford-upon-Avon*, ed. Angela Hewins (Oxford, 1981). Domestic servants are admirably brought to life in Pamela Horn, *The Rise and Fall of the Victorian Servant* (Gloucester, 1986); and Elizabeth Roberts, *A Woman's Place: An Oral History of Working-Class Women, 1890–1940* (Oxford, 1984) has much oral testimony from the 1890s. This is probably also the place to mention the one genuinely proletarian novel of the period: Robert Tressell, *The Ragged Trousered Philanthropists* (1965 edn.) which drew upon the author's experiences as a housepainter in Hastings, Sussex, about 1902.

PERCEPTIONS AND VALUES

Ways of seeing are best explored through autobiographies and memoirs such as those of Beatrice Webb mentioned earlier. But the value of these will be much enhanced by some knowledge of the religious background which underpinned Victorian morality. Here Owen Chadwick, *The Victorian Church, Part II 1880–1901* (1987) is absolutely indispensable. Hugh McLeod, *Class and Religion in the Late Victorian City* (1974) will also be found extremely useful. For a larger perspective see A.D. Gilbert, *Religion and Society in Industrial England: Church, Chapel and Social Change, 1740–1914* (1976); and for statistics of church membership one should consult Robert Currie, Alan Gilbert and Lee Horsley, *Churches and Churchgoers: Patterns of Church Growth in the British Isles since 1700* (Oxford, 1977). Rowntree's *Poverty* has a church census carried out in 1901; and the seven volumes of the Third Series (Religious Influences) of Charles Booth, *Life and Labour of the People in London* (1902) contain a mass of information, including many fascinating case histories. The later chapters in E.R. Wickham, *Church and People in an Industrial City* (1957) cover the religious situation in late Victorian Sheffield; and E.T. Davies, *Religion in the Industrial Revolution in South Wales* (Cardiff, 1965) is a little gem which despite its title contains material relevant to our period. The social context of religious organizations is explored through a case study of Reading c.1890–1914 in Stephen Yeo, *Religion and Voluntary Organisations in Crisis* (1976).

The problems of religious doubt come up, either directly or indirectly, in most of the above works. But the best introduction to Victorian doubt is Noel Annan's brilliant biographical study of the great Victorian agnostic, *Leslie Stephen: The Godless Victorian* (1984). Mrs Humphry

Ward's *Robert Elsmere* (1888) should definitely be read despite its length and occasional turgidity; and there are still plenty of copies about. Shorter and more readable are the novels of Mark Rutherford [William Hale White], *The Autobiography of Mark Rutherford* (1881); *Mark Rutherford's Deliverance* (1885); and *The Revolution in Tanner's Lane* (1887), which deal with the central questions of the Victorian crisis of faith. On this see also David Daiches, *Some Late Victorian Attitudes* (1969).

The anxieties of working people are often reflected in their autobiographies. In addition to those already cited the following reprints are recommended: Margaret Llewellyn Davies (ed.), *Life As We Have Known It, by Co-operative Working Women* (1931; new edn. 1977); Margaret Llewellyn Davies (ed.), *Maternity: Letters from Working-Women collected by the Women's Co-operative Guild* (1915; new edn. 1978); Maud Pember Reeves, *Round About a Pound a Week* (1913; new edn. 1979); Hannah Mitchell, *The Hard Way Up*, ed. Geoffrey Mitchell (1968). As on other topics there is much to be learned from Flora Thompson's *Lark Rise*; but a note of caution about the reliability of this book as an historical source and the sugary nature of some later editions is perhaps in order – see the important article by Barbara English in *Victorian Studies*, vol. xxix (1985), pp. 7–34. On the all-important topic of ordinary people's views about their health very little is known. But a start may be made with F.B. Smith, *The People's Health, 1830–1910* (1979), on which I have relied heavily.

PROCESSES OF CHANGE

The most comprehensive attempt by a sociologist to explain the social changes of the late nineteenth century is Helen Merrell Lynd, *England in the Eighteen-Eighties: Toward a Social Basis for Freedom* (New York, 1945). The book now smells strongly of the 1930s and the New Deal era; but it is still worth looking at – not for the material, which is mostly from secondary sources, but for the way in which it approaches the problem.

The labour movement has been well served by its historians. A start may be made with two books by Henry Pelling, *The Origins of the Labour Party, 1880–1900* (Oxford, 1966); and *A History of British Trade Unionism* (1963). The standard history of trade unionism for this period is H.A. Clegg, Alan Fox and A.F. Thompson, *A History of British Trade Unions since 1889, vol. i, 1889–1910* (Oxford, 1964). Also useful are Alan Fox, *History and Heritage: The Social Origins of the British Industrial Relations System* (1985); Richard Price, *Labour in British Society: An Interpretative History* (1986); Kenneth D. Brown, *The*

Further Reading

English Labour Movement, 1700–1951 (Dublin, 1982); Charles More, *Skill and the English Working Class, 1870–1914* (1980). Bibliographies and autobiographies of Labour leaders are plentiful and the main titles are referred to in the above histories. Likewise the early socialists were extremely articulate and have left plenty about themselves and their views. A good introduction to the various groups and theories are the two books by Stanley Pierson, *Marxism and the Origins of British Socialism* (Ithaca, N.Y., 1973) and *British Socialists: The Journey from Fantasy to Politics* (Cambridge, Mass., 1979). Useful collections of documents are: E.J. Hobsbawm (ed.), *Labour's Turning Point, 1880–1900* (1948); and Henry Pelling (ed.), *The Challenge of Socialism* (1954). An essential work of reference is Joyce M. Bellamy and John Saville (eds.), *Dictionary of Labour Biography*, 8 vols. (1972–87). For a selection of essays on more specialized aspects of labour history one should sample E.J. Hobsbawm, *Labouring Men: Studies in the History of Labour* (1964); and his later *Worlds of Labour: Further Studies in the History of Labour* (1984). An important revisionist essay on 'Working-class culture and working-class politics in London, 1870–1900: Notes on the remaking of a working class' is in Gareth Stedman Jones, *Languages of Class* (Cambridge, 1983). The W.E.A. and adult education are covered in J.F.C. Harrison, *Learning and Living, 1790 – 1960* (1961) which has further bibliographical references.

The bibliography of women's history and feminism is fast approaching the dimensions of labour historiography, and it is easy to get lost in the thickets of controversy, some of which are devoid of historical content. A very good introduction is Jane Lewis, *Women in England, 1870–1950: Sexual Divisions and Social Change* (Brighton, 1984); and for the 1890s David Rubinstein, *Before the Suffragettes: Women's Emancipation in the 1890s* (Brighton, 1986). The essays in Martha Vicinus (ed.), *Suffer and Be Still* (Bloomington, Ind., 1972) are very useful and the book has a good bibliography by S. Barbara Kanner. All of the following contribute something to women's history in our period though usually extending before and beyond it: Patricia Branca, *Silent Sisterhood: Middle Class Women in the Victorian Home* (1975); Sara Delamont and Lorna Duffin (eds.), *The Nineteenth-Century Woman: Her Cultural and Physical World* (1978); Angela V. John, *By the Sweat of their Brow: Women Workers at Victorian Coal Mines* (1980). Women's participation in public life is examined in Patricia Hollis, *Women in English Local Government, 1865–1914* (Oxford, 1987); and Patricia Hollis (ed.), *Women in Public: The Women's Movement, 1850–1900* (1979). For the family see Anthony S. Wohl (ed.), *The Victorian Family: Structure and Stresses* (1978); and Theresa M. McBride, *The Domestic Revolution: The Modernisation of Household Service in England and France,*

251

1820–1920 (1976). The unusual relationship between a Victorian middle-class professional man and a working-class woman whom he secretly married is told in Derek Hudson, *Munby: Man of Two Worlds: The Life and Diaries of Arthur J. Munby, 1828–1910* (1972). The suffrage campaign has been well documented by participants and feminists. Roger Fulford, *Votes for Women: The Story of a Struggle* (1958) is a plain, unpretentious narrative account with a convenient biographical index. Marian Ramelson, *The Petticoat Rebellion: A Century of Struggle for Women's Rights* (1967) is written from a socialist rather than feminist angle. See also Constance Rover, *Women's Suffrage and Party Politics in Britain, 1866–1914* (1967); Andrew Rosen, *Rise Up, Women!: The Militant Campaign of the Women's Social and Political Union, 1903–1914* (1974); S.S. Holton, *Feminism and Democracy: Women's Suffrage and Reform Politics in Britain, 1900–1918* (Cambridge, 1986). The working-class suffragists of Lancashire are at the centre of Jill Liddington and Jill Norris, *One Hand Tied Behind Us: The Rise of the Women's Suffrage Movement* (1978). Opposition to women's suffrage (the 'Antis') is skilfully handled in Brian Harrison, *Separate Spheres: The Opposition to Women's Suffrage in Britain* (1978). A comprehensive study which sets the British movement in a wider context is Richard J. Evans, *The Feminists: Women's Emancipation Movements in Europe, America and Australasia, 1840–1920* (1977). Two histories by participants are particularly worth noting: E. Sylvia Pankhurst, *The Suffragette Movement* (1977 edn.); and R. Strachey, *The Cause* (1978 edn.).

For the social explorers there is an anthology which can serve as an introduction: Peter Keating (ed.), *Into Unknown England, 1866–1913* (1978). Mearns' pamphlet has been reprinted with an introduction by Anthony S. Wohl: Andrew Mearns, *The Bitter Cry of Outcast London*, ed. Anthony S. Wohl (Leicester, 1970). The seventeen volumes of Charles Booth's *Life and Labour of the People in London* (1902) can usually be found in a good municipal, polytechnic or university library, though they may have to be fetched out of storage. Even so, they are well worth pursuing, because a little browsing reveals a wealth of fascinating detail. Seebohm Rowntree's *Poverty: A Study of Town Life* (1901) is of course much more concise; and there is relevant material in Asa Briggs, *Social Thought and Social Action: A Study of the Work of Seebohm Rowntree, 1871–1954* (1961). For Toynbee Hall see Asa Briggs and Anne Macartney, *Toynbee Hall: The First Hundred Years* (1984); and Standish Meacham, *Toynbee Hall and Social Reform: The Search for Community* (New Haven, Conn., 1987). An important book is Gareth Stedman Jones, *Outcast London: A Study in the Relationship between Classes in Victorian Society* (Oxford, 1971). The standard authority on the origins of the welfare state is Bentley B. Gilbert, *The Evolution of National Insurance in Great Britain: The Origins of the Welfare State* (1966).

Histories of education tend to be rather uninspiring; but J.S. Hurt, *Elementary Schooling and the Working Classes, 1860–1918* (1979); and P.W. Musgrave, *Society and Education in England since 1800* (1968) provide a good introduction. A minor classic is G.A.N. Lowndes, *The Silent Social Revolution: An Account of the Expansion of Public Education in England and Wales, 1895–1935* (1937; and later reprints); and there is an excellent chapter on the London School Board by David Rubinstein in Phillip McCann (ed.), *Popular Education and Socialization in the Nineteenth Century* (1977). First-hand accounts of childhood and schooling are provided in Robert Roberts' two books: *The Classic Slum* (1977); and *A Ragged Schooling* (1978); as well as in Burnett, *Destiny Obscure*, already cited. For working-class private schools see Phil Gardner, *The Lost Elementary Schools of Victorian England* (1984); and for a challenging interpretation of working-class childhood experiences, Stephen Humphries, *Hooligans or Rebels?: An Oral History of Working-Class Childhood and Youth, 1889–1939* (Oxford, 1984). On the public schools there is much of interest in T.W. Bamford, *Rise of the Public Schools: A Study of Boys' Public Boarding Schools in England and Wales from 1837 to the Present Day* (1967).

EPILOGUE

The mood of *fin de siècle* is faithfully conveyed in Holbrook Jackson, *The Eighteen Nineties* (1913; later paperback edns.). George Dangerfield's brilliant monograph, *The Strange Death of Liberal England* (1935) is eminently readable, though few historians nowadays would be happy to endorse his interpretation wholeheartedly. A more sober analysis can be found in volume VI of Elie Halévy's *A History of the English People in the Nineteenth Century: The Rule of Democracy, 1905–1914* (1961). Simon Nowell-Smith (ed.), *Edwardian England, 1901–1914* (1964) is a collection of essays on political, economic and cultural aspects of the period by an older generation of distinguished scholars. W. Macqueen-Pope, *Twenty Shillings in the Pound* (1949) is a nostalgic but informative upper-middle class view of the 'golden age' of 1890–1914. The works of Rudyard Kipling are still in print and one might usefully begin with *Barrack-Room Ballads* (1892); *The Jungle Books* (1894, 1895); *The Light that Failed* (1890); and *Kim* (1901). See also Kipling's autobiography, *Something of Myself* (1937); and the standard biography, Charles Carrington, *Rudyard Kipling: His Life and Work* (1986 edn.). On the Boy Scouts and imperialism see John Springhall, *Youth, Empire and Society: British Youth Movements, 1883–1940* (1977). For some of the other social aspects of imperialism see Richard Price, *An Imperial War and the British Working Class: Working-Class Attitudes and Reactions to the Boer War, 1899–1902* (1972); and Bernard Semmel, *Imperialism and Social Reform: English Social-Imperial Thought, 1895–1914* (1960). The Edwardian period is just within the range of oral history and Paul Thompson, *The Edwardians* (1977) should not be missed.

Index

Notes and References and Further Reading are not included in the index.

Index

Index

medical practitioners, 167
menus, 54, 69–71
Merrie England, 148–9
Methodism, 103, 192; *see also* Primitive Methodists
middle class, 14, 16, 19, 42, chap. 3 *passim*; and economic liberalism, 96; education, 203; fear of residuum, 196–9; and imperialism, 211; lower, 59–66; reaction to poverty, 190; and religion, 102, 104–5, 113–14; and social problems, 199; standards and values, 75; stereotype of woman, 160; and suffragettes, 222–3; women, chap. 8 *passim*
Middlesbrough, 75, 97, 134, 167
Midlands, 103
militancy, Irish, 218–19; trade union, 223–5; women's, 176, 219–23
Mill, John Stuart, 22; *Political Economy*, 99; *Subjection of Women*, 174–5
millinery trade, 83–5
Millthorpe, 151
Milner, Alfred (later Viscount), 219
Milton, John, 57
Miners' Next Step, 225
miracles, 121, 122, 124
Mitchell, Hannah, 135, 146, 167, 169
morality, 123–5, 130
Morgan, Campbell, 104
Morris, William, 65, 129, 142, 145, 151, 153–4, 156, 197; *News from Nowhere*, 154
Morrison, Charles, 50
mortality, childbirth, 134–5; infant, 15
music halls, 155, 169, 214
Myers, F. W. H., 123–4

national efficiency, 133
national income, 21
National Liberal Federation, 23
National Society, 199–200
National Society for Women's

Suffrage, 175, 179
National Union of Conservative and Constitutional Associations, 23
National Union of Women's Suffrage Societies, 179
National Volunteers, 219
New Unionism, 142, 151, 209
New Woman, 180–3, 209
New Zealand, 69
Newcastle, 15
Newman, Ernest, 159
Newman, John Henry, 103
Newnham College, 54
Nineteenth Century, 164, 178
noblesse oblige, 42
Nonconformity, 24, 103, 121; and education, 199–200; world of, 115–16
Norfolk, 86, 111
Northampton, 190
Norwich, 197
Nottingham, 15
nouveaux riches, 34

old age, 67, 74, 78, 136–8; pensions, 191; and religion, 116–17
Old Dissent, 103
Oldham, 79–81
Omar Khayyàm, 129
oral history, 75, 138
Ouida, *Under Two Flags*, 46
overcrowding, 15
Oxford University, 31, 45; Ruskin College, 225; and Settlement movement, 194–5; women's colleges at, 170

Paget, General Sir Arthur, 219
Pall Mall, 44, 197
Pall Mall Gazette, 185–6, 198
Pankhurst, Christabel, 177, 222
Pankhurst, Emmeline, 175–6, 222
Pankhurst, Richard, 177
Pankhurst, Sylvia, 220–1
Paris Commune, 126, 196
parish councils, 22
Parliament, 31, 150, 217–18
Parliament Act of 1911, 217–18

Index

Royal Commission on Labour, 97, 195

Royal Commission on the Poor Law, 195–6

Ruskin, John, 16, 98, 99, 129, 149, 151, 155, 157; *Praeterita*, 109

Ruskin College, 225

Rutherford, Mark [William Hale White], *Autobiography*, 109, 124; *Deliverance*, 124, 126; *Clara Hopgood*, 181

Sabbatarianism, 111–14

Sackville-West, Vita, *Edwardians*, 45

St Alban's Church, Holborn, 104

Sala, George Augustus, 185

Salford, 215

Salisbury, Marquis of, 24, 29, 31–3, 185, 211

salvation, 110, 193

Salvation Army, 102, 115, 186, 192–3

sanitation, 70–2

Sassoon, family of, 50

Sassoon, Siegfried, 39, 40

Savile, Lord, 37

schools boards, 147, 171, 200; and attendance officers, 204

schools, elementary, 200–4; leaving age, 202

Schreiner, Olive, *African Farm*, 182–3

science, 97–8; and religion, 120; and women, 158–9

'Season', 44

Secret Ballot Act, 22

secularization, theory of, 130

security, lack of, 73–4, 131–8; search for, 65

Select Committee on Want of Employment, 195

self-education, 149

self-interest, 96

sentimentality, 117

separate spheres, 159, 173, 178–9

servants, 40–2, 52, 57–8

Settlement Movement, 194–5

sexuality, 152–3, 157, 163–4, 180

Shakespeare, William, 57

Shaw, George Bernard, 198, 210

Sheffield, 15, 132, 151, 197

shipbuilding, 19

shooting, 45

shop assistants, 63, 64–5

shopkeepers, 59–66

sickness, 74

Siemens-Martin open-hearth furnace, 18

Sims, G. R., *How the Poor Live*, 185

Smith, Adam, 99

Snowden, Philip, 148

social change, conditions of, 179; evidence in novels, 180; nature of, 166

Social Democratic Federation, 145, 147, 153

social explorers, 196, 199

Social Gospel, 125–6, 193–5

socialism, 66, 80, 120, 129, chap. 7 *passim*; and Bloody Sunday, 197–8; educational role of, 148–9; and imperialism, 211–12; as religion, 144, 147–8; and Ruskin, 151; and social welfare, 192; and women's suffrage, 177

Socialist League, 145, 153

'Society', 31, 42–4, 51

South Wales Miners' Federation, 224

Southsea, 64

Spencer, Herbert, 158, 162

squires, *see* gentry

standard of living, 16, 68

Stanley (Co. Durham), 190

Stead, W. T., 185–6

Stephen, Sir James Fitzjames, 123

Stephen, Leslie, 161; *Agnostic's Apology*, 121–2

Stephen, Vanessa, 161–2

Stepney, 137

Stern, Baron de, 50

Stevenson, R. L., 129

Stratford-upon-Avon, 88, 89

Strikes, 142–3, 223–5

Sturt, George, 133–4

suburbia, 59–66, 80

Index

Rose Elliot

The Bean Book

Beans are an invaluable part of our diet, for not only do they provide an inexpensive source of protein, but they are rich in iron, phosphorus and B vitamins. Throughout history the bean has sustained generations, and here Rose Elliot's flair and inventiveness bring us a host of delicious recipes using more varieties of beans than you ever imagined existed.

Rose Elliot is Britain's top writer on vegetarian cookery and in this classic collection of original recipes the humble bean is utterly transformed. There are spicy dals from India; crisp, tasty rissoles; delectable pâtés and bean salads, shiny with dressing and fragrant with herbs. Delicate bean dishes from France, robust ones from Italy, others from the Middle East, with more than a hint of olive oil, lemon and garlic, full of earthy charm.

Vegetarian or non-vegetarian, nobody can resist Rose Elliot's imaginative and colourful dishes, a sheer delight to the palate and the eye.

A Fontana Original

T. C. Smout

A History of the
Scottish People
1560–1830

'By far the most stimulating, the most instructive and the most readable account of Scotch history that I have read . . . this splendid work carries us from Knox to Neilson, from the hot gospel of Calvin to the hot-blast smelting process – and incidentally seeks to explain the change. For always, in following this lucid narrative, we see an original mind at work, questioning and explaining as well as illustrating.

The illustrations, incidentally, are original and delightful too. The whole book has delighted me. I cannot praise it too highly.' Hugh Trevor-Roper, *Sunday Times*

'This is a fine history of Scotland. It combines rich and deep scholarship with an elegant and lucid style . . . No one who professes an interest in Scotland can afford to miss reading it.' *Times Literary Supplement*

'This remarkable book leaves the reviewer with little to say except that all Scots, and even Englishmen who are interested in Britain's development, should read it. It is admirably proportioned, based on vast reading, and brings all the main topics together.' *Economist*

FONTANA PRESS

EARLY VICTORIAN
BRITAIN, 1832–51

J. F. C. Harrison

For people in all walks of life, the period between the passing
of the Great Reform Bill and the Great Exhibition was one of
turbulence and change, where massive events such as the new
Poor Law, the coming of railways, Chartism, the repeal of the
Corn Laws and the Great Irish Famine were set against a
background of political manouevring and violent economic
fluctuations. Professor Harrison offers a thorough and
entertaining survey of this crucial phase of British history.

'I read . . . with uninterrupted delight, entranced that English
historians could combine so dazzlingly scholarship and art.'
A. J. P. Taylor, *Observer*

Also by J. F. C. Harrison

The Common People: a History from
the Norman Conquest to the Present

The Rise and Fall of the Political Press in Britain

Stephen Koss

In this magisterial book, Stephen Koss traces the evolution of the relationship between journalists, proprietors and politicians from the late eighteenth century to the end of World War Two. He follows the progress of the political press from control by the state through the age of the press barons to the arrival of the mass media and modern market forces. He draws on a mass of manuscript sources, many never previously consulted, to provide a thrilling and vivid account of the history of that most influential and Byzantine of political institutions, the British Press.

'Exceptionally well-written . . . its mind and references are broad enough for it to be enjoyed by the general reader who will frequently read amazed . . . There is nothing but pleasure and instruction here . . . A study of major importance.'

Michael Ratcliffe, *The Times*

'Professor Koss never puts a foot wrong, his scholarship is impeccable and he writes with wit, elegance and humour.'

Robert Black, *Illustrated London News*

'This book is indispensable reading for politicians of all parties.'

Asa Briggs, *New Society*

'Professor Koss knows the ambitions and foibles of every back-bench MP, the hopes and fears for his future of every editor, and half his staff a well, the cheque book stubs, not only of every major proprietor, but of every minor plutocrat who aspired to influence, and maybe towards ennoblement too, through newspaper owner-ship, in almost terrifying depth.'   Roy Jenkins, *Sunday Times*

FONTANA PRESS